The New Church Debate

The New Church Debate

ISSUES FACING AMERICAN LUTHERANISM

Edited and with an Introduction by
CARL E. BRAATEN

FORTRESS PRESS   PHILADELPHIA

Library of Congress Cataloging in Publication Data
Main entry under title:
The New church debate.

Essays presented at a conference on "The new church and its ministry" held at the Lutheran School of Theology, Chicago, Ill.
1. Lutheran Church—United States—Congresses.
2. Lutheran Church—Doctrines—Congresses. I. Braaten, Carl E., 1929-
BX8043.5.N44 1983   284.1'3   83-48008
ISBN 0-8006-1715-0 (pbk.)

366F83   Printed in the United States of America   1-1715

Contents

Introduction:
The New Lutheran Church
and Its Ministry

CARL E. BRAATEN

THE OCCASION

This book on *The New Church Debate* makes available to the wider church public the theological lectures studied and debated at a theological colloquium sponsored by the Lutheran School of Theology at Chicago (LSTC), 6–11 February 1983, on the subject "The New Church and Its Ministry: The Ecclesiological Challenge Facing American Lutheranism." The original idea for such a conference was a proposal I made to President William E. Lesher to convoke a meeting of theologians on the problem of the ministry in all of its most crucial contemporary dimensions. Such a convocation could deal with the ecumenical fact that the doctrine of the ministry constitutes the chief obstacle in the way of reconciling and reuniting the divided bodies of world Christianity. Are Lutherans a help or a hindrance in removing this obstacle? The convocation could also face the crisis of ministry that each of our churches is experiencing. Why are so many ministers burning out and dropping out? Why are so many confused and incompetent? And what about our bishops? Are they really bishops, or such in name only? While all these problems bearing on the theology and practice of Christian ministry would be intrinsically worthy of a week-long seminar of theologians, church officials, pastors, and lay leaders, both Lutheran and others, the thought came to us that we might serve the church better if we oriented our conference around the formation of a new Lutheran church in the U.S.

The interest churchwide in just such a conference proved to be beyond our most optimistic projections. We planned for around two hundred registrations at best, but received nearly four hundred. More than seven hundred persons participated in the conference full- or part-time. In the

1

nature of the case, the majority were white, male clergy from the Lutheran Church in America (LCA), most from the supporting synods of the Lutheran School of Theology. This was to be expected, but we were pleased that so many from beyond the LCA–LSTC constituencies attended, so that a fair sampling of viewpoints could be reflected in the debates and proposals for a new church. The conference itself ran for six days through an intensive rhythm of lectures, question-and-answer periods, panels, working seminars, plenary discussions, questionnaires, and late-night receptions. It was a memorable happening—but now to the issues.

LUTHERAN IDENTITY

William Lazareth was invited to give the keynote address on "Lutheran Identity in an Ecumenical Age." As the executive secretary of Faith and Order of the World Council of Churches he was asked to respond to this question: "What are the theological reasons for continuing to institutionalize Lutheran identity in America, given that we acknowledge the provisional character of these Lutheran institutions on the way to the goal of a visible embodiment of the *una sancta*?"

In answering this question he warned against the danger of "denominational sectarianism" and "ecclesial isolationism." He proposed instead that we speak of our common "Christian" identity and our "Lutheran" identification. Lazareth was right, and he could appeal to Martin Luther who said: "I ask that people make no reference to my name. Let them call themselves Christians, not Lutherans. What is Luther? After all, the teaching is not mine. Neither was I crucified for anyone. St. Paul would not allow the Christians to call themselves Pauline or Petrine, but Christian. How then should I—poor stinking maggot-fodder that I am—come to have people call the children of Christ by my wretched name? Not so, my dear friends. Let us abolish all party names and call ourselves Christians, after the One whose teaching we hold."

The issue is: How should we Lutherans identify ourselves in the years to come? How shall we name our church? From a biblical perspective God's name is the sacrament of his identity. So it is also with his people. The name will bespeak our reality. So what shall we call ourselves as Lutherans in an ecumenical age? The most appropriate suggestion so far is that we are by origin and intention "evangelical catholics." Some Lutherans don't like the word "evangelical" because it has been monopolized by biblical fundamentalists, and others don't like the word "catholic" because it smacks of orientation to Roman authoritarianism or high church Anglicanism. In an editorial in *Dialog* I made the proposal that we call the new Lutheran church the Evangelical Catholic Church of the Lutheran Confession. Of course this is not going to work, and I know it. It is accurate enough theologically, but empirically it is mostly untrue. The evangelical half of the new church won't be catholic enough, and the more catholic half won't be evangelical enough. So we should simply call ourselves "The Lutheran Church/U.S.A." That points to the fact that sociologically speaking we are and act like a typical American denomination, and that should be taken as both an indictment and a challenge to seek a more adequate form of the one, holy, catholic, and apostolic church. Our denominational identity as Lutherans so easily threatens to overshadow our identity as a confessing community of Christians seeking the unity of the universal church in the truth of the gospel. Our true identity stemming from Luther's reformation and the Lutheran confessions lies in Christ and his gospel, but has mostly been obscured by many false identities, such as race, class, culture, and language, which disguise themselves as oaths of loyalty to confessional traditions.

Yet, it would be folly for Lutherans to dream of liberation from their sectarian isolation and doctrinal impediments by becoming less confessional. The church simply stands or falls on its confession of Christ, and it is important for the church to read its own confessional documents in this light. Robert W. Bertram, professor of systematic theology at Christ Seminary-Seminex, was asked to speak on "Confessing the Faith of the Church," to propose a confessional stance for the new church. He did so by stressing the *dynamics* of a confessing church, reaching back to the root meaning of *"confessio"* as the testimony of those on trial in a courtroom situation. Lutherans possess a book of confessions (*The Book of Concord*), but *having* confessions is secondary to *being* confessors of the gospel of Christ. That is finally the only word of authority they can summon to their defense in a time of trial. Bertram compared the church's confession to "sneezing," which is what the body does to clear its head of contaminants. Bertram's leadership role in the confessing movement in the Missouri Synod gave his address a ring of Bonhoefferian authority from personal experience.

LOCAL ASSEMBLIES

Underlying the many controversial issues bearing on the doctrine of the ministry, such as, ordination, apostolic succession, bishops, universal priesthood, and teaching authority, is the nature of the church itself. Bishop Otto Dibelius once said that the twentieth century is the age of the church.

The quest for the true nature of the church has been pursued more vigorously in just the last two decades than in the previous two millennia. Various images have been taken from the New Testament as a starting point for defining the nature of the church, such as, "people of God," "body of Christ," and "communion of saints." More recently the idea of the "kingdom of God" has been used by both Protestant and Catholic theologians as the right starting point for a doctrine of the church. But however the doctrine of the church is systematically developed, Article VII of the Augsburg Confession remains most certainly true, namely that "The church is the assembly of saints in which the Gospel is taught purely and the sacraments are administered rightly." Taken by itself as a full definition of the church, this can lead to a congregationalism in which each assembly is self-sufficient, breeding rampant individualism and parochialism.

Professor Timothy F. Lull, professor of systematic theology at the Lutheran Theological Seminary at Philadelphia, was asked to address the topic of "The Catholicity of the Local Congregation." The point is not to relocate the church beyond the local assemblies, say, in some synodical, national, or international office, giving rise to many layers of massive bureaucracies, but rather to incarnate the sense of the reality of the whole church of Christ within each local community. As Ignatius said, "Where Christ is there is the catholic church." And believers meet Christ as they gather in his name to hear the word and receive the sacraments.

The rub comes when we try to translate such rhetoric into reality at the First Lutheran Church on the corner of Fifth and Main Streets across from the bank. How shall we build the dimensions of catholicity into the structures of worship, witness, and service operating at the congregational level? Some proposals include the following: (1) a committee on ecumenical relationships; (2) occasional Eucharists with other congregations, particularly acting on the interim eucharistic fellowship agreement between Lutherans and Episcopalians; (3) weekly celebration of the Eucharist; and (4) restoration of the role of bishops in the life of the congregation. The two most controversial points have to do with Eucharist and episcopacy. We will deal with the issue of episcopacy later. But what about the weekly Eucharist? The Faith and Order document *Baptism, Eucharist and Ministry* states that the celebration of the Eucharist "continues as the central act of the Church's worship." Many of our congregations do not believe and practice this. They perform the Eucharist not only infrequently, but in a manner as to make it obviously peripheral. I have heard church leaders at the highest level profess that putting the Eucharist at the heart of worship is un-Lutheran; to them it is a Roman Catholic import. Here is an issue where sound theology and local practice clearly collide, and it will not be easily settled in the first rounds of debate.

LAY AND ORDAINED MINISTRIES

It is a theological truism that we cannot deal with the nature of the ministry apart from the doctrine of the church. But within the one people of God, the body of Christ, the fellowship of saints, a distinction going back to the New Testament community between ordained and lay ministries has become a perennial mark of the church catholic. Lutherans have maintained this distinction, but at the present time they seem very confused about its theological justification. This fact became most conspicuously manifest at the "New Church" colloquium. Professor Nelvin Vos, professor of English at Muhlenberg College, was asked to speak on "The Vocation of the Laity." Lutherans have classically affirmed the equal priesthood of believers, yet, as in George Orwell's *Animal Farm,* "some are more equal than others"—and they are the ordained ones. Many feel that the laity are assigned a second-class status in the church, and there is massive confusion about the laity's role in the world between Sundays.

Within the ecumenical movement a theology of the laity has been developing in the interest of overcoming the split between clergy and laity. In its left-wing form the special ministry of the clergy is being called into question. As Mark Gibbs, professional spokesperson for the renewal of the laity, has stated: "There is no fundamental difference in calling between an archbishop and his chauffeur." The appeal is, of course, to the Lutheran stress on the priesthood of all believers. Furthermore, aren't pastors and bishops as much sinners as the lowliest of the laity? Yet, the distinction perseveres in practice, and Lutheran theologians are trying to get hold of its apostolic thread.

Walter R. Bouman, professor of systematic theology at Trinity Lutheran Seminary in Columbus, Ohio, was asked to speak on "The Identity of the Ordained Minister." He surveyed the waterfront of positions and opinions on the subject, but finally confessed that after trying to "get to the bottom" of ordination, he ended in a state of frustration and disappointment. This is not unusual for a Lutheran theologian. This perplexity on the ordained ministry can be traced to a basic inconsistency in Luther's thought. Many Protestants remember Luther as the champion of the laity against the priestly tyranny of Rome. Some historians see the universal priesthood of believers as the great religious principle of the Reformation. This principle meant that each believer has the right to go to God directly, seeking pardon apart from the mediatorial function of the priesthood. So what can the clergy do that the laity cannot do on their own? Nothing, absolutely nothing in principle. However, it is useful and convenient for one person to be delegated by a group to perform certain functions in behalf of all. The group writes the job description and can issue a contract for all parties to sign. Is this what Luther really taught? Whatever the case, it is what a large number of Lutherans today seem to have in their minds.

Two lines of interpretation can be derived from Luther's own writings. One can find quotes from Luther to buttress one's own predilections. The one side derives the ordained ministry from the consent of the congregation, and the other from the word of Christ. If the identity of the minister is derived from the congregation, the minister is a delegated representative of the people. This leads to a democratic congregationalism. When the majority no longer feels fairly represented by their delegate, they can simply get rid of him or her. Whoever pays the piper calls the tune. If they are not getting their money's worth, they can trade their minister in for another. The minister thus loses all authority vested in the office, and becomes nothing but a flunky of those who hold the reins of power in the parish.

Does the ordained person receive the authority of the office from the good pleasure of the congregation, or instead from the institution of Christ and his apostles? Does ordained ministry derive its authorization from below, from the will of the people, or from above, namely, the Lord of the church? Luther scholars are still debating these questions, and the ambiguity of scholarly opinion is glaringly evident in both the theory and practice of all Lutheran churches.

The inconsistency in Luther may be regarded as a tension in his thought created by his situation. He could stress the delegation theory to combat the errors of Rome and to provide a way of continuing the ministry after losing the support of the bishops. He faced an emergency situation. Without bishops he would lose the traditional means for the orderly process of continuing the all-important ministry of Word and Sacrament in the church. In this dilemma he could use the analogy of a little group of Christian laity, taken prisoner and confined in a deserted area, who then choose one of their number by common consent and charge that person with the ministerial office. Is this not what happened in the early church? Today, with more scholarly information, we know better than that. This is by all means not what happened in the early church. However, Luther could throw his weight behind the idea of the ministry's transmission through a succession of ordained pastors and therefore against spiritualists, who rested their ministry on a direct inner call of the Spirit. From our perspective, what Luther said in a state of emergency later Lutherans developed into a state of normalcy. In an ecumenical age, the question we face is whether we can take steps to bring the emergency to an end.

APOSTOLIC SUCCESSION

We come now to the issue of episcopacy. Rarely has a conference of Lutherans spent so much time talking about bishops in the church. Many of the conferees had already settled the issue in their minds. The restoration of the historic episcopacy was a *desideratum* second to none; others continued to have an allergic reaction to prelacy in the church. As we have already stated, Lutherans in America have opted for the name "bishop," but don't really have a clear idea of the reality that the title signifies. Philip Hefner, systematic theologian at the Lutheran School of Theology, addressed the conference on the topic "Can We Have Bishops—Reformed and Evangelical?" This is an issue that the ecumenical movement has foisted upon Lutherans, for which they were unprepared. As Hefner stated: "We have bishops without knowing what to make of them. God has pushed us into cold water, before we even had time to get on our swimming suits." This image stuck, and launched the imagination. Where do Lutherans really stand on the decision to have bishops or church presidents, and what rides on the issue?

The issue, theologically speaking, is whether bishops can contribute to the succession of the apostolic ministry in the church today. Not even Roman Catholic theologians deny that there is a continuation of the apostolic faith in non-Roman ecclesial communities. But can the episcopal ministry witness to the *fulness* of the apostolic faith in the life of the church? This is a question Lutherans need not avoid. Just as the pastoral/presbyterial office in the church needs to be continually reformed in an evangelical way, so also the apostolic/episcopal office can be renewed by the same gospel in every age. The Roman church that Luther sought to reform had fallen in many abysmal respects. Luther had to claim that succession in the apostolic faith was more essential than a continuity of the episcopal office. He was faced with the miserable choice to reform the church without bishops or not to reform the church at all. In this emergency situation he had to break with the classic practice of the ordination of a special priesthood by an episcopacy in continuity with the New Testament apostles through the laying on of hands. Should Lutherans not acknowledge that this emergency situation is drawing to a close in an ecumenical age?

The Faith and Order document on *Baptism, Eucharist and Ministry* asks the member churches whether or not the ancient threefold pattern of ministry—bishops, presbyters, and deacons—has a powerful claim to be accepted by them. Lutherans, along with many other Protestant churches, have gotten themselves boxed into a one-dimensional ministry. Everyone who is ordained is called to be a pastor of a local congregation, and the model of the pastor is of an omnicompetent capable of doing everything. No wonder bishops are complaining more loudly than ever about the "incompetent clergy," but hardly as much as the laity who are their victims. In the New Testament communities there was, in stark contrast, a plurality of ministries, corresponding to the variety of gifts the Spirit so generously distributed among the members. All the ministerial functions of the apostles, prophets, teachers, evangelists, counselors, administrators, healers, deacons, presbyters, bishops, and what not seem now to have collapsed and to be concentrated in the one pastoral office that alone legitimates ordination. It hardly seems far-fetched for our Lutheran churches to respond favorably to the ecumenical call to restore the threefold order of ministry, into which persons would be ordained either as deacons, pastors, or bishops, according to the call of the church.

This would mean that in addition to ordaining pastors, we would also ordain persons to the diaconate as well as the episcopate. What would the restoration of episcopal ordination do for our church? Some fear that this would spell a departure from the "pure doctrine" of our confessional stance. Gustaf Wingren, for example, has stated: "The moment we introduce a doctrine of succession into our view of the ministry, we cease to regard the Church as grounded on baptism and the Gospel. One view is opposed to the other. We have to choose between them" (*Gospel and Church*, p. 131). He also claims that "any question of continuity in regard to ordination is out of harmony with the general drift of the New Testament" (pp. 132–33). His polemics are overcharged by the rivalry in Swedish theology between Lund and Uppsala, and Harald Riesenfeld happens in this case to be the object of his outrage. Wingren's point is valid only so far as it stands as a clear refutation of the high church Anglican claim that "the historic episcopate guarantees the church. Without it, *non est ecclesia.*" This is the kind of nonsense Lutherans cannot tolerate in the church. Episcopal succession is surely no guarantee, but may we not agree with Edmund Schlink, George Lindbeck, and many others, that the historically successive episcopacy can serve as a *sign* of apostolicity in the church? Wherever it is absent, don't we have a right to work for its restoration?

The Lutheran-Catholic dialogues in both Europe and the U.S. should be carefully examined by the Commission on the New Lutheran Church if it wishes to catch up to the theological insights that have already been achieved. The tragedy is, of course, that the results of these dialogues, as Paul Empie so often reminded the church, are the best kept secret in the very churches that sponsored them. How many theologians and bishops have read these dialogues, not to mention the majority of commission members who are by training and vocation ill-equipped to consider them?

ECCLESIAL AUTHORITY

When it comes to the matter of adopting a particular polity for the new church, Lutherans are wont to claim that we are entering into a non-theological arena. Polity matters come under the rubric of *adiaphora*—that is, such matters as are not clearly revealed as core and content of the saving gospel of Jesus Christ. Frequently this useful distinction between what is absolutely essential and what is adiaphoristic has been wrongly interpreted to mean that *adiaphora* are of no theological concern and must always remain matters of indifference.

Both Robert Benne and Robert W. Jenson lifted the sights of the conference to consider very carefully what is at stake in ordering the church in our time. Robert Benne, professor of ethics at Roanoke College, was asked to deal with "The Social Sources of Polity," recognizing that there is no blueprint for the church in the New Testament for all time to come. The formation of the new Lutheran church will have to come to terms with the dynamics of our present social context, such as democratic processes, fair representation, denominational patterns, and bureaucratic organization. How all these factors are combined and shaped into a polity that serves the church's ministry and mission in the world is the issue, and Benne has made some proposals that the commission will ignore to the detriment of us all.

Robert W. Jenson, professor of systematic theology at the Lutheran Theological Seminary at Gettysburg, addressed the question of the locus of authority in the church. In a paper entitled "Sovereignty in the Church" he reflected on the proper place to locate the "last word" in the community's deliberations. There can be no doubt that Jesus Christ is the last Word in the church. His lordship is alive in the church through the living Word that circulates within the assembled body of his believers. This means that those individuals are rightly sovereign in the church only if their authority is a function of the authority of the gospel of the church's sovereign Lord. Every other kind of sovereignty becomes heteronomous and legalistic. As Jenson puts it, "The last word in the church must be the gospel and not the law.'' That means that those who hold authority in the church must be the appointed representatives of the gospel. If this is taken seriously, it will have decisive and far-reaching consequences for the way in which the Lutheran church organizes itself and for the job description of its bishops. Episcopacy, Eucharist, and evangelical authority are intertwined in a polity from within which genuine sovereignty, as the right to the last word, arises. There are suggestions here that could reform the decision-making procedures of the church and go far to overcome its lack of any magisterial authority.

HOLISTIC MISSION

The mission of the church is to proclaim the good news of the kingdom of God in Jesus Christ to the whole world until the end of time. This mission has universal scope; today it is commonly called holistic. The mission is God's bridge to a world that has not yet reached its fulfillment, and it proceeds from the nature of the church as an all-inclusive fellowship. Jesus' ministry of the kingdom showed signs of breaking into every dimension of life—healing physical illness, exorcising spirits, feeding the hungry, speaking out against corrupt public officials and religious authorities, and caring for poor and neglected people. So also correspondingly the church is to be a Christ-like medium of the power and effects of the kingdom of God in this world, bringing its mission into the openness of world history, placing it on the front lines of struggle for the hearts of people, including everything going on in the political, social, and economic realms of human life. This means that the goals and aims of the church for the outside world must begin to be modeled in its own interior life. Kathleen S. Hurty was asked to speak on the topic "Embodying the Gospel in an Inclusive Church." She called for an inclusive church, challenging the new church to embody in its very structures and procedures signs of reconciliation in the midst of the humanity-dividing issues such as sexism, racism, classism, and others. In her final words she said, "We are asking the commission on the New Lutheran Church to be the midwives, helping us to bring to birth a new and inclusive church."

Since the commission itself was formed to determine the meaning of inclusiveness, it has begun to act on the so-called quota system, where color, sex, vocation, and so forth are used as factors to decide the composition of committees. Is this wise? The issue is controversial. Is not the church beginning to rule its inner life by the law, rather than by the gospel? Instead of persuading people within the church by the gospel, we can take a shortcut by laying down the law. It seems that we all agree on the goals, but we argue about the means. Since trusting the gospel leaves too much up to the power of the Holy Spirit to change people's hearts—and that might take too long for us to tolerate—we can take charge right now and create the church we want by a new canon law, reflecting the legalistic spirit of the age. If we proceed in this way the church that we create will be the church we deserve, driven by the rigorous demands for law and justice, rather than by the deeper motivations of the gospel and love. It will be just like every other highly politicized world organization. I believe that the justice the church needs for its mission will be generated by the gospel, and that is the way we ought to move in the new church. A splendid example of this occurred when the LCA voted at its convention in Minneapolis to ordain women. A study of the issue was made; all knowledgeable and responsible persons in leadership agreed; the matter was widely deliberated in the communities; and finally, when the vote was taken, there was not a single dissenting vote. Justice was done, and that was a voice vote for the gospel and the power of the Spirit in the church. This was but a beginning, to be sure, and the goal is still ahead of us. Our controversy is not about the goal, but whether we can still distinguish between law and gospel in the church. If we cannot, it doesn't matter what we do anyway. The living Word will have been smothered in the church, and the church will have become a tool of other principalities at loose in the world.

Elizabeth Bettenhausen, associate professor of social ethics and theology at Boston University, was asked to speak on "Missionary Structures and World Struggles." The issue is painfully obvious: the New Lutheran Church will be predominantly a reflection of the white, rich, privileged strata of the First World. The problem is: how can rich Christians be servants to the poor of the world? How can North American Christians be mobilized to be an instrument of God's mission to nations condemned to fear, poverty, oppression, and hopelessness? How can a church embedded in structures of domination participate in genuinely liberating movements around the world? It is perhaps the most challenging question facing the next generation of Lutherans in the U.S.

Bettenhausen spoke to Lutherans as she pointed out that Lutherans, confessionally strong on justification, have classically betrayed a weakness in the area of sanctification. The doctrine of sanctification has been a problem for Lutherans generally, and when it became the strong suit of Lutheran pietism, it was individualistically conceived. May not the doctrine of sanctification be intended as something more than an index of Pilgrim's Progress to the Promised Land, and become instead a summons to the church as a whole to engage in the struggles of people for liberation and justice? If so, sanctification would become much more objective than subjective, more world-centered than self-centered.

THE PLACE OF THEOLOGY

Robert Benne voiced his suspicion of the notion that theology in the church can make a difference. Many of us who planned and participated in this colloquium were often tempted to embrace such a cynical notion. It leads to theological paralysis. Why do the hard work of theology if it makes no difference at all? In a planning session, I do recall Robert Jenson averring that from his experience, he has reason to doubt that a theological discussion of the issues will make a dent on the bureaucratic mentality that now has a stranglehold on the church. But, in spite of all that, he is willing to give it his best shot. Along came Gerhard Forde to heap coals on the fires of suspicion already burning in the hearts and minds of many lay people and pastors in the church. In an address entitled "The Place of Theology in the Church," Forde of Luther Northwestern Theological Seminary charted the demise of theology in the church and the rise of bureaucratic procedures that pay lip service to theology without taking it seriously. Many people were irritated by the truth, and accused the speaker, who happens to be a theologian, of making a self-serving analysis of the sickness in the church. No doubt Forde's prophecy was out-of-joint with the times, but in the long-run it will prove to have been an understatement of the truth. Forde's essay, incidentally, is not included in this volume but has been published in *Dialog* (spring 1983).

THE FUTURE

The fate of the church is now in the hands of those who are drafting the constitution and design of the New Lutheran Church. As this volume goes to press we have received some preliminary proposals from the task forces at work under the Commission on the New Lutheran Church. It is too early to offer a definitive appraisal; everything is still in a state of flux. The process itself has become political; words or positions are put forth that are calculated to appeal to the majority and to cause the least offense to the minorities. What happens to truth? It will be put to a vote, and right or wrong the majority will win. The hopes and prayers of the faithful who called for something "new" in the New Lutheran Church will be sorely tried in the months and years to come. Some sensitive people opposed the merger of these Lutheran bodies because the condition of its possibility will result in a leveling down of each denomination's strengths to the most innocuous common denominator. In the initial draft of the Task Force on Theology, for example, the parts dealing with "Confession of Faith" and "The Nature and Mission of the Church" have carefully excluded all reference to God as Father, and to Jesus as his Son, even when dealing explicitly with the doctrine of the Trinity. The documents refer to some of the functions of the Triune God, but have quietly avoided using the proper name of the Triune God as "Father, Son, and Holy Spirit." This is the standard name of God in Lutheran piety, in the eucharistic cult, in the ecumenical creeds, and in the apostolic canon. Mary Daly's book, *Beyond God the Father,* has caught the imagination of many who struggle for the liberation of women; some believe they can trace their oppression in the church to its Christian roots in the trinitarian name of God as Father, Son, and Holy Spirit. Obviously, the task force has concurred in this judgment without benefit of serious theological examination.

The work of the commission is facing some unrealistic deadlines, placing in jeopardy the place and function of serious theology in the entire process of shaping a new church body for the future. It was our hope that the colloquium at LSTC could serve as a theological catalyst in a special way for the members of the Commission on the New Lutheran Church, the majority of whom were simply unqualified for their responsibility, if knowledge of theology is considered an important criterion. However, the leaders of the commission had scheduled their meeting for the same week as the colloquium, creating a conflict for members who planned to attend the conference on "The New Church and Its Ministry." A partial compromise was worked out with the consent of the commission to meet at the Hyde Park Hilton, one mile from the Lutheran School of Theology. But as expected, the commission's own agenda was so full as to render the participation of its members all but physically impossible and educationally futile.

POSTSCRIPT

Space has not permitted us to publish all the papers delivered at the conference, nor to include a summary of the proposals and resolutions of the working seminars that wrestled with a myriad of crucial issues. They have all been duplicated and delivered to the Commission on the New Lutheran Church to use as its members see fit. In addition to the lectures published in this volume, there were others that brought the challenge of international and ecumenical perspectives. Father Dulles and Father John Meyendorff spoke from their Roman Catholic and Eastern Orthodox perspectives respectively on the topic "Toward a Mutual Recognition of Ministries." Lewis Mudge, dean of McCormick Theological Seminary, spoke on "Prospects for Christian Unity in the United States," focusing particularly on what is happening in the mainline Protestant denominations that have participated in the Consultation on Church Unity (COCU). Yoshiro Ishida, executive secretary of the Department of Theological Studies of the Lutheran World Federation, spoke on the world mission of the church in the face of new global problems and opportunities. (The essays by Dulles, Meyendorff, and Ishido appear in *Dialog* [spring 1983].)

It is our hope that the publication of this book will serve to highlight the issues and heighten the theological awareness of church people who still face the solemn responsibility to act on the proposals that the commission presents to the national conventions of the uniting bodies in the years ahead.

1
Evangelical Catholicity: Lutheran Identity in an Ecumenical Age

WILLIAM H. LAZARETH

The impending formation of a new Lutheran church body intensifies the passion with which we ask the challenging question: What are the theological reasons for continuing to institutionalize Lutheran identity in America, given that we acknowledge the provisional character of these Lutheran institutions on the way to the goal of a visible embodiment of the *una sancta*? My task is to help us to answer this question against the broad background of worldwide ecumenical developments over the past few decades.

I should first like to sharpen the issues by reformulating both parts of this theme. Wrongly understood, "Lutheran Identity in an Ecumenical Age" could easily invite precisely the denominational sectarianism and ecclesial isolationism that I hope the new church will confidently disavow. Therefore, on the one hand, I propose that we not examine our "*Lutheran* identity"; instead we should clearly distinguish between our Christian "identity" and our Lutheran "identification." More specifically, we will want to analyze our evangelical catholic "identity" (in the Augsburg Confession) as the biblically grounded norm for critically restructuring our Lutheran "identification" (in North American Protestantism). On the other hand, we should not talk about an "ecumenical age," but rather sharply differentiate between the "church catholic" (reflecting its Christic fullness) and an "eschatological age" (in terms of the "already–not-yet" fulfillment of God's inbreaking reign throughout humankind and creation). Moreover, to allow me to proceed sequentially from universality to particularity, I will also reverse the order of these reformulated topics: (1) an eschatological age; (2) the church catholic; (3) our evangelical catholic identity; and (4) our American Lutheran identification.

AN ESCHATOLOGICAL AGE

For some of the most ardent Christians of our day, any concern for the visible unity of the church appears archaic. They believe that there are far more urgent tasks to which the churches are called. Ironically, this impatience can arise from two quite different—and often incompatible—kinds of convictions.[1]

On the conservative right, there are those who are sincerely convinced that the supreme task facing the churches is to bring the saving good news of Jesus Christ to the millions who have never heard it. They believe that nothing should be allowed to hinder this; and that organizational church unity, so far from being a help for this purpose, may actually be a hindrance. The largest churches are often the most lethargic in evangelism, and some of the smallest are among the most active. Church unity is therefore not a priority for Christians unless it can be shown (which in this view, it cannot) that uniting the churches actually leads to more vigorous evangelism.

On the liberal left, there are also equally ardent Christians who are convinced that the most urgent task facing the churches is to show humankind how to live together as one family in peace, to share the world's food among the hungry, to destroy the powers that exploit persons for the profit of others, and to break the shackles of racial domination and social injustice. They contend that the churches will be judged by God, according to their record in meeting these demands. If church unity makes for more effective social action, it is to be welcomed. Certainly most inherited church divisions, however, are irrelevant to any real social issue. Indeed church unity in itself is also socially irrelevant. What really matters, according to this second view, is our effective involvement in the burning societal issues of humankind.

This emphasis on the churches' social involvement presents a perennial source of tension. On the one side, there will always be the danger that concern for visible church unity becomes an end in itself, that we turn our backs upon the world and become totally absorbed in the intricate problems of Christian faith and order which are raised by the quest for church unity. On the other side, there is then the danger of a negative reaction, a sort of impatient nausea regarding the divided churches and, consequently, an attempt to save or serve the world with some sort of evangelistic or political program that leaves the church far behind. It is however the world that sets the agenda, and Christians should be "where the action is."

ECCLESIAL AND SECULAR ECUMENISM

There is a growing discernment that God is indeed at work in the great movements of secular history and the cataclysmic changes in non-Christian religious cultures. This has led many to the conviction that we can become fellow workers with God only by leaving behind our ecclesiastical ghetto and working alongside persons of other faiths or of no faith so that we may do the things that God wants to have done in the world. It is in such groups of fellow servants of God that the real configurations of the true church will be found.

This has also resulted in the growth of what is often called "secular ecumenism" or "catholic universalism," a widespread sense among conscientious persons of all races and creeds that the human family is one, and that everything that in practice denies this common humanity is an offense against God. Therefore many Christians now insist that the real task for our day is to manifest the unity of humankind rather than to realize the unity of the church. Nevertheless, the report of the World Council of Churches (WCC) Uppsala Assembly (1968) continued to affirm that "the restoration and fulfilment of the unity of the churches is the most urgent task for which Faith and Order has to call them" (p. 233). The dialectical tension between church unity and world unity cannot and should not be eliminated. It can be properly maintained, however, only within the bounds of an authentic Christian eschatology.

Already at the WCC Assembly at Evanston (1954), the theme report on "Christ the Hope of the World" made clear that eschatology, as the dimension of God's final purpose and final action of salvation, must not be considered as a mere appendix to the Christian faith, but rather it must permeate the whole life of the church. True eschatology does not put the church to sleep. By witnessing that Christian hope is a proleptical hope, Evanston meant to overcome the gap between the Christian "verticalists" with their tendency to otherworldliness and the Christian "horizontalists" with their propensity for this-worldliness. Quoted again by Dr. W. A. Visser't Hooft at the Uppsala Assembly (1968), the report said:

> The Church is the company of watchmen, who because they have seen the light in the east, know that the new day has already broken and are sounding the trumpets to announce it to all persons. It is the fellowship of those who now in this time are able to recognize the coming King in his hungry, thirsty, naked, sick, captive and refugee sisters and brothers, and are accordingly willing and ready to give them food and drink and clothing, to visit them and company with them. (p. 316)

Since that time, the critical question of *how* Christ's lordship over the world is to be described has been debated extensively. The Faith and Order Commission in Montreal (1963) sharpened the debate by asking: "Is it to be identified *only* with the exercise of Christ's lordship through the Church? Is it a rule *now* exercised even apart from the believing community, and if so, how? How is the tension between the 'already' (Matt. 28:18; Col. 1:15–20; Eph. 1:10, 20–23) and the 'not yet' (1 Cor. 15:24; Heb. 2:8; 10:3; Rom. 8:23, 24; Col. 3:3–4) of Christ's victory to be understood?" (p. 43).

These issues have not been unanimously resolved among advocates of the various eschatologies that lay claim to some biblical foundations. In the course of the ecumenical debates, however, a clearer distinction is increasingly being made between the universality of the world and the catholicity of the church. It underscores the fact that, within the tensions of an eschatological age, the search for the church's visible unity is to be understood as the quest for true catholicity—a catholicity that is continually received as a fresh gift of the Holy Spirit to a servant-church which is also, as its head, willing to abandon its own life for the sake of its mission in and for the world.

UNIQUENESS OF CATHOLICITY

From the ways in which the term is loosely used today, one often gets the impression that "catholicity" is a synonym of "universal" and "ecumenical." This only leads to theological confusion, because all three terms have an additional deeper or broader meaning alongside the common geographical one.

With regard to the term "catholic," the difference is that its original, fundamental meaning is a qualitative, eschatological one. The quantitative, geographical usage represents a later deviation, or still better, an application of the original meaning on a worldwide scale.[2]

"Catholic" primarily signifies totality and wholeness, in the category of a value judgment. It is used in the Christian era for describing the *fulness* of God's action in Christ, who then reveals the truth to all persons, at all times, and in all places. That early Christian writers respected this delicate distinction is also evident in the etymology of the Greek word *katolikos,* composed of *kata* and *olon* denoting a qualitative depth dimension. In the *Martyrdom of Polycarp* (8, 1), for instance, we read ". . . of the catholic church which is throughout the *oikoumene* (*tes kata ten oikoumene katolikes ekklesias*)." Here the church is clearly qualified as catholic, and only as such and because of this qualitative, unique, and distinctive property should it be extended throughout the whole world.

These etymological remarks show why "catholic" refers primarily to the very essence of the church and only secondarily to its geographical extension. It reminds us of the biblical notion of *fulness* (*pleroma*) either in the sense that in Christ "the whole fulness of deity dwells bodily" (Col. 2:9); or that through the Spirit the faithful share in Christ so that they "may know the love of Christ which surpasses knowledge, that you may be filled with all the fulness of God" (Eph. 3:19); or finally, that God has appointed Christ sovereign head of the church, which is truly his body, the complement of him who fills all members with all grace (Eph. 1:22–23). In the Bible, "fulness" is applied first to the nature and action of God, and then it qualifies the nature of the church, which is thus named "catholic" in order to designate its inner coherence with this unique, divine fulness.

Therefore we should not use "universal," "ecumenical," and "catholic" as synonyms. Nor should we speak broadly of "secular ecumenism" or "catholic universalism," thereby confusing the church and the world. We should first make the necessary distinction that the church is catholic as an eschatological reality before the church addresses its message to the universal world or enters into critical solidarity with it. Only in this way can we remain faithful to the uniqueness of God's mighty act in Christ and to the unity and mission of Christ's holy body, the church catholic.

Furthermore, only through the distinctive act of the Holy Spirit do we have the possibility of sharing in the lordship of Christ. The apostolic claim—that the good news of God springs from a particular people, a particular set of events, a particular collection of documents, but that it is also of universal significance, addressed to a universal audience, and seeks a universal allegiance—has always been and continues to be an incarnational scandal, a stumbling block, and offense (1 Cor. 1:23).

Our special calling today is to continue to make the authentic biblical witness so that Christ-centered unity and mission are inseparable and must always be viewed dialectically in the light of God's mercy and judgment. While all persons are sinners before a righteous God, not all persons are victims in an unjust society. This means that we must clearly distinguish between the church and the world without falsely identifying or separating the two. Our Christian hope lies neither in the secularization of the church nor in the sacralization of the world. Rather the church's worldly posture must remain in eschatological tension: nonpartisan in faith as it serves all sinful persons alike in its ministry of Word and Sacrament; but also partisan in love as it struggles on behalf of the poor and the oppressed in its ministry of mercy and justice.

THE CHURCH CATHOLIC

The modern ecumenical movement affirms the inseparability of unity and mission within the church catholic. This dual commitment is grounded in Christ's revelation of God. Having prayed "that they may all be one," Christ immediately added, "so that the world may believe." Christians are called to participate in the unity that the Son shares with the Father. They are thereby incorporated into God's mission: sent into the world by the Son, just as the Son was sent into that same world by the Father (John 17:21; 20:21).

Early in the life of the World Council of Churches, therefore, the Central Committee issued its *Rolle Declaration* (1951) in strong support of "The Calling of the Church to Mission and to Unity." The church leaders said in part:

> We would especially draw attention to the recent confusion in the use of the term ecumenical. It is important to insist that this word, which comes from the Greek word for the whole inhabited earth, is properly used to describe everything that relates to the whole task of the whole Church to bring the Gospel to the whole world. It therefore covers equally the missionary movement and the movement towards unity, and must not be used to describe the latter in contradistinction to the former. We believe that a real service will be rendered to true thinking on these subjects in the churches if we so use this word that it covers both unity and mission in the context of the whole world. (p. 65)

INCLUSIVE MISSION

The cohesion of church unity and mission has long been an issue for Christians. Today there is a growing ecumenical conviction, within the church's inclusive mission, that evangelism and social justice dare not be severed from each other. Their convergence reflects a decade of struggle in the development of holistic missiological strategy and praxis.[3]

In 1973 the Bangkok Assembly of the WCC's Commission on World Mission and Evangelism provided a major opportunity for Third World church leaders to address the tensions between personal salvation and social responsibility within the church's mission. In the name of the new "theology of liberation," their chief aim was to champion "social salvation" in opposition to the pietistic and ethically quietistic individualism which they had earlier inherited from many Western-based missionary societies. Citing the messianic manifesto of Jesus at Nazareth (Luke 4:18), the Bangkok report declared:

Through Christ men and women are liberated and empowered with all their energies and possibilities to participate in his Messianic work. . . . The salvation which Christ brought, and in which we participate, offers a comprehensive wholeness in this divided life . . . It is salvation of the soul and the body, of the individual and society, humankind and the groaning creation . . . As evil works both in personal life and in exploitative social structures which humiliate humankind, so God's justice manifests itself both in the justification of the sinner and in social and political justice. (p. 93)

At the WCC Nairobi Assembly (1975), Section I dealt with the theme "Confessing Christ Today." The report has a reassuring confessional ring:

We boldly confess Christ alone as Saviour and Lord. We confidently trust in the power of the Gospel to free and unite . . . We have been led by the Holy Spirit to confess Jesus Christ as our Divine Confessor . . . His name is above every name . . . Through the power of the cross Christ promises God's right-eousness and commands true justice. As the royal priesthood, Christians are therefore called to engage in both evangelism and social action. We are com-missioned to proclaim the Gospel of Christ to the ends of the earth . . . and to struggle to realize God's will for peace, justice, and freedom throughout society . . . Christians witness in word and deed to the inbreaking reign of God . . . Christ's decisive battle has been won at Easter . . . yet we must still battle daily. (p. 43)

In 1979, at Puebla, Mexico, the Roman Catholic bishops of Latin America reaffirmed the church's "preferential option for the poor." The WCC Melbourne Conference on "Your Kingdom Come" (1980) chose to move in the same direction, and the report stated:

In the perspective of the kingdom, God has a preference for the poor. Jesus announced at the beginning of his ministry, drawing upon the word given to the prophet Isaiah, "the Spirit of the Lord is upon me, because he has anointed me to preach good news to the poor" (Luke 4:18). The Church of Jesus Christ is called to preach good news to the poor, even as its Lord in his ministry has announced the kingdom of God to them. (pp. 171, 175)

Most recently, the WCC Central Committee (1982) adopted an eight-thousand-word document entitled "Mission and Evangelism—an Ecumenical Affirmation." It brings together a wide range of mission insights that draw the churches closer in their inclusive, common witness. A few illustrative ex-cerpts follow:

Conversion. The proclamation of the Gospel includes an invitation to rec-ognize and accept in a personal decision the saving lordship of Jesus Christ . . . God addresses himself specifically to each of his children, as well as to the whole human race. Each person is entitled to hear the Good News . . . God as Father knows each one of his children and calls each of them to make a fundamental personal act of allegiance to him and his kingdom in the fellowship of his people. (p. 432)

The Gospel to all Realms of Life. The teaching of Jesus on the kingdom of God is a clear reference to God's loving lordship over all human history. We cannot limit our witness to a supposedly private area of life. The lordship of Christ is to be proclaimed to all realms of life . . . In some countries there is pressure to limit religion to the private life of the believer—to assert that freedom to believe should be enough. The Christian faith challenges that assumption. The Church claims the right and the duty to exist publicly—visibly—and to address itself openly to issues of human concern. (p. 434)

Good News to the Poor. Most of the world's poor have not heard the Good News of the Gospel of Jesus Christ; or they could not receive it, because it was not recognized as Good News in the way in which it was brought. This is a double injustice: They are victims of the oppression of an unjust economic order or an unjust political distribution of power, and at the same time they are deprived of the knowledge of God's special care for them. (p. 440)

There is here a double credibility test. A proclamation that does not hold forth the promises of the justice of the kingdom to the poor of the earth is a caricature of the Gospel; but Christian participation in the struggles for justice which does not point towards the promises of the kingdom also makes a caricature of a Christian understanding of justice. (p. 441)

VISIBLE UNITY

We have outlined the church's recent struggles for an inclusive mission that encompasses both evangelism and social justice, both eternal salvation and historical liberation. Our focus now shifts to the twin quest for the church's visible unity. This likewise centers on a dual theological convergence: (1) the goal of the unity we seek (conciliar eucharistic fellowship), and (2) the norm of the truth we profess (tradition of the gospel).[4]

The earliest method used in the modern ecumenical movement was that of comparative ecclesiology. Both the divisive and the unifying points of doctrine were carefully identified. By the time of the Faith and Order Commission meeting in Lund (1952), this comparative approach had reached an unproductive dead end. It was therefore replaced by a new "christological method," according to which the qualitative unity of the church is based on the indivisibility of Jesus Christ himself. The churches are called to make this given unity in Christ visible in history. The closer the churches come to Christ, the closer they will also come to each other in Christ. The commission at Lund concluded:

The nature of the unity towards which we are striving is that of a visible fellowship in which all members, acknowledging Jesus Christ as living Lord and Saviour, shall recognize each other as belonging fully to his body, to the end that the world may believe. (p. 37)

The WCC General Assembly in Evanston (1954) further deepened this christological approach by emphasizing eschatology:

> The unity of the Church even now is a foretaste of the fulness that is to be because it already is; therefore, the Church can work tirelessly and wait patiently and expectantly for the day when God shall sum up all things in Christ . . . It is certain that the perfect unity of the Church will not be totally achieved until God sums up all things in Christ. But the New Testament affirms that this unity is already being realized within the present historical order . . . In the upheavals of the present hour, Jesus Christ is gathering his people in a true community of faith and obedience without respect for existing divisions. (pp. 84, 88)

The theological conception of unity appeared in a more concrete form at the WCC General Assembly at New Delhi (1961). The ecumenical model of "organic unity" was affirmed. According to this model, the goal of ecumenism is the "one fully committed fellowship" of all Christians "in each place." The assembly declared:

> The Church is bold in speaking of itself as the sign of the coming unity of humankind . . . This unity of man is grounded for the Christian not only in his creation by the one God in his own image, but in Jesus Christ who "for us men" became man, was crucified, and who constitutes the Church which is his body as a new community of new creatures. (pp. 17–18)

The model of organic unity in catholicity acquired an even more precise formulation at the Faith and Order meetings of Louvain (1971) and Salamanca (1973). The new ecumenical goal was referred to as the model of "conciliar fellowship." Conciliarity was the main topic of discussion at Louvain:

> By "conciliarity" we mean the coming together of Christians—locally, regionally or globally—for common prayer, counsel and decision, in the belief that the Holy Spirit can use such meetings for his own purpose of reconciling, renewing and reforming the Church by guiding it towards the fulness of truth and love. (p. 226)

According to this model, each "truly united" local church, which is an expression of organic unity attained on the local level, possesses in conciliar fellowship with other organically united local churches "the fulness of catholicity" and "the fulness of truth and love." Thus united, each local church participates in the full conciliarity of the Christian church. (For episcopally structured churches, of course, "local church" designates an episcopal diocese.)

A final goal of conciliar fellowship is to prepare the way for a "genuinely ecumenical council" that would represent and serve all Christians and all churches. It was the Uppsala Assembly that had first called the churches "to work towards the time when a genuinely universal council may once more speak for all Christians and lead the way to the future" (p. 17). It has been almost twelve hundred years since the convening of the last of the first seven great councils of the early church (Second Nicaea, A.D. 787). This council is generally acknowledged in both East and West to be not merely regional but authentically "ecumenical" or "universal." The Louvain meeting went on to request the churches to question "whether their life and work are helping to prepare the way for such a 'genuinely ecumenical council'" (p. 228).

After extended debate, the WCC Nairobi Assembly (1975) ratified this decade-long theological development by adopting the following statement as a comprehensive description of the unity to be realized in the ecumenical movement:

> The one Church is to be envisioned as a conciliar fellowship of local churches which are themselves truly united. In this conciliar fellowship each local church possesses, in communion with the others, the fulness of catholicity, witnesses to the same apostolic faith, and therefore recognizes the others as belonging to the same church of Christ and guided by the same Spirit. They are bound together because they have received the same doctrine, and share in the same eucharist; they recognize each other's members and ministries. They are one in their common commitment to confess the gospel of Christ by proclamation and service to the world. To this end, each church aims at maintaining sustained and sustaining relationships with her sister churches in conciliar gatherings whenever required for the fulfilment of their common calling. (p. 60)

Other decisions made at the Nairobi Assembly are also relevant in this context. A new constitution was adopted that states the functions and purposes for which the World Council of Churches exists. The formulation concerning the unity of the church reads as follows: "To call the churches to the goal of visible unity in one faith and in one eucharistic fellowship expressed in worship and in common life in Christ and to advance towards that unity in order that the world may believe" (p. 295). Nairobi went on to clarify that "conciliar fellowship":

> [It] does *not* look towards a conception of unity different from that full organic unity sketched in the New Delhi Statement, but is rather a further elaboration of it. The term is intended to describe an aspect of the life of the one undivided Church *at all levels*. In the first place, it expresses the unity of churches separated by distance, culture, and time, a unity which is publicly manifested when the representatives of these local churches gather together for

a common meeting. It also refers to a quality of life within each local church; it underlines the fact that true unity is not monolithic, does not override the special gifts given to each member and to each local church, but rather cherishes and protects them. (p. 60)

Finally, the Bangalore meeting (1978) of the Faith and Order Commission was able to enumerate in their report three essential elements of the conciliar fellowship of a reunited church: "There was broad agreement that, in order to reach visible unity, three fundamental requirements must be met. The churches must reach (a) common understanding of the apostolic faith; (b) full mutual recognition of baptism, the eucharist and the ministry; (c) agreement on common ways of teaching and decision-making" (p. 40).

A major climax was then reached at the Faith and Order Commission meeting in Lima (1982) when over one hundred theologians—Roman Catholic, Eastern and Oriental Orthodox, Anglican, and Protestant—unanimously voted to transmit to the churches a convergence document, which later appeared as *Baptism, Eucharist and Ministry,* for the churches' official responses. After a half century of research and collaboration, that action marked an ecumenical milestone toward meeting one of the three cited criteria for the calling of a truly universal council.[5]

Highly significant for the "evangelical catholic" self-understanding of Lutheran Christians is the reassuring realization that it has been ecumenically possible to affirm together (as faithful expressions of the church's *sensus fidelium* and as potential bases for the churches' *communio in sacris*): (1) the sacraments as living and effective signs of God's saving grace; (2) infant/ believers' baptismal regeneration and unrepeatable incorporation into the body of Christ; (3) the eucharistic real presence, sacrifice of praise, actualized memorial (*anamnesis*), Spirit-invoked (*epiclesis*), communion (*koinonia*) and normative weekly celebration in Christ; and (4) the apostolic tradition, episcopal-presbyteral succession in the church's order and faith, the threefold ministry of bishop, presbyter, and deacon as the fulsome sign (*plene esse*) of the church's visible unity and continuity, and the universal priesthood of all its baptized members in the church's inclusive mission to the world. There is here not a single word incompatible with the Augsburg Confession, whatever may be the denominational deviations of our present pietistic practices.

The churches are now moving into a period of official study and evaluation ("reception") of the convergences achieved in the complementary bilateral and multilateral dialogues in which they have been involved. The decisive question is whether they can discern in this text, "the faith of the Church throughout the ages." In this regard, the Faith and Order World Conference in Montreal (1963) is commonly recognized as having effected a decisive breakthrough concerning both our self-understanding as Christian traditions and the clarification of the normative criterion for evaluating the apostolic integrity and mutual recognition of each other's ministers and ministries.

> Our starting-point is that we are all living in a tradition which goes back to our Lord and has its roots in the Old Testament, and are all indebted to that tradition inasmuch as we have received the revealed truth, the Gospel, through its being transmitted from one generation to another. Thus we can say that we exist as Christians by the Tradition of the Gospel (the *paradosis* of the *kerygma*) testified in Scripture, transmitted in and by the Church through the power of the Holy Spirit. Tradition taken in this sense is actualized in the preaching of the Word, in the administration of sacraments and worship, in Christian teaching and theology, and in mission and witness to Christ by the lives of the members of the Church. (p. 45)

> But this Tradition which is the work of the Holy Spirit is embodied in traditions (in the two senses of the word, both as referring to diversity in forms of expression, and in the sense of separate communions). The traditions in Christian history are distinct from, and yet connected with, the Tradition. They are the expressions and manifestations in diverse historical forms of the one truth and reality which is Christ. (p. 47)

AUGSBURG CONFESSION:
EVANGELICAL CATHOLIC IDENTITY

In 1980, Lutheran Christians throughout the world engaged in celebrating the 450th anniversary of the Augsburg Confession. For the first time, they had the benefit of viewing themselves and their chief confessional document in the light of the recent ecumenical developments outlined above. For some decades they had been engaged in intensive bilateral theological dialogues with other Christian communions.[6] The common finding: Lutheran Christians, despite their ecclesiastical identification as Protestants, nevertheless define their ecclesiological identity as "evangelical catholics"; that is, as a confessing and confessional communion within the church catholic.

CATHOLIC INTENT

Perhaps the most dramatic reaffirmation of this reality was the series of joint affirmations made successively by the Lutheran–Roman Catholic theological teams on both the U.S. national and Lutheran World Federation (LWF) international levels. For example, bishops and theologians of the international Roman Catholic–Lutheran Joint Commission issued a statement entitled *All Under One Christ*[7] in which they declared together:

> The express purpose of the Augsburg Confession is to bear witness to the faith of the one, holy, catholic and apostolic Church. Its concern is not with peculiar

doctrines nor indeed with the establishment of a new Church (CA VII, 1), but with the preservation and renewal of the Christian faith in its purity—in harmony with the ancient church, and "the church of Rome," and in agreement with the witness of Holy Scripture (CA, XXI). This explicit intention of the Confessio Augustana is also still important for our understanding of the later Lutheran confessional documents. (p. 32)

Joint studies by Catholic and Lutheran theologians have shown that the contents of these statements of the Augsburg Confession in large measure fulfil this intention and to this extent can be regarded as an expression of the common faith . . . Against the background of study and research, we are able to appeal to the Augsburg Confession when we say: Together we confess the faith in the Triune God and the saving work of God through Jesus Christ in the Holy Spirit, which binds all Christendom together (CA I and III). Through all the disputes and differences of the 16th century, Lutheran and Catholic Christians remain one in this central and most important truth of the Christian faith. (p. 32)

A broad consensus emerges in the doctrine of justification, which was decisively important for the Reformation (CA IV): it is solely by grace and by faith in Christ's saving work and not because of any merit in us that we are accepted by God and receive the Holy Spirit who renews our hearts and equips us for and calls us to good works (CA IV, VI, XX). (p. 32)

Together we testify that the salvation accomplished by Christ in his death and resurrection is bestowed on and effectively appropriated by humanity in the proclamation of the Gospel and in the holy sacraments through the Holy Spirit (CA V). (p. 33)

A basic if still incomplete accord is also registered today even in our understanding of the Church, where there were serious controversies between us in the past. By church we mean the communion of those whom God gathers together through Christ in the Holy Spirit, by the proclamation of the Gospel and the administration of the sacraments, and the ministry instituted by him for this purpose. Though it always includes sinners, yet in virtue of the promise and fidelity of God it is the one, holy, catholic and apostolic Church which is to continue forever (CA VII and VIII). (p. 33)

Reflecting on the Augsburg Confession, therefore, Catholics and Lutherans have discovered that they have a common mind on basic doctrinal truths which point to Jesus Christ, the living centre of our faith. (p. 33)

As far as the question of the episcopal office is concerned, here again it has to be noted that, in accord with the historic Church, the Confessio Augustana specifically affirms its desire to maintain the episcopal structure. The assumption here was that the true proclamation of the Gospel is helped and not hindered by this office. The Confessio Augustana affirms a ministry of unity and leadership set over the local ministers (CA XXVIII) as essential for the church, therefore, even if the actual form to be given to this ministerial office remains open. (p. 34)

This basic consensus also comes out and is confirmed by the documents of the official Roman Catholic/Lutheran dialogue today: the joint statements on the relation between Gospel and Church; a broad common understanding of the eucharist; the agreement that a special ministerial office conferred by ordination is constitutive for the Church and does not belong to those elements which the Augsburg Confession denotes as "not necessary" (CA VII, 3). (p. 33)

The theologians go on to add, "Honesty in our dialogue on the Augsburg Confession also compels us to admit that there are still open questions and unresolved problems" (p. 34). These obstruct the path toward a full ecclesial communion between Roman Catholics and Lutherans. However, the "newly discovered agreement in central Christian truths gives good ground for the hope that in the light of this basic consensus, answers will also be forthcoming to the still unsettled questions and problems" (p. 36) so that ecclesial communion between the Roman Catholic and Lutheran Christians will result and that a "common witness" in the world will be possible.

As a major step toward the realization of this goal, the Roman Catholic–Lutheran joint theological team in the U.S. recommended in 1970 that both bodies take the momentous ecumenical step of mutually recognizing the validity of each other's ministers and ministries:[8]

We believe that the unity which is both God's will and his gift to his church is being made visible as all in each place who are baptized into Jesus Christ and confess him as Lord and Saviour are brought by the Holy Spirit into one fully committed fellowship holding the one apostolic faith, preaching the one gospel, breaking the one bread, joining in common prayer, and having a corporate life reaching out in witness and service to all, and who at the same time are united with the whole Christian fellowship in all places and all ages in such ways that ministry and members are accepted by all, and that all can act and speak together as occasion requires for the tasks to which God calls his people.

The WCC General Assembly at Uppsala (1968) further developed the model of organic unity with the addition of the concept of "catholicity." The assembly report stated:

The purpose of Christ is to bring people of all times, of all races, of all places, of all conditions, into an organic and living unity in Christ by the Holy Spirit under the universal fatherhood of God. This unity is not solely external; it has a deeper, internal dimension, which is also expressed by the term "catholicity" . . . The Church is constantly on the way to becoming catholic. Catholicity is a task yet to be fulfilled. (pp. 13, 78)

The concept of "catholicity" also highlighted a further kind of ecumenical approach: the realization of catholicity also reaches out to the world, aiming at nothing less than the unity of all of God's creation in humankind. One of the major documents of the Second Vatican Council

("The Dogmatic Constitution on the Church," *Lumen Gentium,* 1964) had declared in its opening section: "By her relationship with Christ, the Church is a kind of sacrament or sign of intimate union with God, and of the unity of all humankind. She is also the instrument for the achievement of such union and unity" (p. 1). In positive reaction to this text's Christocentric and pastoral orientation, the conference at Uppsala chose to speak in similar—though sacramentally more guarded—tones:

> As Lutherans, we joyfully witness that in our theological dialogue with our Roman Catholic partners we have again seen clearly a fidelity to the proclamation of the Gospel and the administration of the sacraments which confirms our historic conviction that the Roman Catholic church is an authentic church of our Lord Jesus Christ. For this reason we recommend to those who have appointed us that through appropriate channels the participating Lutheran churches be urged to declare formally their judgment that the ordained Ministers of the Roman Catholic church are engaged in a valid Ministry of the Gospel, announcing the Gospel of Christ and administering the sacraments of faith as their chief responsibilities, and that the body and blood of our Lord Jesus Christ are truly present in their celebrations of the sacrament of the altar. (p. 22)

> As Roman Catholic theologians, we acknowledge in the spirit of Vatican II that the Lutheran communities with which we have been in dialogue are truly Christian churches, possessing the elements of holiness and truth that mark them as organs of grace and salvation. Furthermore, in our study we have found serious defects in the arguments customarily used against the validity of the eucharistic Ministry of the Lutheran churches. In fact, we see no persuasive reason to deny the possibility of the Roman Catholic church recognizing the validity of this Ministry. Accordingly we ask the authorities of the Roman Catholic church whether the ecumenical urgency flowing from Christ's will for unity may not dictate that the Roman Catholic church recognize the validity of the Lutheran Ministry and, correspondingly, the presence of the body and blood of Christ in the eucharistic celebrations of the Lutheran churches. (p. 32)

These joint affirmations endorse both the catholic intent and the evangelical content of the Augsburg Confession. Major credit is due to the developing art of confessional hermeneutics, whereby methods and techniques developed for analyzing authoritative scriptural texts are now also applied to the Confession.[9] So, for example, we should not forget that the Augsburg Confession was originally written and presented for purposes far different than those for which it is now read and subscribed to.

Regarding its literary production, we know that the final and the longest article, "The Power of the Bishops" (XXVIII), was written by Melanchthon not last but first. The chief concern was to appeal to the Roman bishops to cease using temporal power, especially against practical church reforms that were instituted in Lutheran territories. Then Melanchthon composed the remaining six articles of Part Two to show that these reforms were really necessary. Finally, the twenty-one doctrinal articles of Part One were added in order to ground these pastoral reforms in the evangelical faith of the Scriptures and tradition of the church. In addition, it also became imperative for the reformers to demonstrate their doctrinal orthodoxy at Augsburg after John Eck published 404 articles which enumerated 380 allegedly heretical affirmations taken from the writings of the reformers, to which he responded with twenty-four theses of his own. It became immediately necessary, therefore, that the originally intended "apology" for the correcting of abuses become more formally a "confession of faith."

It was only after the Diet failed that the Reformation churches suddenly had to acquire a legal right to exist in the Roman Empire. Then what had been intentionally written by Melanchthon as a "programmatic and practically variable *apologia*" was unexpectedly transformed—by official civil recognition—into "a legally binding constitutional document."[10]

Therefore the confessors at Augsburg never intended to write a "Protestant" Magna Charta, to say nothing of a "Teutonic" Declaration of Independence. Theirs was rather a biblically based, patristically reinforced testimony of faith, a confession which condemns what they considered to be the "sectarian innovations" of late medieval Roman scholasticism. That is why Rome was never charged with being "sub-Christian" but always as being "super-Christian." It was never the "traditional Catholic consensus" but the additional nominalistic novelties (for example, Gabriel Biel) that were so roundly condemned. "Rome in 1530 is no longer catholic enough!" charged the evangelical catholics at Augsburg.

Hence, the Augsburg Confession should be read as certainly presenting the heart, but not the whole, of the Christian faith. With 2 percent exposed and 98 percent presupposed, it normatively proclaims only the evangelical tip of a catholic iceberg. The Reformation was fought by biblical theologians who believed that they were not starting a sect, but fighting one. It was precisely the "Roman-izing" of Catholicism against which the reformers protested. They did so in the name of the faith of the church catholic "delivered once-for-all to the saints of God" in the tradition of the gospel (*paradosis* of the *kerygma*). Yet it was done at great cost. Jaroslav Pelikan writes:

> The tragedy of the Reformation consists in the loss by both sides of some of
> the very things each claimed to be defending against the other; its final out-

come was not what either Rome or the Reformers had wanted. Yet the necessity of a Reformation consists in the loyalty of the Reformers to the best and highest in Roman Catholic Christianity and their obligation to summon Rome back to it. Partisans on both sides have difficulty acknowledging that the Reformation was indeed a tragic necessity. Roman Catholics will agree that it was tragic, because it separated many millions from the true Church; but they cannot see that it was really necessary. Protestants agree that it was necessary, because the Roman Church was so corrupt; but they cannot see that it was such a great tragedy after all.[11]

In evangelical fidelity and catholic charity, evangelical catholics view the Lutheran Reformation both as necessary and as tragic.

Evangelical Content

In Part One, Melanchthon wanted to show Emperor Charles V that the doctrine of the reformed communities was the same as that of the ancient catholic faith, and that the reformers' fundamental articles of faith were consequently unassailable. In view of our primary concern here, we shall concentrate our attention briefly on Article VII, "The Church."

It is also taught among us that one holy Christian Church will be and remain forever. This is the assembly of all believers among whom the Gospel is preached in its purity and the holy sacraments are administered according to the Gospel. For it is sufficient for the true unity of the Christian Church that the Gospel be preached in conformity with the pure understanding of it and that the sacraments be administered in accordance with the divine Word. It is not necessary for the true unity of the Christian Church that ceremonies, instituted by men, should be observed uniformly in all places. It is as Paul says in Eph. 4:4, 5, "there is one body and one Spirit, just as you were called to the one hope that belongs to your call, one Lord, one faith, one baptism."[12]

Perhaps the chief thing wrong with the inspired wording of this article is the subsequently added title, "The Church." Actually many other affirmations on "The Church" are also included: Article V on "The Ministry," Article VIII on "What the Church Is," Articles IX to XIII on baptism, the Holy Supper, confession, and repentance, Article XIV on church order, and Article XV on church usages. Articles in Part Two on the power of bishops, the mass, and the veneration of the saints also refer to the church.

Moreover, reflecting its contextual, corrective, and apologetic *Sitz im Leben* (1530), Article VII is also notoriously negligent on other critical issues that are in need of its normative guidance today. It says nothing, for example, about the church's earthly mission or eschatological goal. Indeed, it says nothing either about the church's "holiness" or "apostolicity," and even very little about its "catholicity." It purposely concentrates on only one of the church's four classical marks, namely, its "unity." Consequently the unity of the church is what Augustana VII is really all about, and by purposely concentrating on what was at the center of debate in 1530, it raised "church unity"—ecumenicity—to the level of *"status confessionis,"* making its visible manifestation an evangelical imperative.

When Article VII teaches "that one holy Christian Church is to continue forever" *(quod una sancta ecclesia perpetuo)*, this is by no means to be understood as though the unity of the church is a future goal or a task to be fulfilled. On the contrary, unity is part of the essence of the church. Either the church is the one church of Christ or it is not the church. On the other hand, the *una sancta* is not an otherworldly, transcendent possibility; it is a reality here upon this earth. "We are not dreaming of a Platonic republic [an imaginary church, which is to be found nowhere] . . . but we teach that this church exists [is and abides truly upon earth]" (Apology of the Augsburg Confession VII, 20).[13]

Nor does the unity of church upon this earth exist only, as it were, in the perpendicular, that is, in the ever-new acts of the one Christ and the one Holy Spirit through the gospel and the sacraments. On the contrary, the unity of the church is always at the same time the communion with one another of persons with whom God is dealing through Word and Sacrament. The very definition of the church as the "assembly of all believers" points to this. True as it is that the gospel is preached in the local congregation of believers, nevertheless Article VII immediately looks beyond the largeness or smallness of the local congregation to the whole of Christendom on earth.

The Augsburg Confession speaks not only of the *church* but also of *churches* (I, 1; II, 1; III, 1; etc.). Just as Christendom on earth is the church of Jesus Christ, so the Christian congregation in a particular place is also the church of Jesus Christ. The definition in Article VII does not deny the latter, but at the very outset it puts a check upon any separatistic idea of the church that would isolate the individual congregation (to say nothing of affirming any so-called congregational autonomy).

The word "agree" *(consentire)* in the next sentence of Article VII also points to this idea of unity. The *una sancta* consists not only in the reception of grace by isolated individuals, but also in the consensus of hearing and preaching the gospel and of receiving and administering the sacraments. The unity of the church is grounded in this *consensus de doctrina evangelii*, agreement concerning the doctrine of the gospel. And according to Augustana, this consensus is always twofold, namely, consensus with contemporary, living sisters and brothers and with all other Christians in times past. Moreover, the unity of the church must signify full pulpit and altar fellowship of all believers on earth.

However, it is not essential to the unity of the church "that human traditions, rites, or ceremonies instituted by men should be alike everywhere." The terms "rites," "traditions," and "ceremonies" must not be understood in too narrow a sense here. They include not only definite festivals and festival seasons, but everything in the order of the church that the believers, in the liberty of their faith, introduce and take over from the past, whether in the liturgy or in the order of the ministry.

Hence the idea of the church in the Augsburg Confession contains no canonical prescriptions concerning the form of church organization. At the same time, however, it needs to be strongly emphasized among American Lutherans today that while the forms of church organization are subject to human determination (*adiaphora*), the office of the ministry is not. Article V has already affirmed that "God instituted the office of the ministry" in providing the gospel and the sacraments as constitutive elements of the church. The ministry is developed in Article V in relation to the all-important and governing Article IV on "Justification" and before Article VII on "The Church." The church is the creature of the gospel, and the gospel ministry is "of God" and "to the Church," independent of it and prior to it. Ministers, as such, are not mentioned in Article V because the episcopal succession was everywhere presupposed and nowhere denied in 1530, some five years before the new Lutheran church first had to face the issue of nonepiscopal ordination. The anticonfessional view that the ordained minister is merely a functional concentration of the transferred rights of the universal priesthood of baptized believers (*Übertragungslehre*) was initiated on German Lutheran soil only two centuries later by a jurist named Justus Henning Boehmer (d. 1749).[14]

In this paradoxical bondage to and freedom in the gospel, the church of the Augsburg Confession—despite its seemingly particularistic name of "Lutheran," which is not once found in its confessions—is at the center of all the Christian communions. Its way leads on, between the danger of scrupulous, self-imposed isolation and the danger of irresponsible dissolution to face the day of the Lord.

LUTHERAN CHRISTIANS:
AMERICAN PROTESTANT IDENTIFICATION

We are now in a better position to answer the basic question with which we began: Given that we acknowledge the provisional character of the Lutheran institutions on the way to the goal of a visible embodiment of the *una sancta*, what are the theological reasons for continuing to institutionalize Lutheran identity in America?

We are compelled to admit that neither the New Testament nor the Augsburg Confession addresses the inconceivable situation of intraconfessional church mergers. Among churches that are themselves in schismatic separation from other churches, ALC, AELC, and LCA would all be alphabetical anomalies to the prophets, apostles, and reformers alike. Moreover, if we distinguish properly between theology and doctrine—between our personal views and the church's official teaching—then there are also no valid doctrinal grounds for justifying either the sacramental or institutional separation of any evangelical catholics who proclaim and practice the doctrine of the gospel in the Augsburg Confession.

Yet we know that a lot of water has gone over the dam since June 1530. None of us has remained the same. Probably this is why there has been so little official reception to date of the resultant convergences in the dialogues among the churches' theologians. With no time to analyze any of the contents, let us simply recall the symbolically significant dates of 1545, 1580, 1870, 1950, 1962, and (God willing!) 1982. These events together support the cautious conclusion that "back to Rome" has now largely been mutually repudiated in favor of "on to 'Jerusalem.'" The churches are slowly but surely "growing together in baptism, eucharist, and ministry" in order to bring into realization that unity for which our Lord himself prayed, "that they may all be one . . . that the world may believe" (John 17:21).

In the meantime, a merged Lutheran church in North America—and eventually the Lutheran Church–Missouri Synod will certainly become an integral part of it—will best be able to serve as the servant church of a servant Lord if intentionally its "structure follows function." What might this mean?

FUNCTION

With regard to function, I have been arguing implicitly that the ecumenical future is likely to be found in a restoration and reactivation of the church's evangelical catholicity. This will be distinguished by (1) an "inclusive mission" of salvation and liberation, and (2) the "visible unity" of a eucharistic and conciliar fellowship that is bound together by the authority of the tradition of the gospel.

If this is so, it means that we should actively engage in our own internal renewal and, in so doing, support any and all Lutheran church mergers as intraconfessional "dress rehearsals" for the real interconfessional ecumenical performances ahead. Of course, the danger is always latent that any such intraconfessional ventures will only reinforce sectarian isolationism. (Lutheran chauvinists in the past have often sung "A mighty fortress is our God" while wallowing behind walls as if "a mighty God is our fortress!") Hopefully, however, we have demonstrated that this is because some of our parents in the faith were themselves not confessional enough in professing and practicing the kind of evangelical catholicity inherent in the Augsburg Confession.

STRUCTURE

With regard to "structure," I have also been implicitly arguing for the reformation, restoration, and reactivation among American Lutheran Christians of the historic episcopate. "As it works out," say Gritsch and Jenson, "Lutheran theology calls for a mode of government in the church much like the pastoral episcopacy of the most ancient Church, or indeed of a small Anglican or Roman Catholic missionary diocese today."[15] Such a confessionally permissible and ecumenically responsible move would provide in an incomparable way (1) another sign, though not a guarantee, of the continuity and unity of the church catholic among us; as well as (2) another sign, though not a guarantee, of the kerygmatic-eucharistic community which both constitutes and empowers the inclusive mission of the church's baptized priests in and for the world today.

That organic structure of a pastoral episcopacy might then, in turn, be institutionally reinforced by the kind of frugal and modest "tenting" that is most appropriate for the pilgrim people of God in an age of unprecedented human misery and suffering: (1) eschatologically, it would witness dramatically that "here we have no lasting city" as we both worship and emulate the Word-made-flesh who also "tabernacled" or "tented" among us (Heb. 9:14; John 1:14); (2) ecclesiologically, it would signal in different ways to Christian friends from St. Louis to Canterbury, and from Geneva through Rome to Constantinople that we are not digging in our denominational heels, but rather affirming that our real ecumenical witness, renewed by the power of the Spirit, is yet to come; (3) ecclesiastically, it would immediately astound and perhaps inspire some of those jaundiced cynics who now fear that the Commission for a New Lutheran Church is capable only of repainting the three sets of differently colored deck chairs on a sinking "Titanic" by accepting a challenge that is at once as old as the Seventh Ecumenical Council and as new as the envisioned Eighth.

Finally, you sense that I have purposely not said too much about our "American Protestant identification." At least I can plead some good company:

I ask that men make no reference to my name; let them call themselves Christians, not Lutherans. What is Luther? After all the teaching is not mine. Neither was I crucified for anyone. St. Paul, in 1 Corinthians 3, would not allow the Christians to call themselves Pauline, or Petrine, but Christian. How then could I—poor stinking maggot-fodder that I am—come to have men call the children of Christ by my wretched name? Not so, my dear friends, let us abolish all party names and call ourselves Christians, after him whose teaching we hold.[16]

In this same ecumenical spirit, we join the "obedient rebel," Martin Luther, in offering his 1522 prayer for Christian unity:

O, Eternal and merciful Father! Thou art the God of peace and love and of unity, not of division; yet since the people of Thy Church have abandoned Thee and turned away from the Truth, Thou hast allowed them to be divided and separated, in order that, falling in their pretended wisdom into the shame of disunity, they might return to Thee who dost cherish unity.

We poor sinners pray to Thee, that Thou mayest be pleased by Thy Holy Spirit to gather together what has been dispersed and to unite in one body what has been divided. Grant also that we may be so converted to Thy unity as to seek Thy one eternal Truth and turn from all division, that we may have one spirit, mind and will. And give us to be so governed by our Lord Jesus Christ, that we may be enabled, O heavenly Father, to worship and adore Thee with one voice through our Lord Jesus Christ in the Holy Spirit. Amen.[17]

NOTES

1. Cf. Leslie Newbigin, "Which Way for Faith and Order?" in *What Unity Implies,* ed. Reinhard Groscurth (Geneva: WCC, 1969), pp. 115–32.

2. Cf. Nikos A. Nissiotis, "The Pneumatological Aspect of the Catholicity of the Church," in Groscurth, *What Unity Implies,* pp. 9–33.

3. Cf. Survey: James A. Scherer, . . . *that the Gospel may be sincerely preached throughout the world; a Lutheran Perspective on Mission and Evangelism in the 20th Century* (Geneva: LWF Report 11/12, 1982), pp. 55–183. Reports: *Minutes, Executive Committee,* WCC (Geneva: WCC, 1951); *Bangkok Assembly 1973; Minutes and Report* (Geneva: WCC, 1974); *Your Kingdom Come: Mission Perspectives.* Report on the World Conference on Mission and Evangelism, Melbourne, Australia (Geneva: WCC, 1980); *Minutes, Executive Committee,* WCC (Geneva: WCC, 1982); and "Mission and Evangelism—An Ecumenical Affirmation," in *International Review of Mission* (Geneva: WCC, 1982).

4. Surveys: Miika Ruokannen, *Hermeneutics as an Ecumenical Method* (Helsinki: Luther-Agricola Society, 1982), pp. 9–20; Choan-Seng Song, ed., *Growing Together into Unity* (Madras: Christian Literature Society, 1978); Lukas Vischer, ed., *A Documentary History of the Faith and Order Movement, 1927–1963* (St. Louis: Bethany, 1963). Reports: (A) Faith and Order Commission. *The Third World Conference on Faith and Order, Lund, 1952*

(London, 1953); *The Fourth World Conference on Faith and Order, Montreal, 1963* (New York, 1964); *Faith and Order, Louvain, 1971* (Geneva: WCC, 1971); *The Unity of the Church—next Steps, Salamanca, 1973* (Geneva: *Ecumenical Review,* 1974); *Faith and Order, Minutes, Bangalore, 1978* (Geneva: WCC, 1979). Reports: (B) WCC Assemblies. *The Second Assembly, Evanston Report, 1954* (London, 1955); *The Third Assembly, New Delhi Report, 1961* (New York, 1962); *The Fourth Assembly, Uppsala Report, 1968* (Geneva: WCC, 1968); *The Fifth Assembly, Nairobi Report, 1975* (London, 1976). Reports: (C) Other. *The Documents of Vatican II* (New York, 1966).

5. *Baptism, Eucharist and Ministry* (Geneva: WCC, 1982).

6. Survey: (A) International. Nils Ehrenstroem and Guenther Gassman, *Confessions in Dialogue. A Survey of Bilateral Conversations among World Confessional Families, 1959–1974* (Geneva: WCC, 1975); Lutheran/Roman Catholic Joint Commission, *The Eucharist* (Geneva: LWF, 1980); Lutheran/Roman Catholic Joint Commission, *The Ministry in the Church* (Geneva: LWF, 1982). Survey: (B) National. *Lutherans in Ecumenical Dialogue: An Interpretive Guide* (New York: Lutheran Council in the USA, 1977).

7. "All Under One Christ," in *Ways to Community,* Lutheran/Roman Catholic Joint Commission (Geneva: LWF, 1981).

8. *Eucharist and Ministry,* in Lutherans and Catholics in Dialogue IV (New York: U.S.A. National Committee of the Lutheran World Federation and the Bishops' Committee for Ecumenical and Interreligious Affairs, 1970).

9. Cf. Edmund Schlink, "The Breadth of the Church of the Augsburg Confession," in *The Lutheran World Review* (Philadelphia, 1949), pp. 1–18. Commentaries: Edmund Schlink, *Theology of the Lutheran Confessions* (Philadelphia: Fortress Press, 1975); Holsten Fagerberg, *A New Look at the Lutheran Confessions (1529–1537)* (St. Louis: Concordia Publishing House, 1972); Eric W. Gritsch and Robert W. Jenson, *Lutheranism: The Theological Movement and Its Confessional Writings* (Philadelphia: Fortress Press, 1976); Joseph A. Burgess, ed., *The Role of the Augsburg Confession: Catholic and Lutheran Views* (Philadelphia: Fortress Press, 1980); George W. Forell and James F. McCue, eds., *Confessing One Faith: A Joint Commentary on the Augsburg Confession by Lutheran and Catholic Theologians* (Minneapolis: Augsburg Publishing House, 1982); Gerhard O. Forde, *Justification by Faith —A Matter of Death and Life* (Philadelphia: Fortress Press, 1982); Werner Elert, *The Structure of Lutheranism* (St. Louis: Concordia Publishing House, 1962); Vilmos Vajta and Hans Weissgerber, eds., *The Church and the Confessions* (Philadelphia: Fortress Press, 1963); Harding Meyer, ed., *The Augsburg Confession in Ecumenical Perspective* (Geneva: LWF Report 6/7, 1979), and an unpublished address, "The Augsburg Confession as a Catholic and Lutheran Confession of Faith: A Way towards Unity?" (Rome: Centro pro Unione, 1980); Wilhelm Maurer, *Historischer Kommentar zur Confessio Augustana.* 2 vols. (Gütersloh: Mohn, 1976, 1978); H. Fries, et al., *Confessio Augustana: Hindernis oder Hilfe?* (Regensburg: Pustet, 1979); Eugene L. Brand, *1980: Lutheran-Roman Catholic Kairos?* (Columbus, Ohio: Seminary Bulletin, 1978).

10. Hans Dombois, *Vorträge auf den Michaelskonferenzen der Kirchlichen Sammlung* (1978), p. 69.

11. Jaroslav Pelikan, *The Riddle of Roman Catholicism* (New York: Abingdon Press, 1959), p. 46.

12. *The Book of Concord,* ed. and trans. Theodore G. Tappert (Philadelphia: Fortress Press, 1959), p. 32.

13. Ibid., p. 171.

14. Cf. Schlink, *Theology of the Lutheran Confessions,* p. 244. The alleged "locus classicus" for this view in the confessions is Apology XV, 20, where, however, the reference is to "rites and seasons" and not to the institution of the ordained ministry.

15. Gritsch and Jenson, *Lutheranism,* p. 205.

16. *The Christian in Society,* vol. 45 of *Luther's Works,* ed. Walther I. Brandt (Philadelphia: Fortress Press, 1962), pp. 70–71.

17. Weimar Edition of Luther's Works, 10 II, pp. 477–78. Cf. Jaroslav Pelikan, *Obedient Rebels: Catholic Substance and Protestant Principle in Luther's Reformation* (New York: Harper & Row, 1964).

2
Sovereignty in the Church

ROBERT W. JENSON

THE QUESTION OF SOVEREIGNTY

It is not usual in Protestantism to speak of "sovereignty" in the church, except perhaps in attributing sovereignty exclusively to Christ. But the concept may nevertheless be essential; it may even be that our disuse of it is an important cause of our confusions about the church. The concept of sovereignty is the central concept of political theory. And not only is the church in fact a polity, it should be the most political of polities. My first task is to explain that.

Every community has a political reality; that, indeed, is the difference between a community and a mere collective. A community's politics are simply all its actions of deliberating and choosing its own future, of willing what sort of community it is to be. What shall we teach our children? What acts shall count as crimes, as breaches of the community, and how shall these be dealt with? By what principles shall our resources be allocated? Such are the questions a community must face, to remain a community. Just so, they are precisely *ethical* questions; so that we may further say that a community's politics are the process of its communal ethics, of its communal concern for the good. Then a community's polity is all its arrangements for the action of such concern, for communal deliberation of the good.

There is a possible confusion that must at this point be averted. In the recent history of America we have become accustomed to a very different use of the word "politics." We have become so accustomed that the chief decisions about our common future are in fact made by processes of the mere accommodation of interests, with little or no deliberation of what *should* be done. Thus we regularly use "politics" only for this particular—and really

39

privative—mode of politics. But the original and only useful acceptation of the word is the broader and positive use I have just stipulated, and it is in this sense that I will here use it.

The church is a political body because it must deliberate and choose by what rules and standards it will try to live, and because it has arrangements for this deliberation. Indeed, the mandate of political existence lies more peremptorily on the church than on other communities. The eschatological direction of the church means that the church is indeed always to be reformed, that the church is faithless if it ever supposes that the rules and penultimate values by which it at any time lives need not be reconsidered. Other communities can, if they wisely or unwisely so choose, survive at rest in their status quo, at least for a time; the church cannot. The church must always ask: What should we do in future? When it does not ask this question, it is faithless to the coming kingdom, and the Lord's historical judgments will then compel the church to the communal ethical deliberation it has not undertaken willingly. When we too long fear our political task, we will be driven to it.

The church lives in and by asking: What shall we teach our neophytes? our clergy? our leaders? What sins must count as crimes against the community of faith, and how should these be dealt with? What sides shall the church take in the larger community's struggle about abortion or nuclear armament? Whom shall we ordain? So also, it belongs to the essence of the church that it have *some* polity, some arrangements for arguing such questions.

Therefore when a segment of the church intends new organization, as the American Lutheran Church (ALC), Lutheran Church in America (LCA), and the Association of Evangelical Lutheran Churches (AELC) now do, the peremptory question that must guide their labors is the question about right polity: In the envisaged future time and place, what provisions for communal ethical deliberation will best serve justice and especially the church's particular mission? We should also note that deliberation of the right polity is itself an instance of politics; there is no start here from an apolitical scratch. This symposium is itself an avowedly political act and a good case of what must be arranged for the church.

For years, voices have been heard in American Lutheranism pleading that this time the unification process should be informed by antecedent theological reflection. No doubt a variety of hopes have thereby been expressed, but surely chief among them is hope that this time there should be decisive reflection on right polity. And the negative suggestion of such pleas is true: In the recent past American Lutheranism has altogether too much lacked such reflection. There is a reason for this lack, and disposing of it must be my last preliminary task.

It is one of the few well-remembered items of the Lutheran theological heritage that polity is an "adiaphoron," a debatable variable in the life of the church. There is, we always insist, no such thing as one theologically mandated right polity for the church. And so far, our memory of the heritage is correct. But we have drawn a conclusion from the doctrine of "adiaphora" that is the precise opposite of the doctrine's intention. From polity's character as an adiaphoron, we have deduced that polity is theologically neutral, and have turned the shaping of our polities over to efficiency experts and management consultants. However, the intent of the assertion that polity—as other adiaphora—is theologically debatable is, of course, that it is to be theologically debated. The adiaphora of the church's life are precisely those historical variables that, just *because* they are not laid down in Scripture for all time, are our *responsibility,* to be shaped by all the faithful thought we can bring to them. There is no theologically mandated right polity for all the church's times and places. But just so we are bidden to seek for each time and place the polity then and there most appropriate to the church's mission and being; and that sort of task is the very archetype of a theological task.

Finally I have enough preliminaries out of the way so that I can stipulate the concept of sovereignty. Sovereign in a community are those—if only a group of one—who are expected by the community to *conclude* the community's ethical deliberation of those matters which the community sees as vital—in Lutheran jargon, as having "confessional status"—and to declare the result to the rest of the community. What, in our nation, is to count as crime? Some body of the disputants must have a temporarily last word and be hearkened to for that word. Who are these persons? What, in the church, shall we teach our neophytes? At the moment, each pastor or teacher has the last word on that for his or her group, usually within limits set by the "materials" provided by "experts" at the agencies. Is that how it should be? Such are the questions about sovereignty.

In the tradition of political theory, it is by the location, nature, and conditions of sovereignty that polities are understood as differing from each other. Thus an "aristocracy" is a polity in which sovereignty is held by a self-perpetuating group, but in which the expectations directed to that group are determined by laws and customs not amendable by the group acting alone. An "oligarchy" is the same, except that the sovereign group is not thus restrained. In a "democracy" sovereignty is, somehow, possessed by the whole body of the community's full membership. Our question is: Who are to be sovereign in the church? And how and under what conditions? It is the church's claim about its common life that God's own Spirit is given to it as its communal bond. Therefore our question becomes: Whose voice under what conditions and in what tone may say, as did the fathers of Nicaea, "It seems good to the Holy Spirit and to us . . ."?

It should be noted that sovereignty and power are not the same. In most polities, the sovereign has also the power to compel obedience to the community's last word, if obedience is by some not willingly granted. But it need not be so; power may be located elsewhere or not exist at all. The sovereign instead has *authority*. The English monarch has no power, but she is sovereign so long as it is her voice that must proclaim the law. Should she someday be unable in conscience to ratify a parliamentary enactment, then it would be tested whether England was to remain a monarchy. Our question is not: Who in the church is to have the most power? Our question is: Who in the church is to have the last word?

I turn to substantive questions about sovereignty in the church. I have four. They hang together, but not so that you must agree with all my contentions to agree with any. I will therefore not present them as a system, but simply as a sequence.

THE NATURE OF CHURCHLY AUTHORITY

Sovereignty is the right to the last word. However, the church knows of and tries to speak two radically different kinds of words. The church of course speaks in all the ways the world does; but it also hears and tries to speak the *gospel*, which it understands as a final "promise," and over against which it calls all the other words "law." Therefore, by speaking words of which sort, "law" or "promise," as a last word, is sovereignty rightly constituted in the church? By gospel-insight it appears that there must be two sorts of authority: promise-authority and law-authority. Which sort characterizes churchly sovereignty? Lutherans must above all others press this question and carry its answer into practice, for they above all others have made the difference between law and gospel decisive for the church's life.

To speak law is to lay this pattern on the hearer: "If you do such-and-such, such-and-such will happen to/for you." "If you work hard, you will be promoted." "If you love God, he will love you." "If you fail to fulfill your synodical commitment, synod staff will be happy to discuss your problem." A law-word holds out a desired or feared future and makes its arrival conditional on prior action by the hearer. In this mode of discourse, authority is the capacity to lay down such conditions and make them stick.

To speak promise is so to speak as somehow to establish this pattern for the hearer: "Since I am such-and-such, you may expect such-and-such." "Since I can and will bake, your party will have a cake." Such a word commits the speaker to fulfill some conditions of the future good it holds out, and just so lifts that burden from the hearer. In this mode of discourse, authority is the capacity to be believed in such commitment. Of course no promise made by someone who will die can lift *all* the conditions of a future good from the hearer, to make him finally certain in its expectation. I promised to give this paper, but any of a hundred conditions of my mortality might have prevented me, and the committee knew that. The gospel claims to lift all conditions of future good: "Because Christ lives, you will be fulfilled." Therefore the gospel can be believed only as the word of *God*, who is past death and has all the future. Authority in the gospel mode must be the authority of the homiletical and liturgical spokesman for God, the authority of utterance that begins, "In the name of the Father, Son, and Holy Spirit. . . ."

The foregoing analysis is itself the answer to our question. The last word in the church must be the gospel and not the law, for the gospel claims to be the last of all words, and to believe the gospel is therefore to put none after it. Those who are sovereign in the church—whoever they are—must be sovereign as speakers of the gospel, as preachers, liturgists, and confessors. There must indeed be both law and gospel in the church, and both kinds of authority will be exercised in the church. But right sovereignty in the church has the authority of the gospel, and legal authority must be derived from and legitimated by proclamatory and liturgical authority.

But what does it mean, that legal authority in the church must be derivative from evangelical authority? The meaning, surely, is practical: How is this derivation to be arranged for? So the best way to proceed will be with an example.

Let us suppose that in the new church there are bishops, whether of such units as we now have or of such as I am about to propose or of units of yet another kind, and that their position is such that they have some share in sovereignty. What should their job description be? Their current job descriptions stipulate predominantly administrative and supervisory duties, however "pastorally" these are to be done. Insofar as such duties involve the exercise of authority, the authority is therefore of the legal sort; and there is nothing in itself the matter with that. It is, however, not stipulated that bishops shall regularly preach to their people, or visit congregations in turn to preside at the Supper, or lead theological discussions among their clergy. Bishops are not, that is to say, granted the gospel-sort of authority in their official capacity. Similarly, the legal authority they exercise is dubiously legitimate, even though, given the bishops we actually have, it is regularly beneficial and evangelically intended. If the bishop is to have authority over other ministers and over congregations, however "pastoral," that authority will be legitimate only if it is originally the authority of the gospel—that is, practically, if the bishop's daily chief work is preaching, liturgical leadership, and theological reflection (if he is in fact a *minister of the gospel* in the congregation). Martin Luther always insisted that bishops who will not preach can not be true bishops; that is not our bishops' case—they have no time or assignment to preach. And if the ministry of the gospel should leave the bishop with too little time for daily administration, let that mostly be done by an assistant—the Middle Ages called such a person an archdeacon—under the bishop's oversight and veto. Under any ordering, bishops of course will exercise both law-authority and gospel-authority.

The central point of this section: To whomever in the church sovereignty is to be granted, the authority they are thereby given must first be evangelical authority and only in course thereof legal authority. That is, those called to make vital decisions for the church must be—if they are, as I will next argue, a *group*—persons who gather primarily for proclamation of Scripture, Eucharist, and prayer, and whose official roles, if they have them, are primarily their roles in these acts. Then their decisions must emerge. Let them perhaps preach to one another from what they take to be appropriate texts; let them pray together about the matter in hand, let them praise God; and let them pause in these proceedings to argue their possible consensus. And when they terminate discourse and turn to speak to the rest of the church, let this too be a proclamatory and liturgical act. Let them indeed say to the church: "It seems good to the Holy Spirit and to us." And if their proceedings have not been such as to suggest such language, let them not speak.

There is of course a confusion of law and gospel, opposite to that which currently rules us and which I have just attacked. This confusion, of which some may now suspect me, could appear on such lines as I have been pursuing. I do not intend to say that the church can be ruled by the gospel; rule by the gospel is the definition of the kingdom, yet to come. Those who are sovereign and otherwise authoritative in the church must lay down the *law*. But authority and sovereignty pertain to *persons* and groups of persons, and it must be exercise of the *gospel's* kind of authority that in the church qualifies persons and groups to be in fact sovereign at all.

THE LOCATION OF SOVEREIGNTY

According to the Lutheran confessions, the church is substantially a "congregation," an actual assembly, a gathering of persons at a time and place; see, of course, the Augsburg Confession, Article VII. It is liturgical assemblies that are meant, gatherings of believers to speak the gospel to one another and to respond to the gospel with prayer and praise; as the confession says, the church is "where the gospel is rightly preached and the sacraments accordingly ministered." Business meetings, at whatever level, are another matter.

Since the church has a mission, a continuing purpose, the church is not a mere succession of discontinuous assemblings, but a continuing body that assembles. Therefore most of its actual assemblings will and should be instances in the life of continuous groups of believers: of congregations, synods, denominations, and so forth. When we think of parts of the church's polity, it is such continuing subbodies that we have most in mind. And since these bodies must care for their own continuance, they will and should meet not only to hear and answer the gospel, but also to do business, that is, to arrange for future meetings. Nevertheless, it is worth reminding ourselves from the outset, that these continuing bodies are the *church*—and so can be supposed to make the church's decisions—only insofar as they gather, gathering not only for business but first and foremost (more than decoratively or "inspirationally") around the living gospel for worship.

Assemblies and continuously assembling bodies are not the church's only political constituents. There are also and above all leaders, for continuing bodies must at the very least assign someone to care for the next meeting. There is a form of leadership, conferred by ordination, that is by ecumenical consensus and Lutheran teaching mandated not merely by the community's needs but by God. In addition, there are usually agencies, which under present conditions often develop into bureaus; and if there are bureaus, there are staffs.

There are, therefore, a welter of voices in the continuing discussion that is the church's political existence. Usually, there is also a plurality of forums in which the argument takes place. And often, to complete the complexity, some of the forums appear as voices in other forums, as when in my denomination a synod memorializes the denominational convention.

If a chart is drawn of the relations between all the entities that at a time and place make up the church's polity, or the polity of some segment of the church, the chart will always resemble a pyramid, even if a bumpy and stubby one. There is a reason for this, a reason that lies in the essence of the church and must play a large role in our reflections: the church is *catholic*; that is, in the present context, any actual assembly or any particular continually assembling body is the church only *with* all other such bodies. And, precisely because the church is in substance assembly, there will and must be assembling bodies that encompass local congregations, to incorporate their catholicity.

To whom, in this welter, should sovereignty belong? To whom should we direct our expectation of the Spirit's authority?

In that the church *is* congregation, gathering, sovereignty in it cannot rightly be claimed by leading individuals simply as such. This is generally acknowledged, and the attempt to do so is rare. Nor could sovereignty in *any* body—except perhaps a conventicle of illuminati—belong to an actual assembling simply as such, for there would be no way to know which this was to be. When some meeting suddenly says, "We speak for the whole and all must hearken," the rest of us must be able to test the claim by known standards, that is, by the definition of some continuing body of which this meeting is an instance. And of course agencies are not candidates; indeed the church has sometimes lived entirely without them.

It remains that sovereignty in the church must be vested in continuing assemblies. Since there are none such without continuing leadership, the reference must be to continuing bodies as organisms of people and leaders. And given the divinely ordained character of the ordained ministry, we must say that sovereignty is possessed by continuing assemblies insofar as the specific leadership of ordained ministry is realized in them—the specific definition of that leadership must, however, be bracketed out of this essay.

Therewith we finally arrive at the main problem: In *which* continuing assembly or assemblies should the sovereignty of the church be vested? with *which* laity and clergy? The church's essentially pyramidal shape casts the question: At what level of the gathered people and ministers should sovereignty be placed? The church's typical disagreements about the location of sovereignty are between those who want to move sovereignty's location "down" (to or toward the local congregation) and those who want to move it "up" (to or toward the pyramid's top). That is, the disagreements are between those who urge the character of the church as actual gathering—a sovereignty of the regularly gathering bodies of believers, and not of their mere leaders or representatives—and those who urge the church's catholicity—a sovereignty of bodies that merely represent the mutuality and unity of the local gatherings.

Since both congregational actuality and catholic mutuality are essential characteristics of the church, the tug between them is irresolvable so long as the two are represented only by distinct bodies. If we think of a pyramid with two levels, the urge to see sovereignty at the bottom level and the urge to see it at the top level are both irreconcilably right. Nor is anything helped by intermediate levels such as American Lutheranism now has, since the same sterile opposition appears between each pair of neighboring levels.

Therefore, sovereignty will be right in the church only when located in a continuing assembly that within itself is *both* local and representative of local congregations' catholicity.

As it happens, the church once had such a polity; it is the oldest churchly polity that we know much about. The "diocese" of the most ancient church comprised the believers of a city and its environs, too scattered a group always to assemble as one, yet small enough to do so on great occasions and for great decisions. We could as well call such a unit a "presbytery" or a "synod." No romanticism about the ancient church is needed to see the advantages of such a polity—though we should also realize that the world of the ancient church is more like the world we now inhabit than is any intervening period. Each believer belonged at once to a more local assembly and to an equally actual and liturgical congregation that embodied the catholic unity of a larger territory's believers. The "bishop" of such a diocesan—or "presbyteral" or "synodical"—congregation was its chief pastor, and *not* the pastor only of the other pastors but of all believers in the territory. In this way each believer had various pastors, some for local concerns and one for more catholic concerns, all real liturgical, homiletical, and catechetical shepherds. Thus these "dioceses" are what is needed, at once and within themselves, both locally participatory and representative of catholicity. And it was these units that were sovereign; "higher" levels of the churchly pyramid were constituted by them, and they retained the last word. The unity of the total church consisted in their concord and in mutual ordinations and consecrations.

One may, if one likes, call this polity "episcopacy"; but it must be clear that it little resembles the polity we usually think of under that label. The latter polity resulted when the ancient episcopacy's outward features were imposed on the sparsely populated mission territories of northern Europe. There dioceses were districts too geographically extensive to function as congregations, and necessarily became administrative sovereignties *over* the only actual congregations. It is not this later "episcopacy" that is here advocated. Nor do I here argue what should be the relation between people and bishop; that is the assignment of another essayist. Nor yet do I propose simply repristinating original diocesan polity, which would hardly be possible. But it should not be beyond the wit of believers to devise a fundamental churchly unit that would possess the politically decisive virtue of the ancient diocese: that it encompassed a number of local assemblies, to embody their catholicity, yet was small enough to be itself a kind of congregation. And if we had such a unit, sovereignty in the church would rightly belong only to it.

If creation of an appropriately sovereign assembling body is beyond us, then the pull of locality must be acknowledged over that of catholicity, and the local congregation acknowledged sovereign. For while catholicity is an essential predicate of the church, the church's substance is the liturgical assembly.

It is, finally, important to note what is *not* settled by the decision about where to locate sovereignty, important as that decision is. When we choose at which level of assembly to locate sovereignty, we do not, for one thing, thereby generally decide which levels there shall be. Thus if sovereignty were located as I have said it should be, we could have as many other, "higher," levels in the churchly pyramid as we judged right; we should only not assign them absolutely final authority. Nor need all deliberation of vital matters and even all authority be for all cases initially assigned to the sovereign level of assembly. Thus, for example, if the moment should come when the question of reunion with Rome had actually to be decided, surely this should initially be deliberated by a great council of all who faced the question. The question of sovereignty is that of only the *last* word.

Nor does the decision just discussed necessarily assign responsibilities and power. Thus it is already now decided by the sovereign bodies here represented that there shall in future be one national level of responsibility and power to replace three of those now existing. *What* responsibilities and power this level shall have remains to be decided, and that decision will be bound by the decision about location of sovereignty only insofar as no one in the polity may be given power to *compel* a sovereign body to retract its last word.

THE WORKING OF SOVEREIGNTY

There is to be, then, in the church, a sovereign assembly or assemblies—if not those I have proposed, then others. There may be other assemblies that share in authority, in that they are assigned initial deliberation of certain vital matters. All these assemblies must be proper assemblies of the *church*; that is, first and principally they must be assemblies around the living gospel. Our next question plainly must be: How shall such an assembly come to its decisions?

There are two possibilities that have appeared and competed through history. A group's decision may represent an average of the opinions held anyway by the individuals who make up the group. Or a group's decision may be a *new* thought created by discourse in the group—the conclusion of a common mind that does not exist except as the group argues within itself and that comes to its conclusions in much the same way as an individual mind does. The typical act of the first sort of assembly is the head count. The typical act of the second is acclamation when someone finally voices the needed new idea. With the first sort of group, it makes very little difference whether the members actually meet; they may as well be polled in their several places, so long as all somehow have opportunity to know the issues and arguments. With the second sort of group, it is precisely the meeting that is the deciding mind, and what the issues and arguments are, no one claims surely to know in advance. The one group has the democracy advocated by, for example, Rousseau; the other that once practiced, however imperfectly, by the New England towns. By which model shall we understand decision in the church's assemblies?

As it happens, this choice is one of the few that are unambiguously decided for Lutherans by their confessional position. The Reformation-era "enthusiasts" taught—as have all their like before and since—that the Spirit comes to each individual of the elect equally, privately, and in principle independently of the outward word, that is, of actual discourse among believers. The Lutheran Reformation found in this understanding a perversion worse than any at Rome, and vehemently attacked it, also in confessional writings. The Spirit, said the Lutherans, is the Spirit *of* the actual outward word, spoken by believers to each other and the world, and comes to no one independently of this discourse in and of the church. On the basis of enthusiasm, it will indeed be possible to discover the mind of faith by polling the opinions of the individual believers. But by Lutheran understanding, what could thus be discovered would be at best the mind of the religious Old Adam; the church's mind, the mind of the Spirit, is given only as the living mutual word of the gospel constitutes an actual congregation of the Spirit.

Therefore, by Lutheran understanding, the first kind of democracy is simply wrong and the second kind right, at least for the church. Whatever group is to ponder matters vital in the church, must be allowed and indeed compelled actually to *deliberate,* to think together, to track down the problem and create a solution. A mere head count, even one taken at a meeting after positions have been stated, is not the way in which sovereign decisions may be made in the church. It is also perhaps worth noting that this application of Lutheran anti-enthusiast doctrine to politics is not simply materially appropriate. Historically, a new burst of "enthusiasm" among English Puritans of the 1640s and 1650s seems to have been in fact the origin of the head count kind of democracy in the modern West.

The practical consequences of this confessional commitment are great. Chief among them is a very simple mandate: Whatever assembly is to discuss matters vital for the church must be given *time* for true deliberation. It must be given time to develop a common mind and to exercise that mind on analysis of the problem and on creative solutions and choice of solutions. With most matters of a confessionally significant sort, that kind of time will be a lot of time. To make the point concretely: at recent conventions the ALC and LCA adopted a statement of communion policies, with a few hours total debate, in which five or six theological matters were settled, of the sort to which a council of the ancient church might have devoted each some weeks of discussion.

It is, of course, plain that such conventions as we now have at all levels, doomed to continuous session and with whole books of housekeeping reports to look at, can *deliberate* nothing. The conclusion should not be that deliberation is impractical in the modern church, but that such conventions should not be asked to exercise sovereignty. Perhaps we need housekeeping conventions at various levels. But in any case the church's sovereign assemblies must be other and work otherwise. I am not to propose blueprints for a new church; but surely it again would not be beyond the wit of believers to devise opportunities of assembly that are not asked to keep house and that need not sit twelve hours a day until they adjourn. Indeed, we *must* devise them, for only to such can we faithfully assign the church's ethical deliberation, whether sovereign or more modestly authoritative.

One such method of assembly is commended by the history of the church and deserves special consideration. Probably not one of the Protestant observers at the Second Vatican Council has failed to lament his own denomination's lack of similar deliberative occasions. It has been the church's ancient recourse, when confronted by truly historic questions, to summon such gatherings of the reponsible and possibly wise, to deliberate until they could reach proposed solutions, and then to submit them for "reception"—or rejection—by the whole church. If the church had such sovereign dioceses or presbyteries as it should, "reception" would be their responsibility. The constitutions of American Lutheran bodies now make no provision for such proceedings. Should this not be remedied?

It is apparent that the argument just presented recommends a kind of democracy for the church, the kind sometimes called assembly-democracy. We should perhaps note that such democracy does not necessarily mean one person/one vote. In a living assembly that proceeds by deliberation and consensus, complicated and crisscrossing relationships of individual and group authority always appear. In the church, the institution of ordained ministry assures that it will be so. A deliberating assembly is not a polling list but an organism, of which Paul's description of manifold variation in function and authority holds. Thus if we were to have dioceses and bishops such as I have proposed, assignment of sovereignty to the assembled diocese—and not directly to the bishop—does not mean that we could not also so stipulate the role of bishops in their dioceses that they would in fact have a specific share in the assembly's authority, of a different sort than possessed by other participants. But whether we should so arrange matters, and if so, how, is beyond the scope of my assignment.

THE LIMITS OF SOVEREIGNTY

In no living community is sovereignty unlimited. For a community's self-identity through time is not merely defined as a numerical continuance of the constituent persons, but also by a memory and a purpose. "America" is not merely all Americans plus the apparatus of their governance; it is—as Lincoln put it—a "new nation" "conceived" in a particular memorable event and "dedicated" to a particular "proposition." Those sovereign in a living community decide the community's future in order to preserve the memory of a conception and to pursue a proposition. If they utterly violate this trust, what they in fact do is try to invent a new community altogether—and just so, were they to succeed, they would of course abolish the community in which they are sovereign.

The church's conception is Christ's resurrection and the outpouring of his Spirit, and the church's proposition is Christ's kingdom. This little argument is needed to determine the limits of sovereignty in the church: the church is Christ's, and all its choices must be faithful to him. Moreover, Christ is not merely a remembered founder; for his founding act was to rise from the dead and assume God's right hand from which to move the world with his Spirit. Christ lives; and it is therefore his active will for the church that is the limit of churchly sovereignty. It is this truth that Protestants have sometimes expressed by saying that only Christ is sovereign in the church.

But of course Christ does not appear to chair our meetings. And so there will be other sovereignty in the church, willy-nilly. This will be penultimate authority, limited by its calling to be faithful to Christ's—but there is no reason not to call this sovereignty, for as we have noted, sovereignty in *all* communities is somehow analogously limited. How then does Christ's limiting authority become effective?

Christ's sovereign word in the church is the gospel. Thus the church's fidelity to Christ occurs as fidelity to the gospel. But it is we who speak the gospel. Thus it is precisely whether what we speak as the gospel is indeed the gospel, that is the question. Sovereignty in the church is limited by the church's calling to proclaim the true and pure gospel; that is to say, it is limited by Scripture and the church's dogmatic tradition, by the means which God has provided to make continuance of the true gospel—through the temptations of history—possible. And for our present purposes we may leave it at that; this essay need not analyze the nature of scriptural or dogmatic authority. It is enough to establish that the functional limit of sovereignty in the church is fidelity to Scripture and the creeds; for the consequences of this simple point are quite drastic enough to be going on with.

Indeed, the simplest consequence of this simple point is the politically most loaded, and the only one I will here discuss: sovereign churchly assemblies must be assemblies of persons who *know* Scripture and the dogmatic tradition. How else are their decisions to be limited by fidelity to these? Staying within the customs of Lutheranism, we may put it so: the members of a sovereign assembly must know the catechism well and be able to find their way around in the Bible and the service book. An assembly not so characterized, that claims to decide for the church, can only be regarded as a usurping assembly.

This means, for one thing, that provision for education in the church belongs to the design of its polity. Every community faces the problem of the fidelity of its sovereign persons, and so of their education in the community's "conception" and "proposition." The problem is obviously both most acute and most crucial in democracies of any sort, which must provide the people with the education that befits rulers. Insofar as the church must be one sort of democracy, the church has the same task. Whatever else education in the church *may* be for—development of individual piety or qualification for particular tasks—it *must* be for equipment of the sovereign assemblies. This is too politically decisive a matter to be left to the experts at the agencies. Decision about education must be constitutionally stipulated as a chief exercise of sovereignty, and how to achieve this stipulation must be a foundational concern of our constitutional architects.

And it means, for another thing, that there must be *qualifications* for membership in sovereign assembly. Persons ignorant—to use Luther's habit of language—of the Ten Commandments and the Creed may not deliberate the church's future, whoever or whatever they may otherwise represent or know. No one is thus excluded from the church. No more than the mentally deprived or infantile may be excluded from prayer and Eucharist merely for these disabilities, may ignorance in general exclude from the life of the church. But ignorance of certain sorts must indeed exclude from the church's sovereign assemblies. This too must be somehow established by the designers of a right churchly polity.

AFTERWORD

Not all here present have been persuaded all along that further juridical and administrative unification of Lutheran denominations is the cause to which American Lutherans should just now devote themselves. But those arguments are past. We should now all regard the process of unification as the opportunity it may be, for reform of the church. Doubtless there are many agendas of needed reform. It was my assignment to press the claim of specifically political reform, to consider what theological mandates might govern the design of right sovereignty in the church.

I have argued four propositions. 1) Only those are rightly *sovereign* in the church whose *authority* is the kind that can there be sovereign, the authority of the gospel. 2) It is only a continuing assembly that can be rightly sovereign in the church; and if possible this should be a real congregation that yet embodies the catholicity of plural congregations. 3) Whatever assemblies are sovereign or otherwise authoritative in the church must truly deliberate their decisions; otherwise their decisions are intrinsically tyrannical. 4) Whatever assemblies are sovereign or otherwise authoritative in the church must be instructed in Scripture and the dogmatic tradition.

Finally, an acknowledgment: if any or all of these contentions are right, the political reform of the church has a very great task to accomplish. It may not prove possible to achieve a faithful polity all at once, as the immediate outcome of our present arrangings—though I see no hindrance but our sloth or unwillingness. Should a faithful polity indeed turn out to be beyond us, then let us obey this mandate: let us devise a self-reforming polity, with a stated and structural commitment to not-yet realized political goals, in the hope and confidence that greater churchly authenticity may gradually be achieved as the years of the new denomination go by.

3

The Identity of the Ordained Minister

WALTER R. BOUMAN

It is important at the outset to remind ourselves of the limitations of this study. The title is inclusive, the literature immense, the controversies interminable. To speak of identity at all is to involve sociology, psychology, and anthropology as well as history, exegesis, and theology. I understand the topic to ask not about "identity" in its psychological or sociological sense (although that cannot be completely ignored), but rather to ask what ordination confers on the individual in theological terms. I begin with some current issues as the way to engage our confessional and biblical tradition.

CURRENT ISSUES AND CONCERNS

The first complex of issues and concerns arises in connection with *candidacy* for ordination and the related educational process. The role of the Lutheran parish clergyperson is today a relatively stable institution. Ordination admits one to the exercise of this role. But how does one become a candidate for ordination? The answer of American Lutherans: enroll in a seminary. How students come to enroll in seminaries then determines how they become candidates for ordination.

The first issue here is that most candidates are "volunteers" rather than "recruits." When an application reaches the seminary admissions office, the faculty decides on candidacy. Continued study for LCA students requires endorsement by a synodical committee, and that is an improvement. But the fact is that even in the LCA students are basically "volunteers," to whom the church reacts. Obviously this affects the quality and character of parish clergy.

Currently, seminary education in American Lutheranism has moved away from the European pattern which includes a long period of purely academic instruction followed by a shorter period of "practical" instruction and experience. Seminaries involve students in "field experience" early in the seminary career. Internship normally comes before the final year of academic work. "Preaching calls" are standard for students who have finished their first year of seminary education. But this poses both curricular problems (too much education must be crowded into the two years preceding internship) and questions relating to ordination. The latter are our concern here. The field experiences involve every kind of worship leadership except presiding at marriages. Yet no one "should publicly teach or preach or administer the sacraments in the church without a regular call," says Article XIV of the Augsburg Confession. What is the meaning of "regular call"? Have we conferred the identity of ordination with a new rite: matriculation in a seminary?

A second complex of issues arises in connection with the ordination rite itself. The Lutheran rite of 1982 does not help us in dealing with any of the questions that ordination raises. Four major questions are the subjects of much discussion.

The first question is the theological rationale for ordination. According to Edward Schweizer, the Gospel of John represents the view that no special ministry is needed by the church since all members of the church have "direct and complete union with Jesus Christ."[1] If Schweizer is correct, then the need for a rationale arises already because of, if not in, the New Testament. The assertion that God gives a special ministry to the church may indeed be true, but it is not yet a rationale. The 1982 rite simply begins, "according to apostolic usage you are now to be set apart to the office of Word and Sacrament."[2] That is not a rationale, nor do any of the verses of Holy Scripture cited provide one.

Providing a rationale for a special ministry was the substance of the great inner-Lutheran debate on church and ministry which took place in the middle decades of the nineteenth century.[3] Expressed as simply as possible, the question is whether the administration of Word and Sacrament is the responsibility of the entire community and by means of the call is entrusted to special ministry, or whether the administration of Word and Sacrament is conferred directly by Christ to the special ministry as the contemporary form of the primitive apostolate. The 1982 rite can be interpreted both ways.

The second question is whether the office to which the candidate is admitted by the rite is functional and limited to the function of administering Word and Sacrament or whether a permanent charism is conferred upon the candidate. Again the rite can be interpreted both ways. The repeated emphasis on Word and Sacrament could be read as functional. But with the imposition of hands the ordinator prays that God pour out the Holy Spirit upon the ordinand and "fill him/her with the *gifts of grace* (for the ministry of Word and Sacrament)." The meaning of the "gifts of grace" is not defined or clarified.

A third question left unresolved by the rite is the one which Robert Jenson and Eric Gritsch raise and answer in *Lutheranism*[4] and which Jenson addresses again in *Partners*.[5] The question is what distinguishes the ministry of the ordained from the ministry of the laity. Gritsch and Jenson respond that the whole church has a ministry "done *by* the Gospel . . . to the world." To this ministry every believer is called by baptism. The forms of this ministry are not fixed, but are as varied as the needs of the world and the gifts of the community. The ordained, on the other hand, are set apart for ministry *to* the gospel, to care for the authenticity of the gospel within the community. They fulfill the fixed and designated role of public preaching and administration of the sacrament. The task of presiding at the Eucharist is limited to the ordained. Whatever the merits of such an interpretation, the question as to what, if anything, distinguishes the ministry of the *laity* from that of the ordained is not addressed by the rite.

A fourth question left unanswered by the rite of 1982 is whether all ministries in the church derive from a single ministry, the special ministry of Word and Sacrament. While it is clear that the rite is intended to ordain for that one ministry, nothing is said about other ministries. A bishop presides at the ordination or authorizes it, but is the bishop more than, different than, a minister of Word and Sacrament? Does the diaconate have a separate origin? How are "lay professional leaders" related to the ordained? Neither this rite nor the other related rites in the 1982 *Occasional Services* provides us with answers.

A third complex of issues arises from the actual functioning of the ordained in the parishes and in other ministries. Edward Schweizer's insight and method in *Church Order in the New Testament* is that asking about church order means trying "to understand the Church's essential nature."[6] Behind the actual functioning of ministry lies a conception of church, of its nature and mission. The following issues and concerns arise from the relationship of church and ministry.

In the midst of much valid talk about the ministry of the whole community and the pastor as presiding over that ministry, the fact is that most members of congregations see themselves as the *objects* of the pastor's ministry. "Church" means an organization that is able to support ministerial "chaplaincy." Ministry means providing such "chaplaincy" ser-

vices. By "chaplaincy" here I mean the performance of religious services to
or for others.

This fundamental fact has a profound effect on seminary education. It
means that while we offer a vision of "presidency" and "enabling," we are
required to teach candidates the skills to perform ministry. But "enabling"
and "performing" are not identical skills, and given both the curriculum
crunch at the seminary and the marketability of ministry skills in the
parishes, it is easy to understand why the performance skills receive overwhelming attention.

This conception of ministry is directly related to an attenuated vision of
the church. The Association of Theological Schools' study *Ministry in
America* discovered a significant discrepancy between the expectations of
Lutheran clergy on the one hand and Lutheran laity on the other with
regard to the involvement of the church in social issues.[7] There's the rub. If
the mission of the church is going to enlist persons in the believing of doctrinal formulations which will gain them admission to eternal bliss, then, of
course, involvement in current social and political controversies will be in-
imical to that mission. What *is* the relationship between politics and
religion is another way of asking both what is the mission of the church
and what is the role of clergy leadership.

The present functioning of the clergy has led to an increasing understanding of the pastoral ministry as a profession with parishioners understood as
clients or, if one follows the medical model, as "patients." At Trinity
Seminary, Columbus, we are participants in a program of "interprofession-
al education" with a number of professional schools at the Ohio State
University. We are viewed—and we aid and abet such a view—as one of the
"helping professions" with a role on the "team" that provides help or healing to clients/patients. While this brings to expression some valid dimensions of Christian concern, it does not allow seminary students to exercise
their role as leaders of an *ecclesial* community, a community in which other
participants (whether clients/patients or professionals) in the "cases" might
be members.

We have come back to the beginning of this look at our contemporary
situation. If ministry is a profession, then candidates would normally be expected to volunteer, seek out a professional school, master the skills (and
part of that mastery would be the "practice" of them, as students in schools
of law, medicine, social work, nursing, and so forth, practice under the
supervision of professionals), and eventually receive a "license" to practice.
If this is what ministry is, then ordination is just that license to practice.
And then, of course, one could have one's license revoked for cause, or one

could change professions and give up one's license to practice ministry. We must now ask how the official statements of Lutherans understand ordination.

LUTHERAN STATEMENTS ON THE MEANING OF ORDINATION

THE MINISTRY OF THE CHURCH (LCUSA)

In 1974 the Lutheran Council in the USA issued a document on the Ministry of the Church through its Division of Theological Studies. It is one of the more significant studies because it tries to deal explicitly with the meaning of ordination. It follows the pattern of setting the ministry of the ordained within the context of the ministry of the whole people of God. But it makes the same move as does Robert Jenson in comparing ordination with baptism.[8] It calls the ritual of both baptism and ordination a *kairos,* an "initial significant moment within a continuum" which has past, present, and future dimensions.

Ordination, according to this study, *recognizes* a past dimension by affirming the candidate's call, training, and personal endowments. It is a present event because it establishes a covenant between the ordinand, God, and the church. The ordinand pledges to discharge the duties of the office faithfully. The church pledges its support and prays for the bestowal of God's Holy Spirit as the promise of God to support the pledge of the ordinand. This present event initiates an unfolding process as the promises are kept. "The continuation of the ordinand's ministry depends upon God's calling and sending and upon the minister's faithfulness."

The study faces squarely the question of whether ordination is for life. Its answer is negative. A variety of factors may be involved in the discontinuance of one's ordained ministry. Should a person desire resumption of ordained ministry, a renewed examination of belief, training, and personal qualifications is required, and a renewed calling and sending must take place. All of the past, present, and future dimensions of ordination would again be present and would be "marked by an appropriate liturgical rite." But the document stops short of calling this "reordination." A footnote states that "the logic of this position would call for a repetition of ordination, although this has not generally been Lutheran practice."

THE LUTHERAN CONFESSIONS

If Jenson is right, the problem in dealing with the Lutheran Confessions is a matter of perspective for understanding especially the Augsburg Confession. Is it basically a document for a catholic reform or a constitution for a new church? Whether one consciously opts for the latter view or not, Luther is regularly cited as the way to understand the confessions. Martin Heinecken's reply to Jenson in the *Partners* discussion is an example.[9] In the face of much debate on the matter, I do not finally believe that Luther can be used *against* Melanchthon. He gave his approval to the Augsburg Confession, and his comment that he could not "step so softly and quietly" was directed toward the style, not the substance, of the confession.[10] Hence I limit myself to the confessions.

The best work on the understanding of ministry and ordination in the Lutheran confessions has been done in relation to the Lutheran-Catholic bilateral dialogues. The essays by the late Arthur Carl Piepkorn[11] and George Lindbeck[12] are especially helpful. The following seem to be the crucial points.

1. The confessions teach that the ministry of teaching the gospel and administering the sacraments is instituted by God (Augsburg Confession, Article V). Piepkorn argues that the ministry is viewed "chiefly but not exclusively in dynamic and functional terms" (p. 103). His point is that the functions of gospel proclamation and administration of the sacraments are an abstraction apart from the *persons* who carry out the functions. Lindbeck agrees that the divine institution and power of the office come from the functions which the office serves. But the office should be institutionalized, that is, persons should be set into an office through a rite. The confessions do not just affirm that the gospel *activities* are to take place (p. 594).

2. Ordination is sacramental. Article XIII, 11–13, of the Apology of the Augsburg Confession declares that both the activity of preaching the gospel and the laying on of hands are sacramental. This is the meaning of *rite vocatus* in Article XIV of the Augsburg Confession. The "regular call" here does not refer to the process of *selecting* persons for the office, but rather to the rite of ordination. Both Piepkorn (p. 114) and Lindbeck (p. 601) refer to the fact that *vocatio* and *ordinatio* include the whole process of election and imposition of hands. But the chief question is what "sacrament" means. One thing is certain—it does not mean ontological change, and especially not anything like the indelible character that medieval sacramental theology believed was conferred on an ordinand. The sacramental character of ordination is an example of the "signs and testimonies of God's (gracious) will toward us (i.e., all human beings)" (Apology of the Augsburg Confession, Article XIII, 1). The command and promise which belong to the sacrament are ascribed to the gospel, not to the ordinand (Apology of the Augsburg Confession, Article XIII, 11–12).

3. Ordination will normally be lifelong, but Lindbeck argues that this

does not mean that ordination must necessarily have a permanent character to it. Lutherans have both acted and taught as if the commission of a minister of the word remains in effect even if he or she fails to perform the functions for which he or she was ordained. But Karl Rahner's use of the analogy of marriage is not valid to establish the lifelong *necessity* of ordination. The *proprium* of marriage is a special relation to another person while the *proprium* of ministry is a relation to an office and community. Hence "the length of the term of service for which a (person) is called and ordained into the ministry must be regarded as *de jure humano.*" This means both the possibility of term ordination and the possibility of reordination (pp. 601–2).

4. There is but one ministry to which ordination refers, that of presbyter-bishop. The confessions "desire to maintain the church polity and various ranks of the ecclesiastical hierarchy" (Apology of the Augsburg Confession, Article XIV, 1). But a pastor can ordain, since the distinction between pastor and bishop is by human right only (Treatise on the Power and Primacy of the Pope 65).

5. The authority of ordained ministers includes preaching and administration of the sacraments (Augsburg Confession, Article V), the power to excommunicate and to absolve (Apology of the Augsburg Confession, Article XXVIII, 13), to "judge doctrine and condemn doctrine that is contrary to the gospel" (Augsburg Confession, Article XXVIII, 21), and to meet in synods or councils where decisions are made in accordance with the Word of God (Treatise on the Power and Primacy of the Pope 55–56).

6. The distinction between clergy and laity is blurred. While the church is to obey its ministers, "the church is also above the ministers" (Treatise on the Power and Primacy of the Pope 11). It is to judge doctrine, to withhold obedience where "anything contrary to the gospel" is taught or introduced (Augsburg Confession, Article XXVIII, 23). The churches also have the right to call and ordain because "wherever the church exists, the right to administer the gospel also exists" (Treatise on the Power and Primacy of the Pope 67). In an emergency, the laity can baptize and absolve (Treatise on the Power and Primacy of the Pope 67). There is no mention of laity presiding at the Eucharist, and both Piepkorn (p. 117) and Lindbeck (p. 598) show that Lutherans did not authorize lay-led Eucharists in the sixteenth century because Eucharist was not necessary for salvation, as baptism and absolution were held to be.

This catalog of confessional teaching seems to indicate that ordained ministry is both necessary and instituted by God, that the clergy have the authority of the word in the church, and an ordination rite is necessary. But problems remain which we must now address to the biblical material. Is there a distinction between clergy and laity? If so, where does it lie? What is the relation of ordination to the Eucharist? Is there but one ministry to which ordination refers? Is ordination permanent?

THE NEW TESTAMENT

There are many excellent studies in addition to Edward Schweizer's *Church Order in the New Testament,* to which I have already referred. Arland Hultgren's article "Forms of Ministry in the New Testament" is the best brief survey, and the footnotes have a comprehensive bibliography.[13] The ecumenical dialogues have revealed a remarkable consensus as exemplified in the Lima document of the World Council of Churches[14] and the biblical essays in Lutheran-Catholic dialogues.[15] The long but very rewarding study by Bernard Cooke *Ministry to Word and Sacraments* begins the historical description of each function, or facet, of ministry with a biblical chapter.[16] Edward Schillebeeckx has provided us with a comprehensive and balanced account of New Testament and early Christian developments in the area of ministry.[17] My own focus here must be more narrow—attention only to the question of the meaning of the imposition of hands. For that purpose I rely on the work of Edward Lohse, *Die Ordination im Spätjudentum und im Neuen Testament.*

The first point of significance for our work is that Lohse traces the origins of Christian ordination to Jewish roots. Neither Mandaeanism nor Mithraism influenced the laying on of hands in the New Testament. Indeed the reverse is probably the case (pp. 17–18). We are referred unequivocally to the ordination of Jewish scholar/teachers, that is, scribes. This has significance for a number of issues, especially how one reads the New Testament. It means that we must not so much take the second and third centuries of church life as the starting point and look backwards for signs of "early catholicism" in the New Testament. We must rather understand the New Testament as the witness to a very fluid situation, a time in which some Jews confessed Jesus, the crucified one, as the Messiah in whose resurrection they had experienced the Parousia, the inauguration of the *eschaton.* The New Testament is the evidence of the struggle to understand what this climactic event in world history meant for the relationship of Jesus' disciples to both Judaism and the Gentile world.

In Gal. 3:28 Paul enunciates the agenda if it is true that Jesus is the Christ and if his disciples have been baptized into the Christ: "There is neither Jew nor Greek, there is neither slave nor free, there is neither male nor female." This is a breathtaking vision, and two aspects of it should come as no surprise. First, the emphasis in the first century was on the Jew-Gentile issue.

This must be remembered whenever we read the statements on women in 1 Tim. 2 and 1 Cor. 14 and try to apply them to women in ordained ministry. These statements are part of the church's struggle with the male-female dimension of the agenda, not the final witness to what had happened in Christ. Second, the church came out of the Jew-Gentile issue with mixed success. The goal of the messianic vision was not "church" in opposition to "synagogue" but rather the oneness of Jew and Gentile in the new way grounded in the event of Jesus, the Christ.

The importance for this study is that we need to look at church rites as transformation of synagogue rites under the impact of the event of Jesus, the Christ. Hence, the rituals for the laying on of hands are not part of a developmental scheme in which we are moving from simplicity to complexity, or from charismatic enthusiasm to rigid order. Rather, we can understand the rites as adaptations of what was already available in the synagogue. This may mean renewed attention to an earlier dating of the pastoral Epistles. Joachim Jeremias has argued for something close to Pauline authorship[18] and Lohse follows him in this (pp. 80–81). But whether Paul was the actual author or not, the pastorals come at a relatively early point in the relation of church and synagogue.

Jewish scribal ordination can be summarized as follows (pp. 64–66):

1. It was designed to preserve the purity and continued teaching power of the Torah. This did not mean sterile repetition. A teacher ordained his own students and thus gave them the authority to make independent decisions regarding religious legislation and to function as judges in penal cases (p. 35).

2. Ordination followed upon long and intense study begun in early youth. The ordinand had to be mature, married, and bodily sound, but in contrast to priests, they could come from a variety of tribal/racial backgrounds. The ordinand was recognized only on the basis of learning (pp. 41–43). Ordination involved a close bond between teacher and student, part of a chain of succession.

3. The rite of ordination was simple. The ordinator must himself have been ordained. The ordination was a laying on of hands in the presence of at least two witnesses. The ordination was unrepeatable, but we must not read sacramental or ontological significance into this.

4. The significance was contractual. Rights were conferred. Without ordination one could not make penal decisions or teach in a binding way. A gift of the spirit was given with the laying on of hands, but it was the spirit of wisdom necessary for teaching and legal decisions. It was a sign that God would not allow wisdom to perish in Israel.

5. The teachers who were ordained were often associated with a

synagogue, but they were usually not the rulers of the synagogue. The elders of a village were also the rulers of the synagogue, and the president chose preachers and prayer leaders from among the adult members of the synagogue. The teachers were not to be distracted from their work of learning and teaching.

6. Ordination was regarded as a divine ordinance, a participation in God's ordering of the whole of history. The Spirit that God had given to Moses at the beginning was now being dispensed to teachers who would become part of the *collegium* that God would gather around himself at the end of time. Ordination was therefore a part of an eschatological perspective which looked beyond this world.

With this background we can now look at two key sections of the New Testament. The first is Acts 6:1–6. Amid reports of a peaceful church, a conflict breaks out. The seven are chosen because the apostles were not to "serve tables" (*diakonein trapedzais*). But we never hear of the seven doing such work. Instead, we have the Stephen and Philip stories (Acts 6–8). They are never called deacons but are referred to as "the seven" (Acts 21:8). Indeed, the term "deacon" is not used in Acts at all. Philip is called an "evangelist" (Acts 21:8), a minister of the Word. What seems most probable is that the seven were the leaders of a Greek-speaking community which existed next to the Hebrew-speaking community. The rite of Acts 6:6 was an inauguration into leadership (compared to the installation of Joshua in Num. 27:15ff.). They are recognized as "full of . . . the Holy Spirit." They are presented to the apostles who lay hands upon them. We have here a Christian parallel to a Jewish ordination with a significant addition: prayer (p. 75–77).

The process has two distinct elements: The congregation chooses its leaders. The apostles commission them with the laying on of hands. There are also differences between this rite and scribal ordination besides the addition of prayer. The apostles are not scribes; there is no teacher-student relationship; the laying on of hands occurs through a collegial group rather than an individual scholar. But Lohse comments that the Acts 6 account indicates that this rite could have originated only from Judaism. The account indicates that it was a "Christianized form" of a Jewish rite; it was practiced early and can be traced back to the apostles and the original congregation (p. 79).

The second is 1 Tim. 4:14 and 2 Tim. 1:6. Here and in the pastorals generally we can see more clearly than in Acts the "Christianization of a Jewish rite" (p. 87). It has to do with ordination, whether by Paul (2 Tim. 1:6) or "the Elders" (1 Tim. 4:14). The two are not mutually exclusive. The characteristics of ordination can be described as follows:

1. Timothy is called by "prophetic utterance" (1 Tim. 1:18; 4:14). The "prophet" is not so much one who predicts the future, but rather one who applies the general will of God to a specific instance. In this case, the general will is that there be leaders. The "prophetic utterance" translates that general will to the specific person, Timothy. There are criteria, of course (1 Tim. 3:1–13 for bishops and deacons), but there is no designated process by which these criteria are to be applied. The point is that in the application of the criteria to an individual God does the selecting.

2. Before witnesses he receives a "confessional formulation" of apostolic teaching (2 Tim. 2:2).

3. With a solemn confession—also before witnesses—he has obligated himself to faithful teaching (1 Tim. 6:12).

4. He is ordained with the laying on of hands which confers a charism (1 Tim. 4:14; 2 Tim. 1:6). Lohse is especially concerned to emphasize that "charism" does not confer a special character on the individual. Rather "charism" means a special instance of the one grace by which the Lord redeems (1 Tim. 1:14) and of which he remains sovereign (pp. 82–84). How, then, are we to conceive this if it is not ontological or magical? Lohse's answer: in the "christianization" of Jewish ordination, prayer always accompanies the laying on of hands (p. 92). Prayer in the name of Jesus for the Spirit who confers the charism means that one is set into the struggle between faithfulness to the new reality created by the gospel and all the assaults upon it.[19]

5. The charism therefore has two foci that express the significance of ordination. The first is that the *content* of the leadership, what the leadership is for, is the faithful witness to the gospel (1 Tim. 1:19; 4:6–10; 6:20; 2 Tim. 1:13, etc.). The second is the courage and freedom to *suffer* for the sake of the gospel (1 Tim. 6:11–16; 2 Tim. 1:8–14). What is not mentioned is any kind of sacramental role. The concern behind the admonition to "rekindle the gift," not to "neglect the gift," is the ministry of teaching. In summary, what distinguishes ordination in the pastoral Epistles from Jewish scribal ordination is the *content* of what is to be confessed, taught, passed on: the gospel of Jesus as the Christ. Because the leadership to which he has been ordained is grounded in the gospel, the hesitant Timothy is encouraged to joyful, confident service, even though that service involves suffering.

ATTENTION TO ISSUES

I have tried, up to this point, to present more or less objective material dealing with the problems and resources in the area of the meaning of ordination. This final section remains for analysis and some modest proposals.

I think Robert Jenson is right about the nature of Lutheranism, although he did not express it exactly this way. Lutherans are "catholics without magic." Whether or not that is a contradiction in terms, we continually give expression to this in the tensions evident in Lutheran theology, not least in the question of ordination. It is worth noting that the ALC has produced hardly any studies on the subject of the ministry while the LCA has produced a steady stream of such studies. I think the explanation for both lies in the tension inherent in Lutheranism. The ALC has experienced this tension to a lesser degree than the LCA because it is moderately "low church" and has not had a movement for liturgical renewal in its recent history. The LCA, however, has had both a powerful liturgical movement and a more radical "low church" element as part of its history. The "low church" party reacts emotionally and theologically against the catholic dimension of Lutheranism, and the "high church" party reacts with equal vigor against emphasis on the antimagical dimension of Lutheranism.

We may also discover that in addition to tensions within Lutheranism there may be historical and theological problems in the catholic tradition itself. The result is that we face difficulties similar to that of modern catholic theologians. These are some of the historical problems that we must confront: (1) There is no uniform tradition about the relationship between ordained ministry and eucharistic presidency in the first several centuries of the Christian era; (2) Ordination by bishops only was not performed in the first several centuries; (3) There is no clear-cut line of development in the New Testament; and (4) There is no way ordination can be made a matter of "faith," that is, belonging to the essence of the gospel. With this list of historical problems, it becomes impossible to insist on the catholic tradition as the only way to order the life of the church. And the historical work of both Cooke and Schillebeeckx, in which they identify the late origins of what Schillebeeckx calls a "sacerdotalizing" of ordained ministry, raises theological problems about whether the catholic tradition can be reformed in this area or whether it must simply be replaced.

Given the catholic dimension of Lutheranism, Gritsch and Jenson have demonstrated the best that can be made of the nature of Lutheranism. The analysis is not complicated. Lutheranism keeps the catholic form (ordination for life) and supplies it with a new theological rationale. The elements of that rationale: (1) In order to have justifying faith, there must be gospel;

(2) In order to have gospel, there must be ordained ministry; (3) Only the ordained can publicly preach and administer sacraments. This rationale has given Gritsch and Jenson the basis for distinguishing between the ministries of the ordained and the unordained, as described earlier. Jenson has added that ordination is analogous to baptism. The charism that the ordinand receives through the laying on of hands does not confer an ontologically "indelible character" anymore than baptism does, but it grasps the ordinand with the lifelong claims and promises of God as does baptism. That is reformed catholicity.

This proposal has the virtue of simplicity. But it makes a distinction that, though grounded in the catholic tradition, may not reflect the teaching of the New Testament. The New Testament knows of an "ordination," that is, a once-in-a-lifetime laying on of hands, but not a theologically significant distinction between the ordained and the unordained, nor the identification of the ordained as serving the gospel. This raises a new set of questions, namely the content of the New Testament teaching on the ministry. We must summarize here especially the letters of Paul, the pastoral Epistles, Luke-Acts, 1 Peter, and Hebrews.

There is no special priesthood. Instead, the community that confesses Jesus as Christ is a priestly people. Because Jesus is the end of temple, priesthood, and sacrifice, the priestly people become temple and sacrifice—with the Eucharist as the locus of what they have become and what they are to do and be for the world. However, there is no evident interest in the New Testament concerning who administers baptism and who presides at the Eucharist.

There are many special ministries. There are four listings of ministry gifts in the Pauline letters (Rom. 12:6–8; 1 Cor. 12:8–10; 1 Cor. 12:28–30; and Eph. 4:11–16). They identify a profusion of ministries which do not exhaust the possibilities. Some of these ministries are "commissioned" by a ritual involving laying on of hands (for example, Acts 13:1–3). But whether these ministries are commissioned or not makes little difference. All are given both to build up and to extend the community that confesses Jesus as Messiah.

The once-in-a-lifetime laying on of hands is mentioned in Acts 6 and First and Second Timothy. Its purpose is to provide leadership for the Christian communities. The "gift" given with the laying on of hands has to do with faithfulness in handing on the tradition and the courage to suffer for the faith. But even these characteristics are not limited to the leadership. Rather, the leaders lead the community in faithfulness and courage. The laying on of hands was performed by the apostles (Acts 6) or by elders (1

Tim. 4:14). The elders may have been unordained themselves. If this is a form of leadership taken over from Judaism, as I have argued, then the elders as leaders of synagogues were generally not ordained. As Schillebeeckx points out, there are other instances of lay ordination in the history of the church.

The temptation is to view these three aspects in terms of development. First comes the insight that Jesus is the end of temple, priesthood, and sacrifice; then the free profusion of ministries; finally a move toward order and control. But the argument in favor of such a development lacks a solid historical basis. Often it is argument in a circle. If Lohse is correct, then the existence of ordained leadership is early (Acts 6), existed side by side with the apostles, and also coexisted with the profusion of ministries mentioned in the Pauline letters.

All of this leaves us with the question of how to assess the role of the New Testament with regard to church order, the meaning of ordination, and the identity of the clergy in the church. I can summarize in four statements.

First, the New Testament does not provide us with a "constitution" for the church. And it does not provide us with any historical basis for the later tradition of ordination by bishops only or ordination as necessary for public preaching and eucharistic presidency.

Second, the New Testament witnesses to the "good news" that Jesus, the crucified one, is the Messiah who inaugurates the eschatological kingdom of God.

Third, the community that confesses Jesus as the Messiah is called into being by the event of Jesus and bears witness to the promise of the kingdom by its existence and mission.

Fourth, the ministries—commissioned, ordained, and spontaneously "there"—are "gifts" of the Messiah to the community. The gift of ordained leadership exists in the midst of apostolic and other ministries.

One further point. There is nothing to forbid the development of institutional leadership in the direction of bishops and deacons. The development of a sacramental priesthood is, however, mistaken. No specific development can be made constitutive or normative in the absence of New Testament warrant.

Proposals

1. Lutheranism needs to ask whether its understanding of the gospel is adequate for a full definition of the church and its ministries. Lutheranism has correctly confessed that God's promise of unconditional commitment (grace), grounded in the death and resurrection of Jesus, is to be received by

faith alone and trusted in life and death. But this has also resulted in an individualistic understanding of the priesthood of the people of God, in a "chaplaincy" concept and functioning of ministry, and in neglect of the eschatological vision which animates the New Testament, specifically the corporate witness of the New Testament community, to the promise of the kingdom of God. The confession of the New Testament is that Jesus is the beginning, the way, and the outcome of the coming kingdom.

2. The church bears witness to the good news of the kingdom through attention to forgiveness, compassion, justice, care of the earth, and peace. This is a corporate ministry of the priestly people of God. It is expressed through the many ministries. Lutheranism must examine its tradition of speaking of only one ministry of Word and Sacrament; however, the many ministries of the New Testament do not derive from a single ministry, not even that of the apostles as a formal institution. The many ministries are gifts which arise always as the community catches anew the vision of the eschatological event, that the resurrection of Jesus identifies him to be the crucified Messiah. All these ministries serve the church's witness to the coming kingdom. Some are internal, edifying the community; some are external, directed toward the world. The fact that these ministries are gifts does not mean that the community awaits them passively. They are to be sought, desired earnestly (1 Cor. 14:1), through prayer, cultivation, creation of an atmosphere of freedom in the gospel in which the gifts thrive and flourish. They may be commissioned and supported in advance or recognized ex post facto. This does not mean chaos. The situation in Corinth is the paradigm of how the church both receives and evaluates the profusion of gifts which express the church's eschatological freedom.

3. The church has a right to leadership, writes Schillebeeckx.[20] That is the function of ordination. The laying on of hands authorizes leadership in the church. This has implications in three areas.

Candidacy for Ordination. If ordination means leadership in a community of Christians, then Lutherans need to give sustained attention to candidacy for ordination. Leadership can be given to the church in a variety of ways. But it is difficult to believe that having persons volunteer should be the most normal route or that theological faculties should make the basic decisions as to which volunteers are accepted by the church. At the very least, the church needs to take the initiative in seeking out persons who have the qualities necessary for leadership in the church. This should be a special responsibility of bishops. Volunteers, persons who offer themselves for leadership, should be postulants for a specified time to test their vocation. Seminary education needs to be reconsidered as part of a larger, longer process. I would suggest that the process include postulancy prior to admission to seminary, sponsorship by a bishop while enrolled in seminary, and curacy (a limited probationary period under supervision) after graduation from seminary. The whole process of identifying, educating, and finally ordaining candidates should be a shared venture involving the churches, the seminaries, and the bishops. Creating a structure for such a process could be one of the great gifts to and from a new church.

Ordination and Eucharist. There is no intrinsic relationship between ordination and eucharistic presidency. Schillebeeckx thinks that a distortion of ordination and ministry begins with a sacerdotal understanding of ordination in the high Middle Ages. Bernard Cooke dates the origins of that distortion earlier, already at the time of Augustine. Both agree that it is a distortion and needed reformation. However, the Reformation of the sixteenth century did not produce a clear reform. It did reject what Jenson called the foundation of the medieval understanding of ordination: "the need of identifiable miracle workers to make the Lord's Supper happen." But by linking ordination (*rite vocatus*) to public preaching and administration of the sacraments, the Augsburg Confession did not offer the kind of alternative vision that is needed.

A more appropriate way to understand the connection between ordained ministry and the rituals of the community must begin with a definition of the relationship between the Eucharist and the mission of the community. The Eucharist is the ritual that confers identity upon the church (it is the body of Christ) and shapes its mission (it is for the world). If ordained ministry means leadership of the community, then it means leadership of the community's mission. It is appropriate for such leadership to preside over the ritual of the community's identity and mission. The *Lutheran Book of Worship* has identified functions for both president and assistant in the eucharistic ritual which give expression to their ministries. The presiding minister prays the eucharistic prayer because in its narrative he or she identifies the transcendent ground of the community's existence as Christ's being for the world which is the content of the community's mission. The lay assisting minister leads the prayers—litany, prayer of the church, offertory prayer, postcommunion collect—because in prayer the community offers itself as an agent for mission and struggles with the concrete aspects of its mission.

If Eucharist is understood as the meal of communal identity and mission, and eucharistic presidency means leadership in the community's mission, then perhaps we need to rethink how to substitute for the ordained leader in his or her absence. It is also important to reconsider the leader's ministry in other rituals. The leader presides during the marriage rite, not as the person who "marries" husband and wife to each other, but rather as one who leads the prayers and blessings of the congregation for two persons who are the true ministers of the rite and who marry each other. The presider thus leads the congregation in ministry *to* marriage. Similarly, the leader presides over the baptismal ritual, but the parents might administer the water to their own children; sponsors might administer the water to adults. Thus all rituals might need to be reconsidered so that we give expression to leadership in ministry and mission rather than functioning as local "chaplains."

Ordination for Life? This is one of the most vexing questions related to ordination. In practice, Lutherans have regarded ordination as having lifelong validity. However, the LCA does reordain clergy coming to it from other denominations. And both LCA and ALC have regulations governing the length of time one can be retained on the clergy roster without call. Lutherans are deeply divided on this issue. No Lutheran voices today are urging Lutherans to think that ordination confers an "indelible character." But Robert Jenson has argued vigorously that ordination is like baptism; it involves the ordinand in promises and claims of God that endure throughout life.

I have wanted to accept Jenson's argument, but I have not been persuaded by the analogy. If ordination means leadership, that leadership can have both time and place limitations that are not characteristic of baptism. Baptism and ordination differ in that the claims and promises in baptism are made to the person as such. In ordination the claims and promises are made to a person in relation to certain tasks, or functions. In principle, that means that one can give up and resume leadership. The claims and promises are constant and enduring with regard to leadership functions. But now one does not need them if one is not involved in those functions. The LCUSA document cogently says that under some circumstances reordination is appropriate. The problem is that the LCA has decided to reordain only in cases involving clergy coming to it from other denominations. That is questionable as an ecumenical practice, not as a matter of principle.

4. I have not mentioned ecumenical implications of ordination until now. But they obviously need to be taken into account. We can no longer think and plan and change in a vacuum—if we ever could. But I have not mentioned the ecumenical dimension because I did not find denominational differences significant in my reading. I am increasingly persuaded of the validity of these three conclusions that I came to in the course of my study.

First, a great consensus has developed among biblical and historical scholars as to what can be learned about ministry and ordination in the first several centuries of Christian history. There is agreement that our sources are silent at significant points—for example, who did actually preside at the Eucharist? And there is all but universal recognition that actual history was messier than we like to think, for example, ordinations were not always carried out by bishops, not even always by clergy! Second, Lutherans are learning from the biblical and historical materials, as well as from contemporary needs and problems, to reform their own tradition, for example, the ordination of women. More needs to be done, but the openness to reform is present. Third, other traditions, notably Episcopalians and Roman Catholics, are also giving evidence of openness to reform. There has been considerable progress in ecumenical conversation on ordination. There has been some mutual recognition of ministries, and there have been some actual reforms taking place in other traditions. The pace of reform may vary, but the outcomes in the long run seem to be on a converging path. I hope that Lutherans will continue to be a reform movement within the church catholic, and that our reform efforts may be offered to the whole people of God as lessons to be shared.

We have much yet to learn about the meaning of ordination.

NOTES

1. Eduard Schweizer, *Church Order in the New Testament* (Naperville, Ill.: Alec R. Allenson, Inc., 1961), pp. 117–130, especially p. 124.

2. *Occasional Services* (Minneapolis: Augsburg Publishing House; Philadelphia: Board of Publication, Lutheran Church in America, 1982), p. 193.

3. Holsten Fagerberg, *Bekenntnis, Kirche und Amt in der deutschen konfessionellen Theologie des 19. Jahrhunderts* (Uppsala: University Press, 1952), pp. 101–21.

4. Eric W. Gritsch and Robert W. Jenson, *Lutheranism* (Philadelphia: Fortress Press, 1976), pp. 116–22.

5. Robert W. Jenson, "Ministries Lay and Ordained," *Partners* 3:5 (October 1981): 12ff.

6. Schweizer, *Church Order,* p. 15.

7. David S. Schuller, Merton P. Strommen, and Milo Brekke, eds., *Ministry in America* (New York: Harper & Row, 1980), pp. 423–25.

8. Jenson, "Ministries Lay and Ordained," pp. 12–13.

9. Martin J. Heinecken, "The Ministry of the Word," *Partners* 4:3 (June 1982): 19. "The Confessions must be read in the Light of Luther's theology, out of which they sprung." See Gert Haendler, *Luther on Ministerial Office and Congregational Function* (Philadelphia: Fortress Press, 1981), pp. 9–13, 103–10.

10. *Luther's Works,* vol. 49 (Philadelphia: Fortress Press, 1972), pp. 295ff., especially pp. 297–98.

11. Arthur Carl Piepkorn, "The Sacred Ministry and Holy Ordination in the Symbolical Books of the Lutheran Church," in *Eucharist and Ministry,* Lutherans and Catholics in Dialogue IV (1970), pp. 101–19.

12. George A. Lindbeck, "The Lutheran Doctrine of the Ministry: Catholic and Reformed," *Theological Studies* 30:4 (December 1969): 588–612.

13. Arland Hultgren, "Forms of Ministry in the New Testament," *Dialog* 18:3 (Summer 1979): 201–12.

14. *Baptism, Eucharist and Ministry* (Geneva: World Council of Churches, 1982), pp. 20–32.

15. Lutheran and Catholics in Dialogue IV, pp. 69–100.

16. Bernard Cooke, *Ministry to Word and Sacrament* (Philadelphia: Fortress Press, 1976), pp. 33–57.

17. Edward Schillebeeckx, *Ministry* (New York: Crossroad, 1981), pp. 5–37.

18. Joachim Jeremias, *Die Briefe an Timotheus und Titus. Das Neue Testament Deutsch,* vol. 9 (Göttingen: Vandenhoeck & Ruprecht, 1953), pp. 4–8.

19. Robert Jenson, *Visible Words* (Philadelphia: Fortress Press, 1978), p. 192.

20. Schillebeeckx, *Ministry,* pp. 29–30.

4
Can We Have Bishops—
Reformed and Evangelical?

PHILIP HEFNER

A CURRENT REFLECTION ON EPISCOPACY

North American Lutherans approach the question of bishops as pilgrims, as a community *in via,* on the way. By a winsome act of God, when the merging churches adopted the title of "bishop" a few years ago, we got ourselves into a fix which we cannot avoid by retreating. The way out goes in only one direction—forward. As we go forward from the position that we have already assumed on the questions of bishops and on ecumenical relations, we shall find ourselves subject to the birth pangs of God's history.

PRESENT ATTITUDES

First of all, we must recognize that the New Lutheran Church (NLC) will have an office and persons designated as "bishops." This is a "first" in the history of North American Lutheranism. Within the past six years all three of the merging bodies have accepted such a designation, and we see no reason to believe that the title will not be carried over into the NLC. What that might mean is the real substance of our considerations.

Second, most people in our churches believe that the recent shift to bishops was nothing more than a change in terminology. No constitutional or bylaw alterations of duties, or functions, were involved. It is not clear whether or not there is a desire for a broader significance to the terminology change.

In the minutes of the 1978 convention in Chicago, where the LCA initiated the process that became final in 1980, it is reported twice that "the most firmly fixed powers that are associated with the title 'bishop' are (1) ordination, and (2) visitation in parishes. These powers are already assigned to synodical presidents." As we proceed in our discussion, it will become

73

clear that this opinion is quite a mistaken one. Ordination and visitation (what "visitation" means is left unclear)[1] are indeed two of the most firmly fixed powers, but by no means the only such powers. Furthermore, what Lutherans in the LCA meant by the power of ordination is certainly not identical with what the classical view of the episcopacy asserted. We can only conclude that the drafters of this LCA revision were not only misinformed about the classical office of bishop, but that most of those present believed that little more than nomenclature was involved.

What of the wider expectations? My sense is that a very sizeable group of people in the churches desire the definition of the office of bishop to emphasize the activity of pastoral care for pastors. The clergy in particular are voicing this concern, and they obviously express a very real need in our church life today. It would be unfortunate if we disregarded this concern, because it will be one of the most powerful forces in our NLC definition of the office of the episcopacy.

A second group, smaller but nevertheless important, is calling for the bishop to exercise more influence over the task of monitoring the teaching and preaching in our churches. This is in fact the ancient concern for the teaching office in the church, the *magisterium*. This group, along with those concerned for the pastoral care of pastors, is particularly distressed that the present episcopal office is chiefly defined as administrative.

There are other groups, as we might expect, that are quite content with the understanding of a bishop as an ecclesiastical branch manager, just as the former offices of synod and district president were defined. This is especially true of the ALC, which defines districts in its constitution in a rather formal manner as entities that carry out certain functions "which pertain to the life and program of the American Lutheran Church." The constitution for districts reinforces this character in its statement that "the district shall serve as a segment of the ALC for the purpose of planning, promoting, and executing the program and work of the ALC." In fact, I would hazard the guess that the majority of our people—laity, pastors, and bishops—fit into this third category, because the primary thrust of our traditions has been in this direction of organization and maintenance of the church. Those who hold to different expectations are innovative in the long history of our North American Lutheran practice. A fourth group, much smaller, wishes for our episcopacy to evolve into the classical catholic office, which we shall discuss later.

ECUMENICAL PRESSURES

Besides the previously mentioned elements that are rooted in our own internal histories as ALC, LCA, and AELC, the question of the episcopacy will be affected by certain ecumenical involvements. Of these relationships, our association with the Anglicans is qualitatively most significant in my mind as it is represented in the Interim Eucharistic Sharing agreement with the Episcopal Church. This relationship will affect the question of bishops in at least two ways. First, the position that Lutherans take in the next few years on the classical concept of the ordained ministry will determine whether the interim sharing leads to full intercommunion. This so-called classical ministry is the ministry that is structured by the episcopal succession in the apostolic tradition. We will be increasingly pressured, therefore, by the exigencies of the trajectory we embarked upon with the Episcopalians in the summer of 1982, to declare ourselves concerning the status of the ministry structured by the episcopacy in the Anglican tradition. If we were still in the position of the *status quo ante,* prior to the time in which we Lutherans named our own bishops, then this declaration vis-à-vis the Anglicans would simply be a decision about how we view *their* bishops and the Anglican relation to our own nonepiscopal ministry.

Second, now that we have named our own regional leaders to be "bishops," however, the challenge of the Episcopalian connection is widened. We shall find that our stance on the Episcopalian challenge is directly a matter of our own self-definition—that is, we shall have to ask ourselves how our views of their episcopally structured ministry apply to our own fledgling bishops. If we acknowledge that the roles of Anglican bishops are what the Anglicans claim, then how do the roles of our own bishops differ?[2] Or is it our intention that our bishops should be defined as the Anglican bishops are? If ours differ, how do we first of all understand and second justify that difference? If we desire parity and equality for our bishops, what steps must be taken to bring that condition about? Our more open relationship with the Anglicans could not have come at a more opportune and momentous time. It makes our life, not more comfortable, but much more interesting and relevant to larger ecumenical concerns!

Episcopacy and ministry are also at the heart of the current state of talks with Roman Catholics. Volumes 3 and 4 of the dialogues reached a high level of consensus on the doctrines pertaining to the sacraments. However, the dialogues recognized that the consensus would, in turn, be dependent upon questions about ministry, since the validity of the sacraments is correlated to the validity of ministry and ordination. Volumes 5 and 6 of the dialogues have focused upon authority, teaching authority, and other questions that are related to ministry's validity. Certainly the question of bishops will be high on the priority of discussion as these dialogues unfold. In fact, the issue of bishops may well be one that proves to be an article of standing or falling for further progress.

Our Pilgrimage

As we examine the issue of bishops in the New Lutheran Church, the pilgrimage character of the course we have set out on becomes more vivid. We struck off into new territory as Lutherans in the agreement with the Episcopalians, a fact that the LCMS was not slow to recognize. We stretched the Article VII of the Augsburg Confession to the utmost ("For the true unity of the church it is enough to agree concerning the teaching of the Gospel [*doctrina evangelii*]") when we entered into provisional intercommunion with a major doctrinal obstacle yet unsurmounted. Knowing how difficult and unseemly it is to withdraw steps that one has already taken, it seems reasonable to say that we intentionally entrusted our destiny on this question to historical processes whose outcome we cannot see in any final way. Is it just a coincidence that episcopacy is one of the central issues in this journey with the Anglicans? This question takes on deeper meaning when we recognize that our decisions to change the title of our regional leaders to "bishop" were also taken in risk.

In the moment that we adopted what was for most people simply a change in nomenclature we stepped into a new ball game, and we were not very much aware of the rules of this game. We stepped into the ball game being played by the other churches—chiefly, the Roman Catholic, Orthodox, Anglican, Church of Sweden, and Methodist—that not only use the title bishop, but also that have had a much longer experience with bishops. The history of bishops in these churches is not only of considerable contemporary breadth, but it also goes back many centuries. As we dipped our toes into the swim which these other churches were already immersed in, I think we were relatively unaware of the consequences. Now there is no necessity for us to define our bishops in the way that others do—indeed there are important differences between these churches on the nature and function of the episcopacy. But the challenge of self-awareness is unavoidable. If we choose to define our bishops differently, we shall have to justify that difference. If we choose to think of our bishops in a manner that is similar or equivalent to the other churches, then other implications follow, some of which we shall discuss here. Some of these implications are evident when we ask a few questions, such as: (1) Since bishops are a mark of unity in the church, how do we think of our unity with, and yet our difference from, other episcopal churches? (2) How do we claim authority for our bishops and how do we justify remaining separate from the churches whose bishops derive their authority from their traceable continuity with the apostolic traditions which are now focused in the Roman and Orthodox traditions? This issue of succession is without a doubt the single most pressing issue confronting episcopal churches in their relationships with each other. (3) Were we aware that such questions were, with that vote, being placed on our agendas?

We did not have a full-blown theology and theory of the episcopacy in our group when we voted to designate our regional leaders as bishops. There is no possibility that we will have such a theory and theology by the time of the 1987 merger into the NLC. But we shall not restrain the development of the office because we lack the theory, just as we are not restraining it at this time. Our episcopacy will push full steam ahead, regardless of how well or how little developed our theory and theology are. In 1995, for example, we will find ourselves in the position of having to acknowledge aspects of our theology that have developed in practice without the benefit of the *pura doctrina* that we Lutherans cherish. How very like the apostolic generation in this respect! One would be blind not to see that God has not waited upon our theology. God has pushed us into the cold water, before we even had time to put on our swimming suits! We will feel pain as God's history massages us into pathways that we find strange. We shall also know the mystery, the excitement, and genuine pilgrimage character of Christian church life, if we but hold on. We shall also have the process of theology revealed to us—theology is not projective so much as it is reflective; theology does not come with answers from which church leaders deduce practice, so much as theology comes along to put together the pieces that church practice (hopefully under the influence of the Holy Spirit) strews along the way!

TWO PERSPECTIVES ON THE EPISCOPACY

There are two perspectives on the episcopacy—contemporary function and historical justification. Each of these perspectives is necessary, and each is complementary to the other.

CONTEMPORARY FUNCTION

Every generation of the church that has ever had bishops has had to face the contemporary pragmatic reality that certain functions must be carried out. The functions that have required bishops or their equivalents have varied from time to time and from place to place, but we may begin with the general description of them found in the Lima document on *Baptism, Eucharist, and Ministry:*

> Bishops preach the Word, preside at the sacraments, and administer discipline
> in such a way as to be representative pastoral ministers of oversight, continuity

and unity in the Church. They have pastoral oversight of the area to which they are called. They serve the apostolicity and unity of the Church's teaching, worship and sacramental life. They have responsibility for leadership in the Church's mission. They relate the Christian community in their area to the wider Church, and the universal Church to their community. They, in communion with the presbyters and deacons and the whole community, are responsible for the orderly transfer of ministerial authority in the Church.[3]

The office of bishop may be described in somewhat more traditional terms. The bishop symbolizes the unity of the whole contemporary church and the continuity of this new church with the historical church. The bishop is responsible for the teaching and preaching of the church, presides over the sacramental life, confirms and ordains, governs the church, and serves with peers to form the chief policy-making body of the church. Historical studies have recently shown that a host of other functions, perhaps better termed "social functions," have also been associated with the bishop since early times.[4] These include offering hospitality for traveling missionaries and others who carry out the ministry of the church; supporting and protecting the poor (including maintaining them out of his budget); arbitrating disputes between church members and offering services to Christians who were involved in secular court procedures; maintaining a patronage system, since the bishop controls many lesser job openings; offering good services for political entities in their disputes, and the like. The significance of the bishop's personal life cannot be overlooked, even though it is not technically a "function." Since early times, the status and honor of the episcopal office were linked to the personal character of the person. The bishop was a representative type of the person that all Christians should be. Douglas Powell writes in the context of interpreting Irenaeus on the episcopacy, "If the Church is to be the fullness of him who all in all is being fulfilled, there must be a *traditio,* a handing-on not only of forms of teaching but also of forms of men. It is not merely the handing-on of an office (generally assumed to be mechanical and unspiritual), but also the handing-on of a torch (generally assumed to be dynamic and spiritual), and the two are not contrary to each other."[5] Powell points out that this succession of acknowledged spiritual types is essential to the classical understanding of apostolic succession.

Even if we had never heard of bishops, we would probably need to find persons to perform such a pragmatic set of functions. Two thousand years of church history bear this out. Another factor is added to this pragmatic necessity—all of the functions must be done well. What is the criterion of judging whether they are done well? The primary criterion is that they be done in accordance with the gospel. The Faith and Order document suggests that they must be done so as to serve the "apostolicity and unity" of the church. In short, the criterion of contemporary practice lies significantly (although not wholly) in the early normative events of the church's emergence, in the gospel as expressed in Scripture, in the apostolic generation. This concern for the gospel and for apostolicity is not intruded into the episcopacy, because it is intrinsic to the life of the church to ask about criteria, to be concerned not only to perform functions, but also to perform them properly, correctly, well.

HISTORICAL JUSTIFICATION

Here a familiar argument presents itself, which we must examine if we are to understand the episcopacy.

(1) The revelation of God has come decisively and normatively in Jesus Christ. (2) Our *only* access to this revelation is in the apostolic generation, through the apostles that Jesus himself called together; if it were not for this generation, we would know virtually nothing at all about Jesus Christ and certainly nothing about the divine revelation he brought. (3) The apostles themselves chose their successors, and it is from the apostles and their successors that the early Christian community took its lead in developing around the world of its time.

Scripture attests to the formation of the apostolic group of the Twelve and its mission. (Matt. 28:16–20 is an important instance.) The authority of this group is asserted in Matt. 16:13–19, where Peter is acknowledged as a leading figure within the Twelve and where the keys of the kingdom of heaven, with the power to bind and to loose, are granted to the apostles. The line of authentic bishops proceeds from this succession of the apostles. As the Second Vatican Council says in paragraph 4 of its *Decree on the Bishops' Pastoral Office in the Church:*

The order of bishops is the successor to the college of the apostles in teaching authority and pastoral rule; or, rather, in the episcopal order the apostolic body continues without a break. Together with its head, the Roman pontiff, and never without this head, the episcopal order is the subject of supreme and full power over the universal Church.[6]

The criterion of authenticity arises naturally when we ask, Is the bishop who has succeeded to the office truly faithful to the apostolic faith and practice?

THE INTERACTION OF THE TWO VIEWS

The episcopal office could be arrived at from either the pragmatic contemporary or the historically justified perspective. One could argue that it is essential that these current functions be performed, and hence the office is desirable, even if there were no hallowed historical precedents for it. Contrariwise, given the authority of Jesus Christ and the apostolic witness in the church, one would be inclined to continue the historically posited office, even if contemporary practice did not naturally lead to it. Indeed, the historical precedent would tend to shape our perceptions of the needs of current practice.

The two perspectives are essential. It is intrinsic to the life of the church that the functions we have surveyed be performed. Without teaching, preaching, sacramental life, and the like, as contemporary realities, there is no church. Similarly, if Jesus Christ gave such authority to the apostles, as the New Testament asserts, then the church must respect that witness in order to maintain its identity.

The two perspectives are complementary, just as they are essential. On the one hand, the contemporary practice of the church's life, as manifested in the functions we have mentioned, is empty and demonic if it is not filled with the substance of the apostolic witness. On the other hand, the office that stands in the line of the apostles is dead if it is not vigorous and efficacious in the contemporary life of the church. Continuity with the apostles and current efficacy are two criteria that are applied without fail to the episcopal office and to the person who fills it. These two amount in the end to the same criterion of apostolicity. In the classical expressions this apostolicity was linked to catholicity, that is, to the unity of all the churches of the world and to the historical continuity of the church from the apostolic generation to the present.

Historically, the interaction of these two perspectives in the episcopacy has been very concrete, just as the application of the criterion of apostolicity with its concomitant—catholicity—has been very concrete. In the turbulent second and third centuries, for example, adherence to the true gospel of the apostles and loyalty to the specific communities that stemmed from the apostles were clearly at issue in a concrete manner. The tumult caused by the Gnostics, the Donatists, and the Arians resulted in the formation of many schismatic groups. Often, each group claimed its own legitimate bishops, Scripture, tradition, and gospel. Therefore, it became very important for a group to affirm the correct teaching of the gospel from the correct sources in a community that adhered to a bishop with a valid claim to be in the literal line of the apostolic generation. The classical argument states that both true faith and authorized power to govern in the church go back to the apostolic mandate. In the situation of schism, particularly when each group argues its case with some power and sophistication, the concrete face of apostolicity includes both questions: What gospel do you believe? and With which specific community do you identify yourself? Gospel and community cohere.

An understanding of this historical dialectic is necessary in order to comprehend the true and deepest issues posed by the question of bishops in the church. Note that the issues of administration per se and pastoral care of pastors, for example, hardly figure in the foregoing discussion. Rather the question is that of the concrete vehicle of apostolicity in the church and in its Word and Sacrament ministry. The bishop symbolized and actualized a community in which the true gospel was alive and in touch with the apostolic witness. In this sense, "where the bishop is, there is the church." It is in this light that we can understand the early tendency to speak of the bishop in analogy to God the Father and to Jesus Christ. The bishop was the one who nourished the concrete community on the apostolic gospel of Christ; the bishop was the source of teaching, preaching, sacramental life, and ethical practice that had its basis in the Triune God who had given the revelation in Jesus Christ. In this sense, the church belongs to the bishops. Thus the documents of the Second Vatican Council can say, "in the episcopal order the apostolic body continues without a break" and "the episcopal order is the subject of supreme and full power over the universal Church."

When Anglicans and Roman Catholics challenge us on the episcopacy and the traditional ministry, they are challenging us to ask the questions: Are we concerned with the apostolicity of our ministry? How do we substantiate the apostolicity of our ministry? When we speak of our ministry in these questions, we ask about the ministry of the individually ordained person, the ministry of the specific congregation or agency, and the ministry of the entire Lutheran church of which we are part.

The novelty of the question of apostolicity may blind us to the sense in which episcopacy and succession in the apostolic witness are not questions of church order alone, nor are they adiaphora in the eyes of certain other Christians. If, for example, Matt. 16:16–20 is authentic Scripture, then succession in the line of the apostles is of the substance of the gospel as well as a matter of church order, since it is related directly to what the apostles have bound and loosed in the authority given them by Christ.

Finally, let us remind ourselves of the situation that all Reformation churches are in when they discuss questions of this sort. We claim that our lineage does indeed go back to the apostolic generation. Indeed, as Lutherans we claim that we include within our heritage the entire history of the church. Inasmuch as we did not originally seek separation or schism, we would gladly have remained within the mainstream of the structure of the Western church. We affirm with the originating community of our faith all of the vehicles of continuity except those of physical structure. We claim the same Scripture, creeds, liturgy, piety and devotion, ethical earnestness, and sacramental life. Above all, we claim that our *faith* is the same as that of the apostles!

The absence of the physical continuity of structure, as represented in the episcopal office and the persons who hold it, governs our thinking and our practice on these issues in important ways. First of all, that absence of structural continuity, when combined with our desire to affirm apostolic continuity, compels us to find other modalities of continuity besides the literal, physical, and structural. Second, since concreteness of lineage is an important item, and one that is touched upon in the faith we hold (Matt. 16:16–20), our status and self-esteem are affected by our discontinuity. Both of these factors—discontinuity in physical structural forms and attacks on our self-esteem—can influence our theology. They can, in other words, press us to use our theology to justify our position, and thus our theology may become *ideology*. (This attempt to justify ourselves theologically is perhaps most clearly manifested in our traditional exegesis of Matt. 16:16–20 so as to play down the persons of Peter and the other apostles and to emphasize their faith as the rock on which the church is built and which gives them their authority.) The tendency is also present in our common attempt to define apostolic succession in terms of faith rather than in structural terms and to apply apostolic succession to the whole church rather than to individuals who hold ministerial office.

We must be alert and self-critical so that our theology does not become self-justifying ideology. Today, the consensus of exegetical opinion seems to challenge our traditional interpretation of Matthew 16. However, our traditional theology is credible when we consider that the literal physical succession of the Roman Catholic and the Orthodox churches has proven to be no guarantee of faithfulness to the gospel. The Lutheran gap in succession is nonetheless an exception, necessitated only by the unfaithfulness of the structures. Can the exceptional be lifted up as the rule?[7]

THE ANCIENT EPISCOPAL OFFICE AS MISSION

The significance and possibilities of the episcopacy are not exhausted by the ecumenical, doctrinal, and church-law perspectives that we commonly think of. A great deal could be said at this point which we can only hint at. When viewed in the context of its own times, the early Christian episcopacy was a novel phenomenon in the Mediterranean world. Arnaldo Momigliano writes:

Much can be said about the internal conflicts, the worldly ambitions, the intolerance of the Church. Yet the conclusion remains that while the political organization of the Empire became increasingly rigid, unimaginative, and unsuccessful, the Church was mobile and resilient and provided space for those whom the State was unable to absorb.[8]

The early bishop related to a novel constituency, and in so doing was on the cutting edge of late classical society. Included in this constituency were the poor (bishops played a role in trying to redistribute the wealth), travelers, noncitizen artisans and intellectuals, and women. Concerning the participation of women in the early church, we have the word of Peter Brown:

> For the first time we have a political clientele that explicitly included members of the other sex. To become a bishop meant stepping out of the all-male world of traditional politics to become patrons of women as well as of men. . . . giving to women a public role which they had lacked. This enabled wealthy women, as benefactors of the poor and as builders, to become participants in a ceremonial life from which they had been largely excluded in the all-male definition of the city as a political unit.[9]

The episcopacy was not in its early development solely created as a way of organizing the church. It was also an activity of God in the world, playing a specific role in the way God related to the Mediterranean world. Whatever the episcopacy became, its missional achievements and its betrayals, it is more than an internal organizing activity on the part of the church. Lutherans are not always ready to hear this about the classical office. However, as we contemplate the NLC, we certainly will want to keep this dimension of episcopacy in mind. We will want to respond to the challenge of this new organization so that we may share more fully in God's activity of being God in the world.

PERTINENT ISSUES FOR THE
NLC TODAY

What is the goal of our NLC development of the episcopal office? This is certainly one of the central questions that we must deal with between now and the time of the 1987 merger, and for the first years after the merger. The next ten years, from now until 1993, will certainly be formative ones for the episcopacy in our midst. The persons who hold the office in these ten years will make a decisive contribution to what the office becomes. There are many questions that we should ask ourselves.

1. With respect to our internal life, what ought we to aim for? We should ask ourselves whether the classical functions of the office, as we have

described them on the basis of the Lima document of the Faith and Order Commission and other sources, are those that need attention in our church and whether they should be focused in the office of regional leader. When asking ourselves this question, we must also ask whether and how the apostolicity of our ministry can be strengthened in the carrying out of these functions.

We might begin by reminding ourselves what the regional entities (synods in LCA and districts in ALC) are presently mandated for. The descriptions contained in LCA Constitution, Article 8, Section 7, and the ALC District Constitution, Article D201 are incomplete, but they are not bad places to begin. They suggest that the bishop can indeed, even under present formulations, be understood as one who is responsible for the monitoring of the preaching and teaching in the diocese, as well as providing leadership for the mission of the church. Both ALC and LCA tend to look at their regional entities as branches of the main office, which therefore reduces the office of the bishop.

The role of the bishop in the peer group (or collegium of bishops) as a chief policy maker for the whole church requires some discussion. Synod and district presidents and now bishops have been acquiring this role, through their respective councils of peers. This is a legitimate development, both on theological and church-political grounds. Neither of the present denominations adequately lays the constitutional and bylaw groundwork for this function, however.

The function of the bishop as a symbol of the unity and continuity of the whole church is not envisioned in our present churches. This is one of the most important functions in the classical understanding, and it requires some thoughtful creativity on the part of our NLC planners.

2. If we do not wish to restore to our church the functions classically associated with the episcopacy, should we use the title bishop? Since so many other Christians are accustomed to bishops in the classical mode, and since even the Lima document holds up the classical functions, it would be misleading both to our own people and to other churches if we were to use the title in some other way.

3. What can we expect, ecumenically, from the development of the episcopal office in our midst? The Anglican communion may well find it easier to grow closer to us if we develop the traditional episcopal office. However, we cannot expect, in my opinion, to win ecumenical acceptance of our ministry by instituting the episcopacy, if that acceptance means a surmounting of the age-old objections that our office of ministry is not in physical continuity with the apostolic generation. Setting up a parallel office in the Lu-

theran churches will not meet the criteria for apostolic succession in the Roman Catholic or Orthodox sense.

What may happen from the development of the episcopal office is that our churches will be renewed, and thus it will be clearer than ever that the Holy Spirit can be and in fact is at work to sustain apostolicity outside the physical succession. One might say that the new attention to the episcopal office may contribute to our church order what has been accomplished by the Spirit in our preaching and liturgy in the past decades—namely, that our preaching and liturgy have been pointed back to the apostolic sources in unity and continuity with the whole catholic church. The result is that even though our *Lutheran Book of Worship* liturgy, for example, may not constitute a valid mass on other grounds, it is recognized by other churches as a fruit of the Spirit recovering the ancient faith which we affirm. We will not, however, strengthen the episcopal office in our NLC for the sake of pleasing others or winning their approval. We will hope to renew our roots in the apostolic witness, and approval may be the byproduct of that.

4. Traditionally, Lutherans have affirmed that they could accept the traditional bishops if they were to grant that their authority is *de jure humano,* by human law, rather than *de jure divino*, by divine law.[10] Another expression of this concern is the Lutheran insistence that traditional bishops may be accepted if they allow the gospel to be preached and taught freely. This is the view that bishops must be evangelical. The question arises—what would constitute an episcopacy *de jure humano?* Several suggestions seem to be in the air. First, that the bishop be accorded traditional powers, but that he or she be accountable to the faithful through regular elections in which the bishop may be reelected or set aside. Second, that the bishop be accorded authority, but only in an advisory capacity; that is to say, the bishop's authority could not be enforced. Perhaps this would mean that the bishop's judgment about a parish during the visitation would be taken as advice, but it could not be considered mandatory. What about the other functions? It has been said that the Anglican bishops are of this type, and that therefore they serve as a model of the evangelically functioning episcopacy.

Either of these suggestions may indeed prove practicable for us. There is some question, however, as to whether the bishop can ever be described as holding authority *de jure humano* when considered in the light of Matt. 16:16–20. If we consider that Peter's role and the apostolic power to bind and loose go back, even indirectly, to Jesus, then we must in some sense say that the successors to the apostles bear some divine legitimation. On the basis of current exegetical consensus, this interpretation seems inescapable.

If we nevertheless insist that episcopacy is fallible and in a sense adiaphoron, then we must conclude that even traditions that go back to Jesus may be fallible. Even *de jure divino* shares in human fallibility! The Lutheran churches may not be ready for such speculations, but these kinds of judgments will be just beneath the surface in any decisions we make on the authority of the episcopacy.

5. Lutherans will tend to relate the episcopal office with the pastoral office. Luther accepted bishops as a species of pastor at an earlier time, whereas later he spoke of their authority to enforce sound teaching and preaching in the parishes. In any case, bishops were conceived by him as pastors with "special duties" added. This view roots their authority, like that of the pastors, in the Word of God, but it does not ground their special work of symbolizing unity and continuity and their role as policy makers in the collegium of bishops. If we establish an office of bishop that approaches the classical office, we will simply have to acknowledge types of authority in that office that we are not accustomed to. There is an important question for our careful consideration—what will this mean for this episcopal authority to be nevertheless evangelical? My own opinion is that this will best be done, as I have said, by granting full traditional authority to the bishop, but nevertheless insisting that the bishop be accountable to the people and that episcopal power be in many cases advisory or otherwise accountable within a network of checks and balances.

NOTES

1. Leonhard Goppelt provides a useful description of the term "visitation" in Ivar Asheim and Victor Gold, eds., *Episcopacy in the Lutheran Church* (Philadelphia: Fortress Press, 1970), p. 2.

2. See the essay, "The Apostolic Ministry," in Kenneth Kirk, *The Apostolic Ministry: Essays on the Historic Episcopate* (London: Hodder & Stoughton, 1946).

3. *Baptism, Eucharist, and Ministry,* Faith and Order Paper No. 111 (Geneva: World Council of Churches, 1982), pp. 26–27.

4. Henry Chadwick, "The Role of the Christian Bishop in Ancient Society," in *The Role of the Christian Bishop in Ancient Society,* ed. Edward Hobbs and Wilhelm Wuellner (Berkeley, Calif.: Center for Hermeneutical Studies in Hellenistic and Modern Culture, 1980).

5. Douglas Powell, "Ordo Presbyterii," *The Journal of Theological Studies* 26:2 (October 1975): 326.

6. Walter Abbott, ed., *The Documents of Vatican II* (New York: America Press, 1966), p. 399.

7. As guide to the issues pertaining to Matt. 16:16–20, see Joseph Burgess, *A History of the Exegesis of Matthew 16:17-19 from 1781 to 1965* (Ann Arbor, Mich.:

Edwards Bros., 1976). Also see Hans von Campenhausen, *Ecclesiastical Authority and Spiritual Power in the Church of the First Three Centuries,* trans. J.A. Baker (London: A. & C. Black, 1969).

8. Cited by Peter Brown in his "Response to Professor Chadwick," in Hobbs and Wuellner, *Role of the Christian Bishop.*

9. Ibid.

10. See Bernhard Lohse, "The Development of the Offices of Leadership in the German Lutheran Churches: 1517–1918," in Asheim and Gold, *Episcopacy in the Lutheran Church,* pp. 53ff. On basic historical questions, see Albano Vilela, *La Condition Collegiale des Prêtres au IIIe Siècle,* Theologie Historique, vol. 14 (Paris: Beauchesne, 1971).

5

The Vocation of the Laity

NELVIN VOS

> I believe that I cannot by my own reason or strength believe in Jesus Christ my Lord, or come to him; but the Holy Spirit has called me by the Gospel, enlightened me with his gifts, and sanctified and preserved me in the true faith . . .

No starting point is more appropriate to set our course as we begin to explore the vocation of the laity than to cite Luther's answers to the third article in the Small Catechism. Those powerful verbs—the Holy Spirit has *called* me, *enlightened* me with his gifts, and *sanctified* and *preserved* me—each word denotes an action of the Holy Spirit working in your life and mine.

In hidden and straightforward ways, in seriousness and in playful whimsy, the Holy Spirit makes its presence known not only in individual lives, but also in corporate communities, as the answer to the third article goes on to explain:

> [the Holy Spirit] calls, gathers, enlightens, and sanctifies the whole Christian Church on earth, and preserves it in union with Jesus Christ in the one true faith; in which Christian Church he daily and richly forgives me and all believers all our sins, and at the last day will raise up me and all the dead, and will grant me and all believers in Christ everlasting life. This is most certainly true.

The topic of this essay—"The Vocation of the Laity"—concerns both individual persons and the whole church of Jesus Christ. The vocation of the laity involves an understanding of the nature, purpose, and mission of the church. We are not referring simply to what lay people can do or should do: teach Sunday school, usher, sing in choirs, assist in communion, or even occasionally pray and preach. Important as each of these activities is—and they must continue to be nurtured—the major focus of my discussion will be on the laity in the world, in those arenas of faith and daily life outside the congregation. The term "lay ministry" too frequently has meant a kind of "clericalizing the laity" to assist the pastor. Such a view only confuses the tasks of pastor and people, and still more seriously neglects the mission of the church: to be Christ's living body in the world. The church exists not for itself, but on behalf of the world. We are called, all of us, to be the salt of the earth, not to be the salt of the salt. Only by not being an end in itself is the church faithful to Jesus Christ.

Therefore, the question on which I intend to focus is: What kind of understanding and practice is needed within the proposed new church in order to nurture the ministry of the whole people of God in the world? I will begin with an exploration of the ferment on this question within the contemporary church, including Lutheranism, and then make a brief excursion into lay/clergy issues before examining the meanings of vocation and ministry. The conclusion will suggest some theological emphases as well as several structural implications for a new church which takes seriously the words of Bishop David Preus: "The church is as strong as its laity."[1]

THE PEOPLE OF GOD

The people of God—in those four simple words are contained perhaps the most revolutionary of ideas in church history in the twentieth century. For these four words are used as the controlling image of *Lumen Gentium*, the dogmatic constitution on the church set forth by the Second Vatican Council. Instead of opening with a discussion of the structure and government of the church—as Vatican I did—chapter 1 of *Lumen Gentium*, entitled "The Mystery of the Church," begins with the ringing note, "Christ is the light of the nations," and goes on to speak of the church as the people to whom God communicates himself in love. The groundwork is then laid for devoting the second chapter to the description of the church as "the new people of God." And this term refers to the total community of the church, including pastors as well as other faithful. A later chapter in *Lumen Gentium* speaks directly to those who

> by their very vocation, seek the kingdom of God by engaging in temporal affairs and by ordering them according to the plan of God. They live in the world, that is, in each and in all of the secular professions and occupations. They live in the ordinary circumstances of family and social life, from which the very web of their existence is woven.
>
> They are called there by God so that by exercising their proper function and being led by the spirit of the gospel they can work for the sanctification of the world from within, in the manner of leaven. In this way they can make Christ known to others, especially by the testimony of a life resplendent in faith, hope, and charity.[2]

The entire spirit of the Second Vatican Council is permeated with the sense of the church as the people of God in mission and service in and to the world. Although some individuals continue to ask how much difference this emphasis on the people of God has made in the actual practice of the Roman Catholic church, this ferment within the largest Christian community in our day has clearly manifested itself throughout the church as a whole in various ways. A quick inventory would include: (1) The evangelical academies of Europe as well as *Kirchentag*, rising out of the debris of World War II, were formed to explore connections between Christianity and culture and continue to provide models for us. (2) In 1948 the World Council of Churches was formed and at its first assembly in a report on the laity affirmed that "the Lord Jesus claims the whole of life, and therefore, the Christian faith necessarily demands expression in all realms of life."[3] (3) The rich ecumenical reservoir of books and articles on the ministry of the laity has developed since World War II by such authors as Hendrik Kraemer, Hans Ruedi-Weber, Elton Trueblood, Mark Gibbs, among others.

The listing could go on, but let me turn to current Lutheran manifestations of the ferment. The ecumenical conversations with Roman Catholics have consistently stressed, as the Malta Report of 1972 stated: "The church as a whole bears witness to Christ; the church as whole is the priestly people of God."[4] Just recently, the international Roman Catholic/Lutheran Joint Commission in its report *The Ministry in the Church* reiterated the common theme:

> Through baptism all constitute the one priestly people of God (1 Pet. 2:5, 9; Rev. 1:6; 5:10). All are called and sent to bear prophetic witness to the gospel of Jesus Christ, to celebrate the liturgy together and to serve humankind.[5]

Closer to home, the American Lutheran Church chose as its general convention theme in 1980 "The Unfinished Reformation." Bishop Preus commented that although the Reformation principle of justification by grace through faith in Christ and the principle of the authority of the Scriptures have continued to be crucial in modern Lutheranism, the third fundamental Reformation principle of the priesthood of all believers, as he says, "has not claimed the same loyalty from Lutherans." He concludes: "We understand that the clergy have a ministry, but we are not accustomed to the idea of the ministry of the laity. The Church will operate on less than full power until all its members understand themselves to be called by God to full-time ministry."[6]

In the same year, Dr. James Crumley in his report as President of the Lutheran Church in America stated: "I believe we need to give more creative attention to the Reformation focus on the ministry of the laity in society. Particularly must we emphasize that God calls us to service at some times in the church, but at *all* times in the world."[7]

In 1970, the LCA Commission on the Comprehensive Study of the Doctrine of the Ministry opened its report in these words:

> One biblical affirmation has governed our thinking: all Christians are ministers. Therefore the word "ministry" cannot be reserved for the work of ordained clergy. Ministry is the task of the whole people of God (Matthew 5:13–16; Romans 12:1–8; 1 Peter 1:9–10, 2 Corinthians 5:18–21).[8]

Another LCA document—*A Study of Ministry, 1980*—put the matter succinctly in its key sentence: "Ministry is God's Word in action through the whole people of God."[9] A study on "The Ministry of the Laity in the World and in the Church" is planned to be completed within the LCA in 1984, and an intensive educational program on the ministry of the laity is scheduled to begin the same year. Of course, the organizations of Lutheran Church Women, American Lutheran Church Women, Lutheran Laymen's Movement, the movement of LAOS in Ministry, among others, have contributed in various ways to assist laypersons to respond to their calling. Lay professionals, deaconesses, commissioned ministries, lay associates, and others continue to be avenues of ministry within the church.

The point should be clear: our subject, "The Vocation of the Laity," is in ferment in all the meanings of that word—often confusing, sometimes festering, frequently disturbing, and most of all, always exciting.

THE LAY/ORDAINED ISSUE

One of the issues always in ferment is that of lay/ordained. Indeed, any discussion of laity is expected to enter this entangled thicket. On the other hand, studies on the ordained ministry usually ignore the ministry of the laity or else make a few *pro forma* comments at the beginning about the priesthood of all believers. The extremely significant statements on *Baptism, Eucharist and Ministry* from the World Council of Churches,[10] for example, spend some twelve pages on the ordained ministry in contrast to a single page on "The Calling of the Whole People of God."

My purpose is not to explicate the lay/ordained question once and for all, but rather my three brief observations, I hope, will help to make clear the context of the whole paper.

My first observation is that both clergy and laity are frequently captives in bondage to the institutional church. The church as an institution, as all institutions, tends to be obsessed with maintenance and survival. It spends most of its time and money on itself (think of your most recent congregational meeting or judicatory convention) rather than on the mission of the church to be the body of Christ in the world. A truck driver at a LAOS in Ministry retreat which I led last spring put it well in the last session: "I guess what I've learned this weekend is that I always thought I was in the world to go to church; now I see what I should have seen a long time ago, that I'm in the church in order to go into the world."

The *Laos*, the people of God, both clergy and laity, must help one another to be liberated from the captivity of the institution turning in on itself. To curve in on itself—that is what sin is not only for individuals but also for institutions, including the church. Congregational report forms that inquire only of numerical increases of dollars and bodies and do not raise the question "How *in the world* are you doing?"; pastors who act as if the parish is their world rather than the world is their parish; lay people who think that meaningful Christian ministry can take place only in church buildings; seminarians who enter *the* ministry because in their previous so-called secular activity they did not feel they were "in full-time Christian service"— in such particulars, the body of Christ distorts its mission.

Second, a full and rich understanding of the ministry of the laity in no way lowers the office of the ordained ministry. I am not interested in lay lib, some kind of distorted Americanism which says: we're all alike and no one can tell me anything. If the ministry of the laity encourages that kind of egalitarianism, then the church must respond in clear terms of rejection. The more sophisticated theological argument that baptism is really ordination is an approach that I find only confuses basic theological and biblical matters.[11] The issue in all this is not one of worth and power and status, but one of calling and gifts and response and responsibility.

On a more practical level, there are some clergy who still live out "the Herr Pastor" roles in dictatorial ways. There are also laypersons who are obstreperous in their dealings with clergy. Even more common however are the many clergy who are uncertain of their own identities, and laypersons with great doubts about living out their faith. At its worst, the new church would succeed in being clerical and anticlerical at the same time, failing to meet the actual needs of the laity but also failing to be supportive of the clergy.

Without doubt we all are interdependent and need mutual support, encouragement, and affirmation. If one begins where John Reumann does in his writings on *Eucharist and Ministry* in *Lutherans and Catholics in Dialogue IV,* "the church is a priesthood; it has an ordained ministry,"[12] then both clergy and laity need to be strengthened and undergirded.

Certainly, what Conrad Bergendoff wrote some thirty years ago is still true today: "There is no clear doctrine of the laity in the Lutheran Church . . ."[13] The thrust of this paper is an attempt to take a few steps in this ongoing task.[14]

VOCATION

Vocation is a term that has undergone one metamorphosis after another. The word itself from the Latin *vocatio* is referred to in the New Testament as *klesis*, that is, calling. The nuances of the term include at least two meanings: 1) to *summon* (often by name), to convoke an assembly; and 2) to *choose*, to select or assign to an office or a task. The biblical emphasis at all times is on the God who calls. And the response is God's called-out people.

In the Scriptures, as Donald Heiges stated in the 1958 Knubel-Miller Lectures, *The Christian's Calling*, vocation is essentially corporate.[15] God calls a people. In the Old Testament, this people, this community, is Israel. Many times Israel would rather not have been the chosen one, for the burden of obedience and responsibility was heavy. Yet Israel could not escape its relationship to God. Israel was the chosen community of faith which God summoned together for his service.

Within the community of Israel, individuals were chosen for specific tasks. The calls of Moses (Exodus 3–4), of Samuel (1 Samuel 3), of Isaiah (chapter 6), and of Jeremiah (chapter 1) were regarded not as sources of pride and honor, but rather as summons to particular service.

In the New Testament, Jesus called twelve disciples at the beginning of his ministry. In Jesus Christ, the Word came among us. The call to live in the midst of the cross and the empty tomb is the summons for the new community, the church. Hence, the church itself was appropriately described as *ekklesia*, the assembly of those summoned into the chosen for the body of Christ.

In Paul, the meanings of calling are rich and varied: 1) the general summons from God to each man and woman to the life of faith and love (Rom. 8:28–30; 1 Cor. 1:1–2; 2 Thess. 2:13–14); 2) God's choosing or election of each believer within the corporate body of the church (1 Thess. 1:11–12, Eph. 4:10); 3) the particular summons to specific tasks within the community of faith (Rom. 1:1; 1 Cor. 1:1; Gal. 1:5) and 4) the earthly station of the Christian, allotted by divine will (Eph. 4:1–4, 1 Cor. 7:17–24). In a crescendo of all four themes, Paul in 1 Corinthians 12 and Ephesians 4 describes the newly called community as one in Christ and also as a community manifesting itself in a rich variety of callings.

The biblical witness comes with an all-encompassing vision: the call of

God addresses the whole of life, or as Heiges said, "*The whole life of the Christian becomes, therefore, part and parcel of his vocation under God.*"[16] To each believer the Holy Spirit gives tasks appropriate to the calling and capacities needed for their accomplishment. There is one vocation for all, to serve Christ and one's neighbor, yet each individual also has a distinctive work to do.

In the writings of the early church, the fourth Pauline meaning of vocation, that is, the earthly station of the Christian, gradually came to symbolize "the status of one seeking perfection."[17] The eventual result was the widespread acceptance of a double standard of Christian living: for ordinary Christians, obedience to the commandments; for the seekers of perfection, the contemplative life and the vows of poverty and celibacy. Monasticism (the life set apart from the world) and mysticism (the effort to see God directly) were clearly paths to perfection. Thus, the monk, the priest, and the nun had a calling. Other Christians had no vocation in the world.

The bold claim of Luther, in recovering the biblical witness, was twofold: First, instead of one vocation (the calling of the religious orders), all Christians have a vocation. All are called in their baptism to live in the light of Christ's death and resurrection. Daily living is the arena of one's vocation, as Luther writes:

> You may reply: But how if I am not called? Answer: How is it possible that you are not called? You have always been a husband or wife, a boy or girl, or servant . . . Again: Are you a prince, a lord, spiritual or secular who has more to do than you, in order that your subjects may do right, preserve peace, and wrong is done by no one? See, as now no one is without some commission or calling . . .[18]

Second, instead of limiting the role of priests to religious orders, all believers are priests. As Luther stated:

> Here [God] has crowned, ordained, and anointed us all with the Holy Spirit so that all of us together are priests in Christ, exercise a priestly office, come before God and intercede for one another.[19]

Note that in both of these terms, "vocation" and "priest," Luther not only reinstituted biblical language but he also appropriated the very words that had been used exclusively for religious orders. He insisted that the gracious call of the gospel and the promise of being justified by faith alone meant that all Christians at all times and places were priests with vocations.

Gustaf Wingren in his pivotal study *Luther on Vocation*[20] emphasizes that Luther speaks of the relationship of *Stand* (station) and *Beruf* (calling). Non-Christians do not have a *Beruf* (calling); they have only a *Stand* (station). Christians also have a *Stand* as citizen, prince, magistrate, farmer, husband, wife, parents, child. God has summoned Christians to be his children, and therefore the *Stand* is transformed as a *Beruf* who serves God by serving his or her neighbor. Every Christian has a vocation because every believer exists in one or more stations, and in each station there are opportunities for service.

The biblical and Reformational emphasis on vocation as God's call must now be juxtaposed with a 1977 survey conducted among two thousand clergy and laypersons in the Lutheran Church in America.[21] In this survey the following question was asked and responded to as shown in the chart below:

When you think of the word *vocation*, which of the following come to mind most readily?

	LAY PERSONS	CLERGY
God wants us to live a responsible Christian life in whatever we do	11%	68%
God calls one to enter some specific occupation as doctor or teacher	14%	13%
An occupation	65%	14%
Ordained ministry	1%	
Full-time Christian work	1%	
The word is unfamiliar	3%	

Instead of the term "vocation" being elevated to describe only religious orders (as in Luther's day), we are faced today with the opposite situation—the word has been reduced to a secular dimension only.

So, what should be done? Forsake the term "vocation"? Elevate it, so that life, and particularly one's work, takes on a kind of halo of meaning?

I would suggest that we need to stop equating our calling with what we do for a living. We are called to be followers of Jesus Christ not simply in what we *do*, but in all that we *are*. Vocation involves our relationship with others, with nature, with the world, all seen within the primary call of God in our lives. The chief end of humankind is to glorify God which is not a task, but a gracious way of being. We *are* more than we do. We are called to be "in Christ," to live in the light of his cross. That calling is valid whether we have a meaningful job, a boring job, or no job at all. Vocation involves the whole sweep of life; the call of Christ claims all that we are.

Perhaps one of the reasons the church in this century has spoken of the ministry of the whole people of God has been to appropriate the biblical word *diakonia*, a term always associated with call (ministers have calls), in order to underline the understanding that all Christians are in ministry. The term "ministry" comes, of course, with a lot of baggage and puts off some people: "Who? Me? A minister? I'm only a layperson!" But is there any other term from Scripture and church history which conveys that all of us are called at all times and places to live out our baptism in the world? We are called in the intersections where one's faith in Jesus Christ meets and confronts the concreteness of daily living: in making decisions, in relating to others, in doing justice within our communities, in working to change the corporate structures of society, in being part of a global network of inter-relationships. In all of these arenas, we are sustained and strengthened by the knowledge that God has called us out of darkness into his marvelous light, and in response, we are to be in ministry in the name of Christ.

MINISTRY

An observer might say at this point we all have theology: biblical, historical, as well as contemporary with its emphasis on the people of God. But then why has the church not caught the vision of being the whole people of God in ministry? Why have the laity not had a fuller sense of vocation?

At least three obstacles hinder the nurturing of the ministry of the whole people of God in their relating of faith to daily life. Each of these obstacles is not mutually exclusive; one or more may be found in each of us at different times.

The first obstacle could simply be called passivity. Yves Congar, a French Roman Catholic writer on the laity in the 1950s, tells of a priest who was asked about the position of the laity in the Roman Catholic church. "The laity have two positions," was the answer. "They kneel before the altar, that is one. And they sit below the pulpit, that is the other."[22]

The stance of passivity has various causes: a docility that accepts the meaning of "lay" as second-rate, as a lower status; an apathy that sees the church as a volunteer organization ("Lay ministry? I'm not into that!") rather than as an army whose members are already drafted by the mark of baptism.

Each of these causes of passivity has in common the fact that many laypersons, in Hendrik Kraemer's words, see themselves and are seen by others as objects, not as subjects and agents.[23] Too often, the emphasis of the church is primarily on ministry *to* the laity rather than on ministry *of* the laity. Ministry to the laity implies that ministry is a set of skills certain professional people have who perform them on nonprofessionals. The result is listless resignation (someone has called it "a taming of the pew") and a spiritlessness that denies the living freshness of the Holy Spirit working within the body of Christ who bestows all kinds of gifts among the people of God.

Ministry *to* the laity can be labeled and packaged. But ministry *of* the laity understands ministry more as an adverb rather than a noun, a thing. The servanthood that I have received from Christ influences the *way* I approach everything in my life. Ministry *of* the laity is a way of living in which attitudes, perceptions, and behaviors are informed by faith.

A second obstacle is perfectionism. Did I make the right decision? Did I do the right thing? Is it good enough? Such questions haunt all of us. The search for perfection is self-destructive; the resulting guilt is overwhelming; and this obstacle is far more prevalent than most of us imagine. Last fall, at a five-week seminar on faith and daily life attended by a dozen corporate executives, questions such as these were submitted in writing at the end of the first session: "Doesn't adherence to Christ's teaching preordain continuous frustration?" and "Does the church really understand that I 'must' make 'un-Christian' choices at work?"

Christians need to remind one another that we are not required to be successful, but to be faithful. Faithfulness implies a stick-to-itiveness, or in the old phrase, a perseverance in the faith. Forgiveness and absolution are not abstract doctrines and rites, but tangible and concrete needs for imperfect Christians who are wrestling in their daily lives to live the faith they confess.

The third obstacle to the ministry of the whole people of God is compartmentalization. God is not believed to be present in certain times and places: Sunday morning, yes, of course, but not on Monday in my business or on Saturday in my recreation and leisure. God may be present in my decision making about the use of my income, but not in my political or sexual decisions. God may be present in the shop of the independent storekeeper, but not in the corporate board room or the union hall. God may be present with the nurse and the teacher, these helping professionals, but what about the UPS truck driver or the kid pumping gas? Of course, God is present in the beauty of the sunset and in the walk by the seashore, but what about in the grime of the factory or in the hectic tension of the computer center? Church spires point to the heavens, but what about the skyscraper of glass or the garish neon of used-car lots and fast-food places?

And so the schizophrenia grows. The world is, at worst, the domain of evil and endless confusion; at best, the world is neutral. "This Is My Father's World," and "Beautiful Saviour, King of Creation," we may sing with great vitality, but that is not the way the world strikes us on Monday morning. Out of fear, vulnerability, and a deliberate protecting of self, we believe too frequently in the doctrine of the real presence at the altar, and in the doctrine of the real absence at the desk and assembly line and the kitchen sink.

And at the same time, a deep hunger comes through, a hunger to live all of life in the light of the Christ whom we confess. To see the wholeness of one's commitment to Christ, to be open to the Spirit wherever one is, and to be aware of the Creator in all the places—all these become steps on the journey to understand that all of creation, all of the earth, all of the world, is the Lord's.

BAPTISM, GIFTS, AND CREATION

In the light of the issues concerning the ministry of the laity and in response to the obstacles just noted, what are the theological emphases and the structural implications which a church should explore more fully?

I would like to make a preliminary sketch of three theological emphases which might well make a real difference in a church that understands itself to be the people of God in ministry in the world. This discussion should give us a perspective to consider the practical recommendations in the next section of the paper.

The first theological emphasis is baptism, and there is no other place to begin. We are Christ's, for as St. Paul writes: "We were buried therefore with him by baptism into death, so that as Christ was raised from the dead by the glory of the Father, we too might walk in newness of life" (Rom. 6:4).

My point here is to affirm the emphasis on baptism that the Lutheran tradition has always held and to applaud the more recent efforts to underline its importance. We are and will be richer for it. The church is a community, a fellowship of those who have been promised forgiveness of sins and newness of life through baptism in Jesus Christ. Such a community of believers, such a priesthood of the baptized, lives in the awareness that the cross was the place where the good news was revealed most clearly. We are therefore challenged to live in suffering love for our neighbor. The concluding prayer of the rite of Holy Baptism in the *Lutheran Book of Worship* catches the nuances well:

> Through Baptism God has made these new brothers and sisters members of the priesthood we all share in Christ Jesus, that we may proclaim the promise of God and bear his creative and redeeming Word into all the world.

In brief, baptism is, in Robert Jenson's phrase, "a commissioning to mission."[24]

A second theological emphasis is gifts, the gifts of the Holy Spirit. Out of the Spirit's infinite imagination comes the kaleidoscopic variety of the gifts that the community of Christ possesses. St. Paul's imagery of the church as a body with many members as well as his celebration of the rich abundance of gifts portrayed in 1 Corinthians 12 point to the variety of the gifts; therefore, there is no need to be exclusive in their use. The ministry of the people of God is the use of our gifts to strengthen and support others for the sake of Christ. A vital church identifies, affirms, encourages, and exercises the gifts that the Spirit has given the members of the body.

"God is a great lord and has many servants," said Luther once.[25] Would our discussions of lay professionals, commissioned ministries, lesser orders, and all such matters be different if we put such discussions within the framework of the multitude of gifts within the body of Christ? Would our examination of the functions of the laity be different if the stress were placed on the many callings the Spirit presents to us? "The vocation of the Church is to sustain many vocations," wrote Richard Neuhaus.[26] No number of committees or no amount of studies will once and for all delineate with perfect clarity the relationships of the ordained and those of the laity, the distinctive nature of each, let alone all the other callings within the church. Living persons within a living church cannot be so circumscribed. While we will need to spell out carefully such specific matters as endorsement, certification, and pension plans for those who work in the new church, such discussions are primarily internal management with principles of good order and justice to be observed. Of absolute importance is a full understanding of gifts as a framework for all discussions of ministry, for the nature of the Spirit's richness is to bestow an abundance of variegated gifts to God's servants.

In addition to the doctrines of baptism (Whose we are) and gifts (who we are), I would submit that we need to underline the doctrine of creation (where we are). If baptism emphasizes our relationship to Christ, and the teaching of gifts stresses the Holy Spirit, then the doctrine of creation gives prominence to the first article of the Creed.

For Luther, the creation as such was good. The created world is not a lower order of being but is itself the instrument of divine goodness. When God now chooses to reveal himself, he does so in and through the creation itself. The finite is capable of revealing the infinite. God is throbbingly alive in his world.

And the world is the arena for our ministry, for our various callings. The earth is the Lord's; there is no sacred and secular division. The seemingly ordinary and the allegedly mundane world in which women and men cultivate fields, design computer programs, empty bedpans, and vacuum carpets—this world is the *locus* of where we are in God's creation, and where we are to be participants in the ongoing and interdependent work of his creation.

The world, the arena of God's activity, is full of ambiguity and opaqueness. That means motives are mixed; compromises must be struck. Yet, it is in the very stuff of life that God calls us to be partners and colleagues, to participate in the care and nurture of our life together as humankind in creation.

Perhaps one of the most important things that I have learned in the last several years working with laypersons in conferences and retreats is to begin inductively, concretely. Start where you are. Out of the cauldron of actuality come questions such as: What challenged you last week? What haunted or bugged you? What sustained you, gave you joy? At what points and in what ways did your daily living *intersect* with your Christian faith? How do the words and feelings of your daily living (pressure, tensions, competition, success, compromise, conflict) intersect with the language of faith (discipleship, prayer, the presence of God)? What did your life tell of the goşpel yesterday? What will it mean to live by grace tomorrow?

You are already in ministry. You are already part of God's intricate network of creation.

Baptism, the gifts of the Spirit, and creation—nothing new here, one might say. But these three doctrines, deeply rooted in the Scriptures and in the tradition of the church, begin to bridge the gaps and meet the obstacles discussed. To passive Christians neglecting their vocation as God's servants in his world, what could be more challenging and renewing than the awareness of their baptism as their never-ending bond with Christ? To Christians futilely searching for perfection and overwhelmed with guilt, what could be more crucial than the gifts that the Spirit has already given them, as well as the forgiveness of sins which the Spirit promises? And to Christians torn between the sacred and the secular, what could be more helpful than a theology of creation that sees the world as the arena of God's Word in action?

Baptism, the gifts of the Spirit, and creation—these three doctrines could be pivotal in a church that takes the ministry of the whole people of God with great seriousness.

THE NEW CHURCH

I now put before us some suggestions for a church which understands itself as the whole people of God in ministry. Not one of the suggestions is elaborated in detail; I only identify some critical places where structural entities will be affected.

First, concerning institutions related to the church—the colleges and seminaries.

1. The colleges. Students of the 80s are highly career-conscious. Some Lutheran colleges have, through both the curriculum and extracurricular areas, confronted students not only with what career to pursue, but also with the importance of why they want to follow a particular occupation. Vocation in all meanings of the term is exactly what the church-related college is about.

2. The seminaries. A friend of mine from the business community who knows several seminaries quite well reports that when he asks what the end product of seminaries is, seminary leadership usually responds something like this: a well-educated and fully committed clergy. His rejoinder is that such a response is too narrow. It is as if the leadership at a service academy, he says, would limit their vision to well-trained officers rather than to goals of producing a fine army which is aware of the responsibilities of war and peace. The end product of seminaries, he suggests, is a well-equipped and fully committed church.

I would also plead that scholarship and research are urgently needed on the subject of the ministry of the laity. With a few notable exceptions, most of the present writing is exhortatory and popular. Meanwhile, has Lutheran theological scholarship looked at questions such as these? What is the understanding of *laos,* of *diakonia* in the New Testament and early church? What is Luther's understanding of the laity? In the ecumenical groundswell concerning the phrase, "the people of God," where do Lutherans stand? What kind of models for shared or mutual ministry of pastor and congregation is already practiced? Unless the best theological minds engage in careful thought on such questions, the ministry of the laity will just be another passing fad, or worse yet, follow paths and create structures that distort the mission of the church.

There are three areas (briefly) on how we go about the work of the church: (1) Advocacy. Have we really heard what the Evanston Assembly of the World Council of Churches said some thirty years ago?

> The time has come to make the ministry of the laity explicit, visible and active in the world. The real battles of the faith today are being fought in factories, shops, offices, and farms, in political parties and government agencies, in countless homes, in the press, radio and television, in the relationship of nations. Very often it is said that the church should "go into these spheres"; but the fact is, that the Church *is* already in these spheres in the persons of its laity.[27]

(2) Education. The Lutheran tradition has always stressed an educated clergy and a well-trained laity. The educational resources of the new church might well have as part of its mandate: to enable persons to identify, be equipped, and be supported in their ministries. How will the material assist persons to see that the church, as Daniel Berrigan once said, is the place to go from? (3) Ecumenism. Whether in inter-Lutheran or interchurch dialogue, the subject of ministry is always on the agenda, as well it should be. My question is that in such discussions, will the ministry of the laity receive no more than lip service? Will issues such as ordination and recognition of ministries, important as such matters are, receive such overwhelming attention that no time, energy, or resources are left for study and recommendations on the ministry of the whole people of God?

A word on congregations.

Luther spoke of the "mutual conversation and consolation"[28] which the Christian community of believers experiences and lives. That is the difference between seeing the congregation as a group of persons gathered around one minister or as a ministering community, both to one another, and to those around them. The church building is not first of all a shrine or an assembly hall, but in Trueblood's words, the church building is the "headquarters" of the army of the committed.[29] The building in its worship, education, and fellowship is the base of operations. The field is the world.

Thus, the structure of the congregation gathered needs arenas for dialogue where members can engage in "mutual conversation and consolation" for support and encouragement in order that the church scattered (individually and corporately) may be the body of Christ in the world.

I end this section with comments on the institutional structure of the church.

A church which understands itself as the people of God might well avoid two extremes: (1) To create a Department of the Laity. I say emphatically No! If that is what my listeners assumed was coming, I have failed in all that I have said. The ministry of the laity is not to be reduced to a program of the church. (2) The other extreme is to take a business-as-usual approach. "After all, everything we do in the church is ministry of the laity!" That, as I have attempted to spell out earlier, is just not true.

Rather, when questions (large and small) such as the following are raised, the awareness that the church is the people of God will so permeate our thinking that the answers will reflect an openness to exploring the various implications.

1. What time will the meeting be held? The answer to that seemingly routine question, whether of the Commission of the New Lutheran Church,

or of a congregational meeting, or of this gathering pretty well determines who will participate. A friend of mine, a chemist in Kansas City, assumed before the dates for this weeklong conference were announced that at least part of the sessions would be on a weekend.

2. Who will be considered for positions in church leadership? Whether elected or appointed, except for the office proscribed by the documents, the needs of the position and the gifts of those being considered would, I assume, be the criteria.

3. What kind of representation will be set up for judicatories, committees, councils, and national conventions? Let me cite three kinds of models: First, I begin with my home territory, whose predecessor body was the Ministerium of Pennsylvania. At the first Lutheran synod formed in North America under Muhlenberg in Philadelphia in 1748, the assembly involved six pastors and twenty-four laymen representing ten congregations. The laymen were simply visitors, with no vote. Second, the general practice at present, with a few exceptions, is the fifty-fifty principle: 50 percent clergy and 50 percent laity. Third, I cited a moment ago the first Lutheran assembly in North America in 1748 and now I would like to point to the most recent North American Lutherans who are in quest of unity: the Canadian churches. Their discussions thus far have approved a formula for arriving at eligible voting members of the convention in which approximately three-fifths of the delegates will be laypersons.

Let me be clear: I am not arguing at this time for any particular kind of governance or polity. I am raising these matters in this context because at the crucial points of decision, the questions should include not only: What has been the polity in the Lutheran tradition? but also: What kind of governance is needed in light of the gifts and needs of the body of Christ?

I end this paper by reminding all of us that what Conrad Bergendoff called for in 1951 still needs to be done: the development of a doctrine of the laity, a theology of the whole people of God.

In his provocative book *The New Reformation?*[30] Bishop J. A. T. Robinson points out that the resource for theology in the twentieth century is precisely that: the church as the people of God in the world. He traces the sources of theology in the history of the church: in the early church after the New Testament, episcopal theology, the feeding and nurturing of the flock, was central. Later, monastic theology emphasized the contemplative, and medieval theology with its university setting focused on scholastic theology. Since the Reformation, the training of a professional clergy has meant a centering on pastoral theology, the development of the skills of the ordained. Robinson's point, and mine, is that each of these strands can and should continue to be sources for theological reflection. But the church of the twenty-first century will find that their thinking about the power of the gospel will be in the context of the lives of the people of God in the world.

Theology of the laity certainly does not mean anticlericalism nor theology made simple and easy. Rather, theology of the laity will take seriously such difficult words as experience, contextual, *praxis* among others. It will bring to expression the life of the people of God as they express the body of Christ in the world.

We must find the arenas and the methods to begin to talk about what such theology of the *laos* might look like, what the gospel means as it is lived in the lives of the whole people of God. What could be more exciting than such an undertaking for a new church?

The vocation of the laity, the ministry of the whole people of God, the body of Christ giving itself to the world in the name of Jesus Christ—that has been, is, and will be the mission of the church.

NOTES

1. David Preus, *The Lutheran Standard* (September 16, 1980): 45.

2. *Lumen Gentium,* chapter IV, section 31.

3. W. A. Visser't Hooft, ed., *The First Assembly of the World Council of Churches* (New York: Harper & Bros., 1948), p. 155.

4. Report of the Joint Lutheran/Roman Catholic Study Commission on "The Gospel and the Church" ("Malta Report"), *Lutheran World,* XIX, 3 (1972), pp. 259ff.

5. *The Ministry in the Church* (Geneva: Lutheran World Federation, 1982), pp. 6–7.

6. Preus, *Lutheran Standard,* p. 45.

7. LCA *Minutes,* 1980, p. 31.

8. LCA *Minutes,* 1970, pp. 428–29.

9. LCA *Minutes,* 1980, p. 141.

10. *Baptism, Eucharist and Ministry* (Geneva: World Council of Churches, 1982), pp. 20–32.

11. One of the best defenses of this position is Peter L. Kjeseth, "Baptism as Ordination," *Dialog* 8 (Summer 1969): 177–82.

12. John Reumann, "Ordained Minister and Layman in Lutheranism," *Lutherans and Roman Catholics in Dialogue IV: Eucharist and Ministry,* ed. Paul C. Empie, T. Austin Murphy (New York and Washington, D.C.: USA National Committee of the Lutheran World Federation and the Bishops' Commission for Ecumenical Affairs, 1970), p. 232. This lengthy essay, the most substantial study of the relationship of the ordained and lay in the Lutheran tradition which I have found, deserves more attention.

13. Conrad Bergendoff, "Wanted: A Theory of the Laity in the Lutheran Church," *Lutheran Quarterly* 3 (February, 1951): 82.

14. This paper, as most such endeavors, is indebted to many others. In addition to those cited within the paper, I would express my gratitude to several others who have been extremely helpful in their writing, speaking, and conversation for developing more fully my understanding of the ministry of the laity: Robert Brorby, William Diehl, Franklin D. Fry, Barbara Hanst, Timothy Lull, Roland Martinson, and Michael Root.

15. Donald R. Heiges, *The Christian's Calling* (Philadelphia: Muhlenberg Press, 1958), p. 21.

16. Ibid., p. 40.

17. Robert L. Calhoun, "Work and Vocation in Christian History," *Work and Vocation,* ed. John Oliver Nelson (New York: Harper & Bros., 1954), p. 103.

18. "Church Postils," *The Precious and Sacred Writings of Martin Luther,* ed. J. N. Lenker (Minneapolis: Lutherans of All Lands Co., 1950), pp. 242–43.

19. Cited in Paul Althaus, *The Theology of Martin Luther,* trans. Robert C. Schultz (Philadelphia: Fortress Press, 1966), p. 314.

20. Gustaf Wingren, *Luther on Vocation,* trans. Carl C. Rasmussen (Philadelphia: Muhlenberg Press, 1957).

21. "Lutheran Listening Post Survey Number Three," Office for Research and Planning, Lutheran Church in America.

22. Yves Congar, *Lay People in the Church,* trans. Donald Attwater (London: Geoffrey Chapman, 1957), p. xi.

23. Hendrik Kraemer, *A Theology of the Laity* (London: Lutterworth Press, 1958), pp. 18–19.

24. Robert W. Jenson, "Baptism for Ministry," unpublished paper presented at the Colloquium on the Ministry of the Laity, 23-26 May 1982, sponsored by LAOS in Ministry.

25. Cited in Paul Althaus, *The Ethics of Martin Luther,* trans. Robert C. Schultz (Philadelphia: Fortress Press, 1972), p. 36.

26. Richard John Neuhaus, *Freedom for Ministry* (New York: Harper & Row, 1979), p. 203.

27. *Evanston Speaks* (New York: World Council of Churches, 1955), pp. 64–65.

28. Smalcald Articles, part Three, 4, cited in Reumann, "Ordained Minister and Layman," p. 236.

29. Elton Trueblood, *The Company of the Committed* (New York: Harper & Row, 1961), pp. 72–75.

30. John A. T. Robinson, *The New Reformation?* (Philadelphia: Westminster Press, 1965), pp. 60–63. One of the most extensive efforts to develop a theology of the laity is found in John Macquarrie, *The Faith of the People of God: A Lay Theology* (New York: Charles Scribner's Sons, 1972).

6
Embodying the Gospel in an Inclusive Church

KATHLEEN S. HURTY

> "When *I* use a word," Humpty Dumpty said, in rather a scornful tone, "it means just what I choose it to mean—neither more nor less."
>
> "The question is," said Alice, "whether you *can* make words mean so many different things."
>
> "The question is," said Humpty Dumpty, "which is to be master—that's all."
>
> —Lewis Carroll, *Through the Looking-Glass*

Definitions are key positions. What we mean is shaped by what we believe and where we stand. Meanings grow out of our experiences as human beings and are translated into terms and concepts that can be shared within the human community. This paper will focus on the meaning of inclusiveness in relation to an expanded definition of the concept of power. The frame for this exploration of the interaction of inclusiveness and power is the church as organization—an organization with the good intention of embodying the gospel in the way it acts, decides, communicates, and worships.

Embodying the gospel in an inclusive church is, at root, *receiving a gift already given.* We are accepted into the community of faith by the living risen Christ. Neither sex, nor race, nor class, nor age, nor geographical location, nor organizational wit, nor theological expertise, nor strength, nor vulnerability, nor any other specification determines our full participation in this community and its organizational manifestation, the church. Rather it is determined simply by grace—a gift. Therefore, to struggle with the concept of inclusiveness is not to invent it but to be about the task of discerning and implementing the gift, of finding a new organizational expression of grace for our time, of praying and working for the perfect reign of God. Secondly, the answers to these questions will be voiced only when *all*

106

members of the community become listeners. To name the distortions of our past is both to listen and to share in the experiences of hurt, pain, and frustration of those excluded. It requires a sharing of stories over the next decade, a collecting of the data from the "outsiders"—the nonincluded. This talking and listening, this sensing and sharing of the other's pain and joy, will shape the response to these questions. In other words, we cannot construct or pronounce inclusiveness by fiat, for it is a proffered gift. Nor can we shape a new church without gathering more data through the *"mutual conversation and consolation of the saints,"* a very Lutheran methodology which includes listening, sensing, and speaking together in trustful ways. This implies a continuing search in these next years—in commissions and task forces, in congregations and councils, in homes and work in ad hoc interest groups—for what it means to be *gracefully* and inclusively the church.

In order to define clearly what it means to be an inclusive church, it is necessary to look at the concept of power and its interaction with the concept of inclusiveness. I have chosen to concentrate on power from two angles of vision: organizational and experiential. Several presuppositions are basic to the examination of meaning within this topic: 1) inclusiveness is organizationally possible; 2) inclusiveness images and embodies the gospel; 3) inclusiveness and power are interactive; 4) power informs structure; 5) power, though frequently ignored in ecclesiological research, is a central concept within the church. From this perspective my thesis is that *the new church—to be new—must struggle with the interaction of power and inclusiveness and must employ the principle of coactive empowerment in order to participate in the emergence of unity.* Part of my task is to look at the divisive issues that impede this process of embodying the gospel. My experience with and research in the area of gender stratification prompt me to choose this as a focus although clearly all of the "isms" of inequality—racism, classism, ageism, ethnocentrism, as well as sexism—are interrelated and complex. I speak out of my experience as a woman and a feminist. But to use gender as a "prototypic" division is not to ignore the other profound and divisive structures of oppression and brutalization that exist.

The word "power" derives from the Latin *posse:* "to be able." By the eighth century, this form in vulgar Latin was supplanted by *potere. The Oxford English Dictionary* devotes nearly three full pages to the word "power." Defined primarily as a quality or property, power is said to be the ability to do or effect something or to act upon a person or thing; physical or mental strength; might, vigor, energy; force of character; possession of control or command over others; dominion, rule; government, domination, sway, command; control, influence, authority.

Most of our later definitions of power have shifted considerably from the original notion of power as *posse,* "to be able." In the earlier sense, power seems more akin to a *capacity to do* than a *property to have,* yet we now tend to define power predominantly as a finite resource that can be objectified. In this definition, when one has more, others have less. Note how this is evident in organizational theory.

Organizational theorists, building on the work of Max Weber, an early twentieth-century German sociologist, describe power as an attribute of the powerful whose organizational positions are marked by *control over* others and the ability to justify that control as legitimate authority (Etzioni, 1964). Power in organizations has thus come to be attached to concepts of authority, might, domination, legitimacy, and influence. A frequently cited definition of power stipulates: A has power over B to the extent that he can get B to do something that B would not otherwise do (Dahl, 1957; Etzioni, 1964). This definition of power is a cornerstone of the bureaucratic model—the most predominant organizational model of the mid-twentieth century—and churches, along with corporations, public agencies, and many other institutions, have chosen that model together with the definitions it provides. To have power is to have *control over* people and resources (including theology and ecclesiology) with little attention to the interactive relationships within a power setting.

What is becoming evident, however, is that power defined in this way is problematic. The concept of power in organizational theory is being reexamined (see, for example, Bennis, 1973; Kanter, 1978; Pfeffer, 1981). There is a malaise in institutional power settings as seen in labor/management disputes, affirmative action conflicts, divergent claims of authority. In the churches these conflicts sometimes occur between laity and clergy, between women and men, between "white" and "minority," between those who cite "authority" and those who cite "experience" to justify truths, and between bureaucrats and theologians. There is dis-ease among the presumed powerful and the presumed powerless. Elizabeth Janeway captures the broad sweep of the power dilemma:

> The analytical vision of power from Aristotle [onward] . . . has been directed to matters that concern the powerful. But that's only half the story, it's the eagle's view of power from above, sharp and definable, but separated from the ordinary processes of living.
>
> To be content with this view alone is to agree that power belongs to the powerful as an attribute or a possession, a kind of magic wand that compels obe-

dience. Such an appraisal leaves out the deeply grounded relatedness in which new human creatures find their own identities through the intervention of others, whose presence mediates and interprets the whole ground of reality . . . This vision of relatedness modifies our understanding of power. If it is a process of human interaction, it is much more than a static structure of dominance and submission. (Janeway, 1980)

It is the structure of domination and subordination that is being challenged today. The hierarchical arrangements we call "bureaucracy" and the institutional managerial practices constructed around that theory were originally intended to prevent the abuses of power that had become prevalent in the early days of the Industrial Revolution. They were developed for another era and the context has changed. The time has come for new meanings to be developed, new structures to be explored and shaped.

Other meanings are beginning to appear. Carol Gilligan, in her book *In a Different Voice* (1982), shares what she hears as a distinction: two ways of speaking about moral problems and two modes of describing the relationship between other and self. The association of these two modes with male and female voices in psychological and literary texts is clear. This association has led to the somewhat typical assumption that men's development and language are the norm, while women's way is deviant. Women, seen from that view, fail to fit existing models of human growth or current measures of competency. The problem can rather be defined as a limitation in the conception of the human condition or an omission of certain truths about life. Gilligan lifts the argument into the broader area of inclusiveness and power:

The different voice I describe is characterized not by gender but theme. Its association with women is an empirical observation, and it is primarily through women's voices that I trace its development. But this association is not absolute, and the contrasts between male and female voices are presented here to highlight a distinction between two modes of thought and to focus a problem of interpretation rather than to represent a generalization about either sex. . . . Clearly, these differences arise in a social context where factors of social status and power combine with reproductive biology to shape the experience of males and females and the relations between the sexes. My interest lies in the interaction of experience and thought, in different voices and the dialogues to which they give rise, in the way we listen to ourselves and to others, in the stories we tell about our lives.

In this spirit, then, it is to the writings of some women that we now turn in order to ferret out a wider range of meanings for the concept of power.

Mary Parker Follett, working in the early part of this century in the field of business administration, drew a distinction between "power over" and "power with," coercive and coactive power. Her arguments freed the latter from the dysfunctional association of power with domination. The roots of *integrative bargaining,* being explored in my school district and others to-day (as a step beyond the adversarial tendencies of collective bargaining) are found in the work of Follett. Dorothy Emmet (1954), acknowledging her debt to Follett, expanded the meaning of the concept of power by developing a typology that might be utilized more effectively in understanding human actions and sociopsychological conditions. She suggests that there are notable differences, for example, between the power of manipulation, direction, and control and the power that is manifested in creative, coactive relationships. In this latter power situation, the effect of power of B on A will be to stimulate A to such firsthand effort as he or she is capable of. This need not take the form of B conforming to the opinions or practice of A. Those who have had the good fortune to come in contact with effective teachers who open windows of vision for students and seek not conformity but originality and invention know the difference between these two kinds of power: power as domination and power as creative collaboration, or, to use Letty Russell's term, power as partnership.

Jean Baker Miller (1976) defines power as the *capacity to implement.* This capacity to do a job (power) is seen by Miller not as a possession of "the boss" but as an empowerment process within a relationship based on *mutuality.* This definition bears clear resemblance to the meaning of power from its Latin root *posse,* "to be able"—and leads us in the direction of power as possibility. It is also compatible with the Greek word for power *dynamis,* and its English derivative *dynamic,* characterized by the concept of energy. Miller explores the problems of domination/subordination from the perspective of psychology:

> A dominant group, inevitably, has the greatest influence in determining a culture's overall outlook—its philosophy, morality, social theory, and even its science [and, I would add, its theology]. The dominant group, thus, legitimizes the unequal relationship and incorporates it into society's guiding concepts. The social outlook, then, obscures the true nature of this relationship—that is, the very existence of inequality. The culture explains the events that take place in terms of other premises that are inevitably false, such as racial or sexual inferiority.

Miller bases her book on the premise that the "subordinate" has something to say about the human condition and to the dominant/subordinate paradigm within it. The psychological characteristics found most commonly in women and identified as "weaknesses" by the dominant are redefined as strengths: the willingness to acknowledge vulnerability, emotional connectedness, cooperativeness, and creativity. Her challenge is to serve without subservience. She rejects the definitions of power based on dominance and explores ways to move beyond weakness to new meanings of power.

Bell Hook's work in showing vividly the inseparability of racism and sexism (*Ain't I a Woman: Black Women and Feminism,* 1982) focuses also on the tragedy of domination as an ideology. As she examines the impact of sexism on the black woman during slavery, the devaluation of black womanhood, the sexism of black males, and the racism within the recent feminist movement, she keeps our eyes focused on the need to eradicate this "ideology of domination that permeates Western culture on various levels—sex, race, and class to name a few." Both Hooks and Miller are clear that the elimination of the domination/subordination paradigm is not just for the benefit of women, or people of color, or working-class persons—but the fundamental goal is the liberation of all people. Hooks recalls the words of Anna Cooper who in 1892 proudly voiced the black woman's perspective:

> Let woman's claim be as broad in the concrete as in the abstract. We take our stand on the solidarity of humanity, the oneness of life, and the unnaturalness and injustice of all special favoritism, whether of sex, race, country, or condition.

Such a view preempts domination as the primary relationship.

The language of domination is subtle and pervasive. Theologian Rosemary Radford Reuther (1975, 1982) firmly believes that language is the prime reflection of the power of the ruling group to define reality in its own terms. She sets her argument in the context of a challenge to patriarchy which has shaped human history until now. Note the patriarchal dichotomy, suggests Reuther, between "the transcendent masculinity of God, who alone possesses all initiative and power, and the abject passivity of the Christian, represented by the femininity of the church." The way we talk about the relations between Christ and the church, between pastor and people, images the "rigid hierarchical complementarity of male over female." Thus our language of faith reflects the definition of power as *control over* persons along sexist lines. Reuther's vision is that:

> The entire psychodynamics of relationships must be entirely transformed, so that activity is not identified with domination, split from a receptivity as dependency. We must envision a new model of reciprocity . . . This demands not only a transvaluation in psychic imagery, but a revolution in power relations between the sexes, representing all power relations of domination and

subordination. The symbol for this is not an "androgyny" that still preserves sexist dualism, but that whole personhood in which women can be both I and Thou. (Reuther, 1975, p. 58)

Questions about the relationship between language and power are the focus of Dale Spender's recent work. Like Reuther, she casts her discussion in the framework of sexism and patriarchy. Both men and women inhabit a male-decreed reality and make sense of it through male meanings, argues Spender. Women's silence and/or acquiescence leave this unchallenged. When it comes to power, for example, male meanings have been studied and male types of power have come to be accepted as the only "real" power, thereby placing women's meanings on the periphery of knowledge and reality. Today, however, feminist sociologists, linguists, theologians, educators, psychologists, and others are calling for redefinitions of power. With Spender, these people are saying that power could have many different and useful meanings if the experiences of women were to be taken into account.

Rosabeth Moss Kanter (1978) exemplifies this process of formulating meanings through her careful research on men and women in the corporation. She defines power as the ability to do, using the classic metaphor of power as energy, and thus power means having access to whatever is needed to be done. She includes in the discussion of power the elements of powerlessness, blocked opportunity, and tokenism. *Empowerment* is, in Kanter's analysis, a viable and productive strategy:

> To empower those women and others who currently operate at a disadvantage requires attention to both sides of power . . . Empowerment must also start with, and rest fundamentally on, modification of official structural arrangements. Flattening the hierarchy—removing levels and spreading formal authority is among the more general and important strategies.

Kanter rightly warns against the dangers of *not* dealing with the structures of power and opportunity. Strategies such as job enrichment, the sharing of discretion and autonomy among levels of the organization, and enlarged participation in decision making can be merely mechanisms for adjustment, not justice, when definitions of power, opportunity, and representativeness are not attended to.

The work of these "other voices" and many others that could be cited calls forth new meanings of power: power as a process of interrelating, power as shared capacity to implement, power as coactivity, power as empowerment, power as reciprocity, power as partnership. Now we have a Humpty Dumpty situation—an upside-down, off-the-wall logic of formulating meanings—that confounds the theoretical assumptions that pervade our social, political, and ecclesiastical life. The time has come to reject both Alice's naive powerlessness and Humpty Dumpty's scornful superiority. The time has come to begin the process of reconciliation and reconstruction through communication and discussion as we give new, enriched meanings to power *together*. We should work together in a shared humanness—women and men, people of color, people of varied ethnic backgrounds and in diverse economic situations. Such conversations are only possible when we listen as well as speak, when our decision-making bodies are fully representative of the diversity within the community of faith, and when we reject the *"we/they" dichotomy* that has characterized so much of the church's action in mission.

It is in the biblical perspective that power can clearly be seen as *empowerment*. Power and empowerment are threads woven into the stories of concern throughout Scripture—stories about people's struggle with the everyday, people who were empowered by and in partnership with the God of action and possibility. God's incarnation—becoming flesh in Christ—then energizes us to embody the gospel in and through the church. But what must be explored more deeply is the radical and refreshing meaning of power/empowerment articulated in the gospel. The hierarchical orderings of individuals and groups based on the "authority" of knowledge and achievement are replaced by the inclusive concept of brotherhood (familyhood)—we are children of God, sharing a common inheritance. As the German theologian Dorothee Soelle stated:

> The manner in which Jesus thought and acted *de facto* broke open and transformed the social structures of the world in which he lived. Thus, in light of the new brotherhood, familiar associations and limitations lose their traditional status as orders of nature (Mark 3:31–35) . . . Even the most significant of all social classifications, the division of men [sic] according to their level of culture—those who read and write and are religiously informed versus those who belong to classes that are culturally and educationally deprived—is stripped of its dignity and significance. "You are not to be called rabbi . . . Call no man your father on earth . . . Neither be called masters." Sovereign authority is abolished, and in place of a society constructed on a patriarchal model appears one structured according to the spirit of brotherhood. Matt. 23:8–10 indicates that this practice inaugurated by Jesus was continued by the community. (Soelle, 1974)

God's power is chronicled from Genesis to Revelation, and, though overlayed with centuries of patriarchal interpretations, the central concept embedded in the biblical message is still this: the gospel is the power of God for the salvation of everyone who believes (Rom. 1:16). It is this gospel—*the power of God for all*—that we are challenged to embody in an inclusive church. It is this power I am calling *coactive empowerment*.

Biblical religion celebrates the revelation of God-with-us as "advocate of the oppressed, as overturner of the unjust social order, as bringer of wholeness" to use Soelle's phrases. The gospel—the key message, the good news, the unqualified promise—is the story of Christ's divine-human life exuberantly and gracefully lived by the rubrics of compassion and cooperation, service and sacrifice, for the benefit of all and with the participation of all. The gift of the gospel is given not in a vacuum but in a relationship: the receiving of grace is matched with the call to be saints (Rom. 1:5)! It is a call to faith-lived-responsibly-in-community with God and within the human family. It is this *holy with-ness* that is the clue to empowerment. Together, God and people *are* the hungry and *feed* the hungry, *are* the stranger and *welcome* the stranger, *are* the sick and *visit* the sick (Matt. 25:31–46). God's presence here mediates and interprets the whole ground of reality. God here is *with us in need and in service.* Those who need and those who serve are not in a subordinate/dominant relationship but both are involved in the common and complex dilemmas of hunger, strangeness, and disease. God's presence is God's working-with managerial style—partnership, not lord-it-over-ship. It is this God-human interaction of shared receptivity and shared responsibility that marks most clearly the biblical perspective of power. This then becomes the basis of the principle of coactive empowerment from a religious perspective.

We have been talking mostly about power—what about inclusiveness? What about organizing and planning for a new church that is inclusive? As our thesis states, the new church—to be *new*—must struggle with the interaction of power and inclusiveness and must employ the principle of coactive empowerment in order to participate in the emergence of unity. So far I have tried to establish that power, often defined as "control over," is more productively understood as coactivity, *"power with,"* and as such is faithful to the biblical concept of empowerment (that is, the gospel defined as the power of God for the salvation of all believers and exemplified in the serving ministry—the life, death, and resurrection—of Jesus, the Christ). The organizational implications of this concept are many and varied. Specifically, now, we must deal with the knotty problem of inclusiveness.

Few would argue with the premise that the gospel's invitation is inclusive—open to all. Of course! Where we run into major difficulty is in organizing ourselves to live out that basic inclusivity in our church life without reverting to patriarchal and hierarchical structure. Let's look at some of the elements we need to consider in organizing an inclusive church.

There is little mention in the Scriptures concerning ways to organize a church, let alone prescriptive chapters on organizational development and change. What we do and have done over the centuries is our best guess about what God might want. The problem is: *who makes the decisions?* the disciples? the clergy? the church fathers? the theologians? the seminary professors? the church administrators? the elected committees? If that is so, did you notice a dilemma? Did the observation that this group is predominantly white, male, and "middle-class" strike you as limiting in any way? If, on the other hand, decisions are made by the *believers*—the whole people of God—is the experience base, the perspective and insights available for decision making, enriched? How do you organize for such participatory decision making?

Coactive empowerment is an alternative paradigm for the decision-making process. It is based on participation rather than domination. Flattened hierarchies may be a first step, as Kanter suggests. This means removing levels and spreading formal authority, creating more autonomous units, increasing the discretion and latitude of leaders, implementing team concepts and carrying out work through task forces and project groups, opening communication channels and making system knowledge more routinely available for everyone (Kanter, 1978).

Sheryl Pearson (in Florisha and Goldman, 1981, pp. 59–74) focuses specifically on aspects of communication in her model which she calls *co-orientation*. Her suggestions include: 1) less autocratic downward communication contributing to an attitude of respect for the other party; 2) integrative decision-making and group problem-solving behaviors, ruminating toward conclusions, recognizing the power of personal narrative to stimulate inquiry; 3) nondefensive communication techniques and conflict-resolution skills using provisional language and integrative responses (uniting speaker and listener); 4) listening skills, receptivity to variant views, audience analysis, and orientation toward interchange. These approaches include participants in the grappling-toward-a-decision-together that is a mark of an inclusive church, and they imply face-to-face exchange. They do not rule out conflict and tension but seek, rather, reconciliation through participation. When we sit down together, in *mutual* conversation, we do not allow *Robert's Rules of Order* to get in the way of full participation, nor do *we* make decisions *for them*—that is, for women, blacks, Hispanics, Asians, the poor, homosexuals, or for any groups that are excluded. When I am sitting across the table from you, eye-to-eye, you must take me into account. When I am involved in shaping the questions to ask, gathering data, and acting as a partner in the decision, then I am empowered. We may not agree, but we can test our disagreements in the arena where the decisions are made—conjointly, coactively, consensually.

I remember the dramatic moment when Joseph Kibira was elected president of the Lutheran World Federation in 1977 in Dar es Salaam, Tanzania. To the ecstatic tremolo of the vigelegele he was ushered to the podium to accept the gavel. With delightful reverence, however, he laid down the gavel, and said he would choose, instead, the fly whisk—the symbol of tribal decision making. In this process the leader, assessing that the conflict is not yet resolved, or the decision not yet consensual, simply waves the whisk and the talking continues. Such a vivid model of participatory decision making serves us well as we move into unity talks!

In addition to organizing for participatory decision making we must also know our history and deal with the tensions that are a part of our past. Martin Marty focuses our attention on these elements in his book on American Protestantism, *The Righteous Empire.* This work describes well the constant tension both within the biblical record and throughout the history of the church—the tension between what it means to be both *a chosen people* and *an inclusive church.* It is a history we must understand, for the dilemma is a real one. How do we reconcile the exclusive commitment of being "the chosen people of God," or the "new Israel," and the overriding ethic of American Protestants to attract the allegiance of all people and set up a spiritual empire within a new nation? For us as Lutherans it relates to our attempts to define ourselves as church over against other churches and the larger world. Our struggles throughout this process have been both internal and external: questions of what languages to use, how to adhere appropriately to sixteenth-century formulations, how much to amalgamate into the American culture, how to deal with revivalism, modernism, fundamentalism, pluralism. To name the distortions in our history, to understand the limits of exclusiveness, is to probe our history, as Protestants and as Lutherans, among the other histories that we share. To deliberately plan an inclusive church means to be brave enough to critique our history and to struggle openly and honestly with the tensions that pervade it.

Another factor pertaining to inclusiveness is the sensitive gathering and analysis of data. Research is not a substitute for action but is itself a form of action—of seeking to know what is, while planning for what might be. Both qualitative and quantitative data can help us in defining the problem of exclusivism. For example, to know that the membership of the Lutheran churches in the U.S. is approximately 57 percent female, while only 25 percent of the decision-making positions (appointed and elected) are held by women, is to recognize exclusiveness. To know that American Indian, black, Asian, and Hispanic members combined make up less than 2 percent of our total membership while our population statistics show a much more diverse profile is to name our exclusiveness. Data on economic stratification within the church are almost nonexistent but would be informative in helping to recognize that here, too, we are most likely far more alike than different—far more monolithicly middle- and upper-class than inclusive of the broad spectrum of economic situations among U.S. citizens. With the increasing feminization of poverty, however, balanced against the predominance of women in our membership, that may change within the next decade.

With regard to our exclusivist tendencies there are two dangers in the use and analysis of data that should be noticed. I'll call these: *one-eyed interpretation* and *the conspiracy of silence*. When the Consulting Committee on Women of the LCA started their work a number of years ago it was impossible to get figures for male/female membership. The data were not there, the questions had not been asked. It took nearly three years to get spaces for male/female to be recorded on the congregational report form. This is not alone a church problem, for the term "conspiracy of silence" comes out of the work of historians David Tyack and Elizabeth Hansot who used it to describe the hiddenness of the decrease in the number of women in educational administration. The difficulty of obtaining data in many sensitive areas of our common life in organizations is well documented. Why are data not available? Do racist and sexist assumptions conspire to keep people uninformed and thus quiescent?

One-eyed interpretation is a metaphor for looking at data through the lens of only one group's experience. Exclusiveness exists when that data—quantitative or qualitative—is not reviewed by a broad spectrum of interests. For example, missing from historian Marty's *Public Church* (1981) is an accounting of women's participatory work in building the public church through ecumenical women's organizations and other groups. Women are quite hidden from this particular history, but that omission in itself has a certain eloquence for it points to the possibility that our histories to date are views of the patriarchy—not the whole people of God—and therefore are ripe for new research. New visions may grow from old roots if we reexamine our history as a public church using gender as a factor of importance.

Yet another element of inclusiveness is the integration of public and private worlds. The public world has been traditionally seen to be the world of economics and politics, of government and business. By extrapolation, the domains of theology and ecclesiology were also seen to be a part of the public world. The private world consisted of home and family and, in church life, devotion and duty. The public world was the arena of men; the private world the place of women. Vestiges of such a belief structure are still obvious. For example, adherence to a rigid view of the "orders of creation" makes one gasp in the presence of the gospel of inclusiveness; yet subtle beliefs, attitudes, and actions still persist. Many are calling today for the integration of the public and the private and the abandonment of stereotypes that prevent full stewardship of one's gifts.

Florisha and Goldman (1981) argue that to join work and relationships is to join the public and private worlds. In their view women have a distinct responsibility in this process of designing new social organizations: in many ways when women—trained to operate in the interpersonal sphere—achieve power, they become models of the integration of power and love (task orientation and people orientation) in the workplace. The key question then is not, How can women make it in the men's world? or How can people of color make it in an ethnocentric and basically white world? but rather, How will the presence of women and people of color alter and enrich the world we all share? And, how might this be true, especially, in the leadership of an inclusive church?

Let's look again at the biblical record in our discussion of inclusiveness. Though the Bible overwhelmingly favors male metaphors for deity, there is in Gen. 1:27 a basic metaphor of equality: the image of God as male *and* female. Phyllis Trible, in her signal work entitled *God and the Rhetoric of Human Sexuality* (1978) helps us explore this rich imagery and others as well. Important to our discussion of inclusiveness is her careful exegesis from a scholarly feminist perspective and her conclusions that male and female, though different, are nonetheless harmonious sexes; that unity embraces sexual differentiation while not imposing sexual identicalness; and that sexual differentiation does not mean hierarchy but rather equality. Created simultaneously, male and female are not superior and subordinate; neither has power over the other; in fact, both are given equal power. This is Gen. 1:27 interpreted afresh. We could go on through the Old Testament and find, hidden among stories of conquest and stories of exclusiveness, still other visions of a more inclusive way—the stories of Ruth and Jonah, for example. These are stories of crises, of mundane existence, and of timidness and vulnerability in the face of challenges to inclusiveness. In the New Testament Jesus' ministry is a model of inclusiveness as he meets, eats, talks with, and loves-into-partnership the outsiders of his day (prostitutes, tax collectors, women in general, lepers, rich, poor). And the exquisite breakthrough of Gal. 3:28 where Paul formulates the gospel on the principle of inclusiveness gives us a clear vision of inclusivity:

> There is neither Jew nor Greek, there is neither slave nor free, there is neither male nor female; for you are all one in Christ Jesus.

Bold and beautiful words—a manifesto of inclusiveness. The patterns of inclusiveness that are embedded in these words and in Jesus' work and life once again emphasize *partnership—the holy with-ness* that we discussed earlier, in relation to Matthew 25. So it is that we come full circle in our discussion of inclusiveness as we discover that the aspects of the gospel that require us to be inclusive are the same elements that speak to us about power. We cannot evade the interconnection. When power and inclusiveness are juxtaposed, there begins to emerge such gospel-centered values as mutuality, cooperation, collaboration, trust, service without subservience, and creativity.

Since Lutherans take sin seriously, it would be helpful to look at the sinfulness we share when we are not inclusive. I suggest that we take seriously—and publicly confess—the sin of *primacy*. I refer to the craving—sometimes subtle, sometimes naked—to be first, to be on top. Using old definitions it is the "will to power" or the "drive for power" and it is evidenced in the desire to dominate, to control. It is found everywhere: in organizations, in families, between interest groups, in churches. Primacy asks such questions as: which came first, men or women? class society or male supremacy? property or rape? production or slavery? which is the primary contradiction? Primacy establishes one group as the definers of reality, one language as the language all speak, one set of pronouns to cover all humans. Primacy says: my experience is *the* experience, my authority is *the* authority, my knowledge is *the* knowledge, while inclusiveness asks: what is my experience, what is your experience, and what can they together bring to the whole? Primacy chooses either/or. Inclusivity values both/and. To allow the values of inclusiveness and empowerment to emerge and take specific organizational shape we must *together* confess the sin of primacy.

We must also consider some of the counterarguments to inclusiveness. One is the argument of *relativism:* if all are included, anything goes and criteria for judgment cease to exist. Relativism, however, need not rule out evaluation. All beliefs are not equally true or desirable. All patterns of action are not appropriate. All people do not have the same gifts. Judgments, however, should not be based on stereotypes. Criteria should be developed interactively and from a perspective of deep appreciation and respect for other views. The gospel becomes the key touchstone which we use to validate the authenticity of our interpretations.

A second argument is *time:* if everybody participates in decision making it takes too long. Granted, it does take a long time to make consensual decisions if all interests are included in the discussion. But in our haste to decide, in our quest for efficiency, and in our hallowing of time-management studies, we have lost something. Peter Drucker (1971), in describing what we can learn from Japanese management, discusses the differences in time perspective between the consensual model and the hierarchical model. The Japanese debate a proposed decision throughout the organization until there is agreement on it. This involves *defining the question* together, exploring alternatives, focusing on the problem, not the answer. Such a process may take several years—but when the decision is made it is implemented immediately. The American style is quite the reverse. We tend to make speedy managerial decisions and then spend several years convincing people that it is the right decision. Time—used differently—carries different values.

Another difficulty with inclusiveness as a principle is what some call *quota-ism:* there is ambiguity about the strategy of using categories on ballots or when making appointments. The criticisms are that "quotas take us too far too fast" or that "quotas rule out competence." But quotas are essentially channels of choice as we act our way into embodying the gospel. They are the traffic rules that assist us to be our most fair selves. When we are in a hurry, they irritate; when we'd rather rule the road they chastise us. Following them does not ensure our salvation nor our safety! But they contribute to fairness and since we are coming to recognize that sin includes a social dimension we can acknowledge that quotas—like traffic signals—have our best interest in mind. Specified ballots, like specified budgets, shape our decisions and show where our commitments lie. In a similar vein, race- and sex-specific employment practices such as affirmative action give credence to our professed values. But they are just a first step. We will need to alter our narrow views of competence, passionately seek diversity of thought and imagination, and tenderly guard the notion of fairness.

The principle of coactive empowerment leads to some specific and practical suggestions for embodying the gospel in an inclusive church. I recommend:

1. that the concept of power be carefully defined in our documents to reflect the empowering aspects of the gospel;
2. that varieties of experience be accorded respect and presence in all meetings focusing on the formation of the new church;
3. that a participatory style of leadership and decision making be developed and adopted;
4. that the art of asking questions broadly before coming to conclusions be developed and honed;
5. that communication channels among committees, agencies, congregations, and so forth, be designed to allow for the "mutual conversation and consolation of the saints";

6. that the language of our liturgies and our legal matters be inclusive of and sensitive to people of color and to women;
7. that our educational materials reflect a commitment to inclusiveness;
8. that the councils and committees of the new church seek to maintain representativeness that does not penalize any group, and that the fifty-fifty lay-clergy requirements for many committees be re-examined in the light of these issues;
9. that a pluralism of viewpoints be honored in the organization;
10. that a balance of tradition and inventiveness be sought—and that both tradition and invention be tested against the principles of inclusiveness and empowerment;
11. that this list be kept open to the creativity of the Spirit as we move toward the embodiment of the gospel in an inclusive church.

Power as coactive empowerment is the placenta of our birth struggle toward the already-but-not-yet new church, conceived in love, trust, and coactivity. We are asking the members of the Commision on the New Lutheran Church to be the midwives, helping us to bring to birth a new and inclusive church. But they do not work alone. The creation of new meanings, the redefining of terms, the shaping of questions and the development of an inclusive church—all are our common tasks. And, in the fulness of time, that birth will come.

SELECTED BIBLIOGRAPHY

Arendt, Hanna. *On Violence.* London: Allen Lane, Penguin Press, 1970.
Bennis, Warren. *Beyond Bureaucracy.* New York: McGraw-Hill, 1973.
Booth, Wayne C. *Modern Dogma and the Rhetoric of Assent.* Chicago: University of Chicago Press, 1974.
Champlin, John R., ed. *Power.* New York: Atherton Press, 1971.
Cobb, John B., Jr. *Christ in a Pluralistic Age.* Philadelphia: Westminister Press, 1975.
Dahl, R. A. "The Concept of Power." *Behavioral Science* 2 (1957): 201–15.
Daniels, Roger, and Harry Kitano. *American Racism: Exploration of the Nature of Prejudice.* Englewood Cliffs, N.J.: Prentice-Hall, 1970.
Deutsch, Morton. *The Resolution of Conflict: Constructive and Destructive Processes.* New Haven: Yale University Press, 1973.
Drucker, Peter F. "What We Can Learn from Japanese Management." *Harvard Business Review* (March–April 1971).
Eckstrom, Vance. "Pluralism and Lutheran Confessionalism." *Lutheran Quarterly.*
Emmet, Dorothy. "The Concept of Power." *Proceedings of the Aristotelian Society* 54 (1954): 1–26. Reprinted in Champlin, 1971.

Etzioni, Amitai. *Modern Organizations*. Englewood Cliffs, N.J.: Prentice-Hall, 1964.

Florisha, Barbara, and Barbara Goldman. *Outsiders on the Inside*. Englewood Cliffs, N.J.: Prentice-Hall, 1981.

Follett, Mary Parker. *Creative Experience*. New York: Longmans, Green & Co., 1924.

Gilligan, Carol. *In a Different Voice*. Cambridge: Harvard University Press, 1982.

Hansot, Elizabeth, and David Tyack. "The Dream Deferred: A Golden Age for Women School Administrators." Policy Paper No. 81-C2. Institute for Research on Educational Finance and Governance, Stanford University Palo Alto, Calif., 1981.

Hooks, Bell. *Ain't I a Woman: Black Women and Feminism*. Boston: South End Press, 1981.

Janeway, Elizabeth. *Powers of the Weak*. New York: Alfred A. Knopf, 1980.

Kanter, Rosabeth Moss. *Men and Women of the Corporation*. New York: Basic Books, 1977.

Mansbridge, Jane. *Beyond Adversary Democracy*. New York: Basic Books, 1980.

March, James G., and Johan P. Olson. *Ambiguity and Choice in Organizations*. Oslo: Universitetforlaget, 1979.

Marty, Martin. *Righteous Empire*. New York: Dial Press, 1970.

_____. *The Public Church*. New York: Crossroad, 1981.

McClelland, David. *Power: The Inner Experience*. New York: Irvington, 1975.

Miller, Jean Baker. *Toward A New Psychology of Women*. Boston: Beacon Press, 1976.

Ouchi, William. *Theory Z*. Reading, Mass: Addison-Wesley, 1981.

Pfeffer, Jeffrey. *Power in Organizations*. Marshfield, Mass.: Pitman Publishing, 1981.

Reumann, John. *Jesus in the Church's Gospels: Modern Scholarship and the Earliest Sources*. Philadelphia: Fortress Press, 1968.

Reuther, Rosemary Radford. *New Woman, New Earth: Sexist Ideologies and Human Liberation*. New York: Seabury Press, 1975.

_____. *Disputed Questions: On Being a Christian*. Nashville: Abingdon Press, 1982.

Russell, Letty. *The Future of Partnership*. Philadelphia: Westminister Press, 1979.

Sanday, Peggy Reeves. *Female Power and Male Dominance: On the Origins of Sexual Inequality*. Cambridge: Cambridge University Press, 1981.

Soelle, Dorothee. *Political Theology*. Philadelphia: Fortress Press, 1974.

Spender, Dale. *Man Made Language*. London: Routledge & Kegan Paul, 1980.

Thompson, Betty. *A Chance To Change: Women and Men in the Church*. Philadelphia: Fortress Press, 1982.

Thorne, Barrie, and Nancy Henley. *Language and Sex: Difference and Dominance*. Rowley, Mass. Newbury House, 1975.

Trible, Phyllis. *God and the Rhetoric of Human Sexuality*. Philadelphia: Fortress Press, 1978.

7

Confessing the Faith of the Church

ROBERT W. BERTRAM

So hazardous is confessing, as in those fateful "times for confessing," "the time of trial," that our Lord bids us pray to be spared that ordeal. However, his church's only preventive against such times is a faith that at all times is, if necessary, confessable. That is the faith that for the integrity of his church, his one gospel-and-sacraments, is all the authority it needs, ever.

CONFESSIO: STERNUTATIO ECCLESIAE

Can it be that confessing is "the church's (form of) sneezing?" Doesn't that trivialize confessing? Well, consider what sneezing is. It is (1) the body's protest against contaminants in its head, (2) protesting within an inch of its life. Moreover, sneezing is (3) apparently an overreaction, though only apparently. It is (4) not optional yet (5) whenever possible it is to be averted. So, in all these five respects, is confessing.

Confessing is the body of Christ protesting against contaminants in its head (1). It is a conflict situation, the most serious conflict being internal. Confessing, in this primary sense, is not just any genial declaration of faith—for example, the way candidates for baptism might "confess" their faith amidst an approving congregation, or the way a Christian friend may "confess" the reason of her hope to a confidante, or the way a new denomination might vote into its constitution a "confessional" preamble, maybe unanimously and to standing ovations.

No, confessing is more embattled and adversarial than that. If faith were likened to breathing in, as we shall suggest later, confessing is not just the automatic reflex of that—breathing out. Confessing may mean that, too, but then only in a derived, domesticated sense. Then it describes a quite natural, noncontroversial venting of one's faith. Just as sneezing is not

123

some ordinary exhaling done at one's ease but is rather in the nature of an uprising, so is confessing, in the sense employed here. In fact, as often as not it comes off looking like disobedience, civil and/or ecclesiastical disobedience.

Confessio in its classical sense is the forensic counter-testimony of defendants on trial, *martyres,* implying that at that historic moment they—and with them the whole church—have been arraigned on a witness stand (*in statu confessionis*) by a superior critical tribunal, to all appearances divinely ordained, from whose authority the witnesses must nevertheless dissent.[1] Such a kairological moment, a fateful time of last resort, is what our tradition, the tradition of the Confessio Augustana, has called "a time for confessing" (*tempus confessionis*) or "a case of confessing" (*Fall der Bekenntnis*). But notice, that is always also "a time of persecution" (*Zeit der Verfolgung*).[2] What is being persecuted is not just the confessors but the gospel of Christ, the body's head. And those who persecute the gospel are secular authorities, though not only those in civil government but in church government as well—those in ecclesiastical positions who have been authorized publicly to speak for and to look like the head in their leadership of his body. In fact it has been powerful coalitions of ecclesiastical authority with the forces of secular society that confessors have been up against, right within their Christian communions, in the Confessing Church under Nazism, in the Second Vatican Council of the Roman Catholic church, in the Minjung martyrdoms in South Korea, in the confessional stand against apartheid in South Africa and in the U.S. "Times for confessing," we might generalize, are those singular occasions when Christians have had to disobey secular authority, including the church's own, in order to testify that for the integrity of the church of Jesus Christ his one gospel-and-sacraments is authority enough. *Satis est.*[3]

What is it about secular authority in the church that is objectionable—though objectionable, notice, only in those rare "times for confessing"? Ordinarily, secular authority does have validity in the church: divisions of labor, chains of command, grading systems, elections and promotions, legal contracts with sanctions, some Christians with titles, full-time staffs, promotional media, spending power, contracts, and above all influence, and some other Christians whom all that authority is meant to motivate or to pressure or even to censure. *De facto* churches could scarcely function without some such secular power.

The objection, even in "times for confessing," is not that secular authority is not sacred. It is, even though it is that "left-hand" administrative style in which the Creator merely minors, not majors. Nor is the objection that in secular authority the Creator creates by appealing to sinners' self-interest. That is of course what makes it "secular," a necessity of this outdated *saeculum,* this old aeon, which new-age Christians, however, do not for that reason abandon. The confessional objection is not even that secular authority promotes evil, as it notoriously does, for example, in the case of the German churches' anti-Semitism or the South African churches' apartheid. But such evil already stands condemned by just good secular authority, the divine law. It does not first need the Christian gospel or some doctrinal *status confessionis* or even a churchly trial of "heresy" to define it as sin. Just ask the victims, Christian or otherwise.[4]

There are other, quite ethical modes of combatting social sin—other, that is, than something so exotic as a uniquely Christian *confessio*—and these other modes (public outcry, for instance, and organized resistance) are incumbent upon the church but not on the church alone. "A time for confessing," however, *is* a distinctly Christian occasion, since what is there at stake is the priority of the *gospel's* authority, the Creator's major. That is exclusively the agenda of the church, for the defense of which the church may just have to go it alone.

Perhaps in historic fact there is no "time for confessing" which is not simultaneously a time of fierce social oppression, though there might be a time of oppression which is not, in our sense of confessing, a *tempus confessionis.* I am not sure. How about Paul's confessional protest against circumcision in Galatia ("for the truth of the gospel") or Jesus' confessional protest against Sabbath restrictions?[5] Were those also ethical protests? Maybe. But if so, the ethical concern hardly exhausts the point at issue. The point at issue in "a time for confessing" is that the headship of the body of Christ is being misrepresented, therefore so is the whole body, by an alien kind of ecclesiastical headship—the kind we have called by its traditional (awkward) name, secular authority. Again, there may be nothing wrong with such authority as such, but there is everything wrong with it as the usurper of the authority of Christ—that is, when what was once allowable in the church as the Creator's minor now assumes, in the church, the operational importance of the Creator's major.

What necessitates confessional protest is the confusing of two very different styles of authority, "secular" with "spiritual," both of them all the more powerful for being grounded in deity. When these become miscombined, misaligned, misprioritized, so that the old creation saps the radicality of the new creation and the law conditions the promise, then we face a *tempus confessionis.*[6]

What distinguishes the one authority from the other is their contrasting approaches to justice or, perhaps more accurately, to righteousness or, more loosely, to fairness. Secular authority, shall we say, is God being fair, giving people what they have coming to them, if not immediately then sooner or later. But that is the trouble: though we all have a right to be treated fairly, when sooner or later the Creator's final day of fairness arrives, none of us will be able to stand that much fairness. God's secular authority is something we cannot live without, but neither can we live with it. Fair enough it is, but in the end it is just not viable.

Whether Jesus, by contrast, is entitled to upstage God's secular authority depends on whether he can deliver on his promise of a new, viable kind of fairness. By secular standards his fairness is quite unfair at least to himself and to God: he takes what sinners have coming to them (criticism and death) and they receive what he has coming to him (approval and lasting life). This is the strange fairness of "the happy exchange," as Luther and the medievals called it.

It is not that Jesus' followers are exempt from God's day of fairness but rather that they are undergoing that day now, ahead of time, by sharing in Jesus' pre-apocalypse, his already finished death and resurrection. Thus, through their cruciform faith-lives his believers have for all practical purposes trumped the old secular authority by acquiring it in advance, in Christ. Of course Christians' only authority for believing is Jesus' word, as that word has been fleshed out in his cross and Easter and, ever since, in the pentecostal relay of his gospel and sacraments. That being their lifeline, one can understand why they, the body, are so partial to that one and only authority from their head: *die reine Lehre des heiligen Evangeliums,* "the fresh teaching of the holy good news."[7]

How can one know when the church's secular authority, which might well have begun as the gospel's servant, has in the meantime expanded into the gospel's partner and finally into its rival? What are the symptoms of such creeping contamination in the head? Answer (as the reformers put it): when the members' submitting to that alien authority is touted as "necessary."[8] Necessary for what? It is necessary for their own "righteousness," that is, for their basic value and sense of worth, for their status as saints, for their acceptance within the fellowship—in short, necessary for their Christian survival. Even when the church's secular authority does acquire that sort of soteriological (salvational) clout, that might at first seem quite harmless. It might seem downright admirable, especially if this power which church authority has for enforcing its will—rating its members according to their cooperativeness or their ethical sophistication or whatever, elevating or marginating them accordingly—is exercised precisely to enforce "the fresh teaching of the holy good news." Can that be all bad, enforcing the gospel by means of the law?

What is not at first apparent is the contradiction: employing retributive sanctions to coerce conformity, whether doctrinal or institutional, when by the very nature of the church that can be gained only by the inherent winsomeness of the "holy good news." Indeed, such enforced, secularized orthodoxy—theological, organizational, liturgical, moral—may actually impress legalists as desirable, who perceive such a church as having, thank God, "real standards" and as "putting some teeth" in the gospel. Before long, however, such subtle ecclesial secularization—enforcing an unenforceable Christian faith and ethos—brings with it still other standards and conditions that are less integrally Christian though perhaps more heroically pious or elitist or robust: standards of ancestry (genetic or cultural), maleness, literateness, ordained-ness, cleanliness, or, for that matter, a normative slovenliness or anticlericalism or antinomianism.

The possibilities are infinite but the sorry effect is the same, to reinstate in the church that reactionary feature of all secular authority: people are to get what they have coming to them, what they have coming to them now being defined by some norm other than the gospel. The indiscriminately merciful authority of Christ, the good news of his happy exchange, is superseded by admission requirements.

Confessional protest has a strongly liberationist ring to it, hence an ethical ring, though the intention is as much soteriological as ethical. Secularized religious authority is a legitimation structure on which people depend for their worth, their plausibility. As such, it can rival the gospel as a value-ascriptive authority. It is then a system of enslavement that can be countered only by the freedom of the gospel, by the gospel's revaluing those who have been disvalued, the oppressed, both the undervalued and the overvalued. Another way to say it is to define Christian *confessio* as protesting against gospel-plus. Whenever some other condition or qualification has been added to the gospel, however well meaning—whether to dignify the gospel or to reenforce it or even to safeguard it—then the gospel has in fact been diminished and subverted. More is less. Or as a Jewish saying puts it, when there is too much, something is missing. Then, as Paul said about embellishing faith with the addition of circumcision, the gospel has degenerated into "another gospel."[9]

The confessors' sternutatory protest, this "sneeze of the church," though it is meant to rid the body of contaminants in its head, precipitates the body to the very brink of death (2). I have it on good medical authority that when we sneeze we are momentarily very close to death. Not that sneezing is mortally dangerous as practiced, though it would be if it lasted longer. For that split second, without air and with blood pressure and spinal-cerebral fluid excessively high, the conditions are fatal if they were to be prolonged. Timing is everything.

Confession is *martyria*. While the term "martyrdom" should not be taken here to connote, as it often does in ordinary usage, an exaggerated, self-pitying sense of persecution, neither should it lose the connotation of extreme—yes, ultimate—jeopardy.[10] Emil Fackenheim, marveling at the defiant faith of the Holocaust martyrs, calls them "witnesses to God and man even if abandoned by God and man."[11] That, also for Christian confessors, suggests what their ultimate jeopardy is: witnessing to a God who to all appearances is abandoning them, exactly because of the way they are obliged to witness to him—for God against God.

That confessional risk has longstanding biblical precedent, all the way from Job's "Behold he will slay me; I have no hope; yet I will defend my ways to his face" to Jesus' "cry of dereliction": "My God, my God, why have you forsaken me?"[12] At Augsburg, likewise, the confessors were not unaware of that same risk. As Melanchthon reminds his accusers, "Certainly we should not wish to put our own souls and consciences in grave peril before God by misusing his name or Word."[13]

The life-and-death dilemma faced by confessors is that the God of authority to whom they appeal to vindicate their witness is the same God who has installed their opponents in positions of authority and who now seems to vindicate that authority instead. In face of that ultimate impasse the only recourse of Christian confessors is the promise of the Matthean Jesus—"So everyone who confesses me before human beings, I also will confess before my Father in heaven"—but also the threat of the converse—"whoever denies me before human beings, I also will deny before my Father who is in heaven."[14] Those two options, and the fact that they are the only options, merely underscore all the more just how high the stakes are: either fidelity or apostasy, either divine acceptance or divine rejection.

Thus, the risks to the confessors, but then also to the body in general, are not just the loss of order or of reputation or even of life but, worst of all, blasphemy. It would be as if, by having to sneeze to clear one's head, one risked losing one's head. As one confessor, Bishop Desmond Tutu, testified on the stand before South Africa's Eloff Commission of Enquiry a few months ago, "The most awful thing that [the authorities] can do is to kill me, and death is not the worst thing that can happen to a Christian." Then what is the worst thing? Tutu explains, "Woe is me if I preach not the

Gospel.''[15] But if we do preach the gospel, then in "times for confessing" there is woe too.

Sneezing is not, contrary to appearances, an overreaction. Neither is confessing (3). True, confessors have always dramatized their situation as if it were a case at court. As if, behind and above the intimidating secular authorities of church and society, sat some unseen, still higher authority who waits for the witnesses' testimony to be spoken—not into his ear secretly, as in the safety of prayer, but publicly and vulnerably throughout his world, "before human beings."[16] Indeed, it is only because of that imagined ultimate tribunal *coram Deo* that the confessors picture their human critics, their ecclesiastical authorities, as likewise sitting in the forensic role of minijudges, the way a secular magistrate might.

The ecclesiastical authorities, for their part, may well disclaim that that is what they are being, namely, judges, and may attribute such high-flown metaphors to the confessors' own self-dramatizing paranoia. For that matter, there may literally be no ecclesiastical trials, actual forensic proceedings with formal charges and evidence and judicial verdicts. No, the metaphor of the courtroom (or the courtroom word, "confessing") is no more than a theological construct—and no less!—representing the actual human situation according to the perceptions of faith. To call that situation by such a prestigious name, a *status confessionis,* a *martyria,* is to take what is to all appearances a ridiculous and petty ecclesiastical squabble and dignify it with the image of a cosmic tribunal—which in truth it is.

Confessing is no more optional than sneezing. Or it is what William James would have called a "forced option" (4). Before that daunting tribunal it is really the whole church which is being arraigned. Not just the immediate confessors but the church everywhere is here and now being asked, in view of its secular authoritarianism whether it does despair after all of the gospel's being "enough"—whether it does lust after all for the gospel to be shored up by other, secular authority. With that as the question, the court waits for a reply. The moment for the church to answer this interrogation, its "time for confessing," is agonizingly short and not postponable. That is quite literally so for the immediate, historic "confessors."

In that fleeting historical moment the ecclesiastical authorities—often miserably inarticulate and without credentials—have no choice but to seize the microphone and to speak for the whole church, to be its *satis*-sayers, and thus to do what otherwise they would never dream of doing, renounce their own authorities, and then only because these were displacing the one gospel-and-sacraments. Their confession, of course, includes taking the consequences, although—as Luther reminded—"never in silence."[17] For their answer is too good to be silenced, in view of whose it finally is. "There is," as we sing in that fond old Reformation potboiler, "no other God"—and therefore no other option.

So nonoptional is confessing at those times that, though it cannot be planned for in advance in the church's organizational structure, it must somehow be allowed for, as the Faith and Order Commission's new *Baptism, Eucharist, and Ministry* attempts to do: "There have been times when the truth of the Gospel could only be preserved through prophetic and charismatic leaders . . . only in unusual ways. . . . The whole community will need to be attentive to the challenge of such special ministries."[18]

Considering the odds we can understand why that sort of confessional confrontation is—far more than sneezing is—if at all possible to be averted, nipped in the bud, rendered unnecessary (5). That is why the body prays, and on rather high recommendation, "Do not put us to the test." "Save us from the time of trial." Not only did Jesus authorize his followers to petition for such exemptions. When faced with his own ordeal, he prayed that the bitter cup of being put to the ultimate test might be spared him as well.

But suppose the confrontation finally turns out to be unavoidable and the offensive testimony simply has to be given and the consequences taken. Then the confessors will have to rivet their attention upon that formidable judge behind the judges and boldly affirm, as they did at Augsburg: "I will declare Thy testimonies before kings and shall not be put to shame."[19] Still, even then the selfsame Luther who added that verse from the Psalter as the superscription over the Augustana retained a godly (shall we say) "confessional restraint." God, he dared to say, would be hard-pressed to get him ever to do it again.[20]

A current case in point is the peace movement among East German Christians. Some of them are ready to declare nuclear warfare a confessional issue for the church. But many Lutherans there, every bit as much engaged in the same struggle on the same side, are inclined to forestall that next step. Their confessional restraint, so far as I can judge, is due exactly to their recognizing how ultimate the jeopardy is in such a fateful step of last resort—an insight for which they have compelling precedent.[21]

FIDES: INHALATIO ECCLESIAE

So "confessing the faith of the church" is not just any constructive, unpolemical airing and sharing of the faith, as natural as ordinary exhaling, but is rather the body's strenuous counteroffensive revolution, like sneezing. But then there is all the more need of faith. Any good sneeze assumes prior, good inhalation, which is the relation of faith to confession. Ironically, a faith which the church can confess, if it has to, is the only faith which can prevent such hazardous "times for confessing" from befalling us. What are the marks of such a confessable, preventive faith?

Isn't it true of inhaling (1) that no one else can do it for us, (2) it is only as good as the air a person breathes, and (3) it abhors a vacuum? Isn't much the same thing true of faith?

True it is, no one can do our believing for us (1). Not even the Holy Spirit claims to. Neither should the church. But then it is likewise true, though frequently ignored, that what believing we do—I mean, believing in Christ—we do not by someone else's compelling us or legislating for us or even holding us to some previous covenantal promise of our own. That would be as extraneous and imposed as artificial respiration, and not the spontaneous, self-involving faith that confesses *"We* believe."

Is that what the new Lutheran church will be doing, institutionalizing faith and thus imposing it? We all know we shall have to legislate for our new constitution some doctrinal clause, a "confession," as legally binding and compulsory. But then can that kind of church be "new"? Isn't that rather the style of the old *saeculum*? Maybe, and maybe not. Isn't that what Bonhoeffer worried about in Barth as legislated faith (*Glaubensgesetz*) and what Lutherans generally have deplored as forced faith (*Glaubenszwang*)? Not necessarily, though the danger is enormous, especially if we neglect a fundamental distinction.

But first, before we get to that distinction, we are reminded of how enormous the danger of forced faith is when we recall what was said earlier about confessing. The twin hazards it poses, apostasy and blasphemy, are so fatal that "times for confessing" are conscientiously to be averted whenever possible. So if confessing in that sense is not deliberately to be sought, wouldn't it be the final folly to imagine it could be legislated, let alone programmed? Yes and no, depending on an important distinction.

Anyway, the worst thing about legislated faith is not that it forces us to believe against our consciences, which most of us independent moderns would probably not do anyway. Rather the illusion is created that that sort of socially defined believing—believing what is denominationally expected, under peer pressure, by force of habit and tradition—is all there is to faith, thus confirming the worst suspicions our Roman Catholic critics have long harbored about cheap *sola fide.* Then we in turn, sensing the vacuum in such superficial faith—such artificial respiration—might rush to fill the void with . . . well, what? With programs and causes? "Good works"?

Gospel-plus? I cannot imagine a riper, more inflammatory "time for confessing"—from which, good Lord, deliver us.

Isn't it embarrassing that even the Augsburg Confession slips back into the lingo of legislated faith right in its opening article "that the decree of the Council of Nicaea . . . must be believed (*credendum esse*)"? As if faith could be decreed! Not really. That unfortunate wording appears only in the Latin text, not in the original German. And all subsequent references to faith, not only in the Augustana but in the whole *Book of Concord* describe faith evangelically as the free response to the fresh good news, including the good news of the Nicene Creed.[22] Even the so-called Athanasian Creed, the lowest on church-people's popularity scale precisely because of its legalistic ring, somehow gets reclaimed in our Smalcald Articles as downright winsome, "the sublime articles of the divine majesty."[23] Luther knew how to take liberties where the liberation of believers was at stake.

It is time to recall a venerable distinction: between unconstrained faith and constrained doctrine. *Lex credendi*? No. Not if that means obligating people to believe. But obligating preachers to preach, *lex praedicandi*? Sure. Proclaiming the Word of God, not something else, is what the church has a legal right to demand of me, and I have a legal duty to provide. One dimension of my call-ordination is its legality, which within limits is enforceable.

What is not enforceable is faith, either my own or my hearers. Indeed, it is only as a means to that prior evangelical freedom, letting the good news do its own persuading and sinners their own believing (or disbelieving), that church law has a function, albeit subordinate. As a pastor my legal duties are merely a derivative from the church's "right," as our confessions call it: the church's right to have what Christ gave it, his gospel and sacraments, which are gratis, as air is ours for the breathing.

When in the above quotation Melanchthon speaks of the churches' "right," superseding even the authority of bishops, he clearly includes local congregations as "churches."[24] Is that an argument for congregationalism? I doubt it. What it does argue, though, is that it is the people who are the end of the food chain and so it is to their feeding by their pastors—that is, to the preaching of the gospel in their hearing and for their believing—that all the church's other supervisory, teaching, and programmatic authority is subordinate and accountable.

In his "happy exchange" Christ takes responsibility for us, but he does so in order to free us for a whole new responsibility of our own, the response of faith. That, as his new creation, he will let no one else, no proxies, no mercenaries, no paternalism, do for us. "We are no longer slaves but heirs." Fostering that sort of free faith amongst the church membership may seem to be inviting trouble, giving the natives restless ideas, tempting them to plot disruptive things like confessing. True, such firsthand, responsible faith does equip believers to spot oncoming "times for confessing" and, if necessary, to take the stand. But the same bold faith is what equips them also to obviate "times for confessing" and so to render confessional protest unnecessary.

Believing like breathing is only as good as the air that a person inhales (2). No amount of pulmonary expanding and contracting can fetch life breath if an individual is not breathing oxygen. So it is with faith. Everything depends on whether the individual receives the Christ of the gospel. Therefore when the topic is "Confessing the Faith of the Church," the implication is not that "the faith" is whatever the church believes and confesses. Churches, including ours, have been known to believe all sorts of nonsense. No, the faith is not the faith because the church believes it. But rather the church believes it because it is The Faith, "the fresh teaching of the holy good news."

The best faith for the church, therefore, is a faith that clearly identifies the gospel, that discriminates between the gospel and its trappings. It is a faith that is not taken in by cheap imitations, but one that does develop fastidiously expensive tastes for the very best in gospel teaching and practice. Really discriminating faith, which could mount a *confessio* if necessary and thus knows how to forestall one, appreciates what it is about the classical confessions and creeds of the past that gave them rare immortality. These confessions and creeds were nothing more than the scriptural Word, that "sole rule," ruling history in some later place and time (Nicaea, Chalcedon, Augsburg) in order to bring that new situation as well into captivity under Christ. The confessions are but a biblical echo, Scripture meeting itself coming back.[25]

Good faith has such a nose for the gospel—the distinctive breath of fresh air—so that faith prizes the gospel even in the Scriptures, namely, their "fresh teaching of the holy good news," the Baby whom they swaddle. It is the good news not because it is in the canon; the canon is canonical because it dispatches the good news.

It is only because faith is so preoccupied with the Scriptures' Christian gospel that it presumes to distinguish the Scriptures, Christianly, as those which are "old" and those which are "new,"[26] as the confessional statements of all three of our uniting denominations do. That intrascriptural distinction is almost as radically evangelical as the Formula of Concord's, which further distinguishes those "writings of the Old and New Testaments" which are *prophetic and apostolic.*[27] That is something more than the old/new distinction. (After all, the New Testament also has prophets.) "Prophetic and apostolic," I take it, is in contrast to the Mosaic-Levitical ceremonial law, which of course is also Scripture. Exclude *Scripture*? Does that mean then that when faith is so biblically finicky and selective it limits itself to a very small canon? Quite the contrary. True, there is a sense in which, as the Formula of Concord says, the same Scriptures which are the church's "rule, judge and plumb line" are themselves regulated by another, internal *forma doctrinae,* their kerygmatic structure: the good news.[28]

However, far from reducing Scripture to some minimalist gospel, the Spirited impulse is rather to approach *all* Scriptures through the prism of that *forma doctrinae* and to rediscover it—that is, to find Christ—in the most unlikely narratives and passages of the Hebrew Scriptures, even in the ceremonial legislation.

A faith with such cosmopolitan biblical tastes, capable of drawing oxygen from what seemed like smog, converting exegetical sow's ears into silk purses, may make the authorities in the field nervous. It would not be the first time. Remember the religious authorities who, as Jesus observed, searched Scriptures in quest of eternal life. And well they might. But "they are they"—the life-yielding Scriptures, that is—"which testify of me."[29] Evangelical scripturalness is a "search" more than a dogma, but the search knows in advance, more or less, for what and whom it is looking. Such a single-minded sniffing out of the gospel might also, I admit, sniff out not only "times for confessing," but also their prevention.

Faith is like deep breathing: it abhors a vacuum (3). The intaken oxygen spreads not only to every cranny of the lungs but through them into the blood and on to the body's remotest tissues, for their response. Similarly faith, churchly faith, will not rest so long as any of the body's cells, its believers, are left out of the action.

Still, isn't that the one issue in the new Lutheran church that—if any issue does—holds the grimmest potential for worsening into a confessional issue among us: that volatile gap between the church and us its professional leadership, by whatever crude epithet that gap is coming to be called ("church bureaucracy," "hierarchism," "paternalism," "organizational fundamentalism")?[30] For thousands of our fellow believers won't that be the barometer of our "confessing the faith of the church": how we confess the faith *as* church? But that extends beyond the credal preamble of our constitution into the constitution itself, the structure of how we believe *together,* the participatory body.

Seeing the issue of our internal governance, or foreseeing it, as a confessional issue is not the danger. That may well be the preventive as long as we do so in good time before it is too late. Rather the danger is in seeing that issue merely nonconfessionally or subconfessionally. Then the debate degenerates into the transparent misrepresentations we have seen from our critics in *Reader's Digest* and "Sixty Minutes"—as if the real objection were the churches' social programs, as if the churches' efforts against injustice are ever immune to exploitation. Those critics, of all people, should know that.

Even if their complaint against the churches' "bureaucracy" does come closer to the point, how hollow that complaint rings when in league with military-industrial interests (whether socialist or capitalist) whose own bureaucracies pace all the rest.

But what if the danger in our corporate organization of the church were seen confessionally: for instance, that that organization could become so "necessary," as the reformers said, that ordinary Christians would depend on it to relieve them of responsibility which only Jesus the Christ by his cross can bear for them, and he, only so that they in turn can shoulder their own crosses behind him? What if believers then got the phony consolation that their cross bearing is all being done for them far more expertly than they, the amateur Christians, could ever manage, and that all that is left for them is to support (above all financially) and to implement the programs which this highly efficient system labors to make easy for them? Thanks to the professional Christians, including seminary professors, who then might even be hired to do the church's confessing. That *would* be something to sneeze at.

To keep such "a time for confessing" from befalling us, lest a whole soteriological, mediatorial system moves in to usurp that glory which the Father jealously reserves to his Son, let the new church say from the outset, also in the order of its common life, that that Son is "ample"—*satis*. So altogether ample is he that he shares his headship with his body altogether.

NOTES

1. Some of the materials in the section of this essay headed Confessio: Sternutatio Ecclesiae appeared earlier in my "A Time for Confessing: When Is the Church a Confessional Movement?" in *The Cresset Occasional Papers III*, ed. David G. Truemper (Valparaiso, Ind.: Valparaiso University Press, 1978), pp. 78–85.

2. Formula of Concord, Solid Declaration, Article X, §2, 3, 10, 25, in *The Book of Concord*, ed. and trans. Theodore G. Tappert (Philadelphia: Fortress Press, 1959), pp. 610, 611, 612, 615; Hans Lietzmann, Ernst Wolf, et al., eds. *Die Bekenntnis-*

schriften der evangelisch-lutherischen Kirche, 6th ed. (Göttingen: Vandenhoeck & Ruprecht, 1967), pp. 1054, 1057, 1062.

3. Augsburg Confession, Article VII, §2, in Tappert, *Book of Concord*, p. 32; Lietzmann, *Die Bekenntnisschriften*, p. 61.

4. Of course in the case of both examples here cited, in the Christian protest against National Socialism as well as against apartheid, the issue does assume the proportion of "heresy" and the confessors see themselves, in so many words, in a *status confessionis*. A copy of the Barmen Declaration of 1934 appears in Julius Bodensieck, ed., *The Encyclopedia of the Lutheran Church,* vol. 1 (Minneapolis: Augsburg Publishing House, 1965), pp. 191–93. On apartheid, see Arne Sovik, ed., *In Christ—A New Community: The Proceedings of the Sixth Assembly of the Lutheran World Federation, Dar-es-Salaam, Tanzania, June 13–25, 1977* (Geneva: LWF, 1977), pp. 179–80, 210–14; relevant documents from the Twenty-First General Council of the World Alliance of Reformed Churches, Ottawa, Canada, 17–21 August 1982, in *Reformed Press Service* 206 (September 1982): 14–17; articles reporting similar actions against apartheid as "heresy" by Reformed, Presbyterians, Methodists, and Anglicans in southern Africa, in *Ecunews* (News Service of the South African Council of Churches) 10 (December 1982): 5–13, 18–19.

5. Galatians 2; Mark 2, 3; Matthew 12; Luke 6.

6. Augsburg Confession, Article XVI, in Tappert, *Book of Concord*, pp. 222–24.

7. Formula of Concord, Article X, §10, in Tappert, *Book of Concord*, p. 612.

8. Ibid., §12–15, pp. 612–13.

9. Gal. 1:8, 9.

10. See Paul Ricoeur, "The Hermeneutics of Testimony," in *Essay on Biblical Interpretation*, ed. Lewis S. Mudge (Philadelphia: Fortress Press, 1980), pp. 119–54; Robert S. Bilheimer, "Social Ethics, Evangelism and the Confessing Act," *Perkins Journal* (Autumn 1981): 28–31.

11. *God's Presence in History* (New York: Harper & Row, 1970), p. 97.

12. Job 13:15; Mark 15:34; Matt. 27:46 (Ps. 22:1).

13. See the concluding summary of the Augsburg Confession, Article XXI, in Tappert, *Book of Concord*, p. 47.

14. Matt. 10:32–33.

15. Desmond Tutu, *The Divine Intention* (Braamfontein, South Africa: South African Council of Churches, 1982), pp. 35, 28.

16. It is this character of confession as publicly accountable which, I would think, challenges or at least weakens the description of "confessional" theology which David Tracy appropriates from H. Richard Niebuhr's use of that term, namely, a theology arising within the community of inquiry "of a particular church tradition." *Blessed Rage for Order* (New York: Seabury Press, 1975), p. 15. In modern church history it may well be those kairological moments of confessing that, just because of their public character, press toward universal significance and do for the church what in earlier centuries was done in its juridical "definitions" of dogma. See Bernhard Lohse, *A Short History of Christian Doctrine*, trans. F. E. Stoeffler (Philadelphia: Fortress Press, 1966), pp. 230ff. For a theologically suggestive discussion of "the public realm," "the common," see Hannah Arendt, *The Human Condition* (Chicago: University of Chicago Press, 1958), pp. 22–78.

17. *D. Martin Luthers Werke: Kritische Gesamtausgabe*, vol. 28, (Weimar: Her-

mann Böhlaus Nachfolger, 1883), p. 361, 11, 37f.

18. Faith and Order Paper No. 111 (Geneva: World Council of Churches, 1982), p. 28.

19. Augsburg Confession, in Tappert, *Book of Concord*, p. 23; Lietzmann, *Die Bekenntnisschriften*, p. 32.

20. *Table Talk,* Vol. 54 of *Luther's Works*, ed. Jaroslav Pelikan and Helmut T. Lehmann (Philadelphia: Fortress Press; Saint Louis: Concordia Publishing House, 1955-), pp. 12-13.

21. Paul Bock, "The Nuclear Debate within German Protestantism," unpublished essay presented at the annual meeting of the Society of Christian Ethics, Indianapolis, 15 January 1983.

22. Lietzmann, *Die Bekenntnisschriften*, p. 50, §1.

23. Smalcald Articles, Pt. 1, in Tappert, *Book of Concord*, pp. 291-92.

24. Treatise on the Power and Primacy of the Pope, "The Power and Jurisdiction of Bishops," in Tappert, *Book of Concord*, pp. 330-32.

25. Formula of Concord, Epitome, "The Comprehensive Summary, Rule . . . ," in Tappert, *Book of Concord*, pp. 464-65.

26. "Confession of Faith," in *Handbook of the American Lutheran Church* (Minneapolis: ALC, 1979), p. 45; *Preamble to Constitution and By-Laws of the Association of Evangelical Lutheran Churches* (Saint Louis: AELC, 1979), pp. 1-2; Article II, "Confession of Faith," in *Constitution and By-Laws, Lutheran Church in America* (New York: LCA, 1978), p. 3.

27. Formula of Concord, Epitome, "The Comprehensive Summary, Rule . . . ," in Tappert, *Book of Concord*, p. 464.

28 Formula of Doctrine, Solid Declaration, "A General, Pure, Correct . . . ," §3, 9, 10, in Tappert, *Book of Concord*, pp. 501, 505-6.

29. John 5.39.

30. See *The Christian Century*'s recent series, "The Churches: Where from Here?" especially the installments on the United Methodist Church (45:29 [September 20, 1978]:850-54), United Church of Christ (45:19 [May 24, 1978]:561-65), the Episcopal Church in America (45:2 [January 18, 1978]:41-47), "northern" and "southern" Presbyterians (45:5 [February 15, 1978]:158-64), the Southern Baptists (45:21 [June 7-14, 1978]:610-15), American Baptist churches (45:12 [April 5, 1978]: 354-60), Roman Catholicism (46:2 [January 17, 1979]:42-45). Eric W. Gritsch and Robert W. Jenson, *Lutheranism* (Philadelphia: Fortress Press, 1976), pp. 204-5. Richard G. Hutcheson, Jr., *Wheel Within the Wheel: Confronting the Management Crisis of the Pluralistic Church* (Atlanta: John Knox Press, 1979), pp. 67-149. Ross P. Scherer, ed., *American Denominational Organization: A Sociological View* (Pasadena, Calif.: William Carey Library, 1980), esp. Part Three, "Strain and Change in Denominations."

8
The Catholicity
of the Local Congregation

TIMOTHY F. LULL

INTRODUCTION TO THE PROBLEM

What is most remarkable about Lutheran parishes in North America is their very existence. On this continent there was a great deal of indifference to the establishment of Lutheran churches. For instance, the early Swedish settlers in the Delaware Valley of Pennsylvania gave up Lutheranism and became Anglicans. And others must have been tempted to lapse as well.

This story has often been told, but it has special relevance to the theme of catholicity of the local congregation. Two examples may perhaps stand for all of the frustrations and obstacles faced by the leaders of the Lutheran church on this continent in the eighteenth and nineteenth centuries. The first is the account of Muhlenberg's arrival in New Hanover, Pennsylvania, in 1742. Although he had expected a welcome, he received a mixed greeting that first Sunday. Some members of the congregation were attached to the incumbent pastor, even though he lacked proper ordination. Some doubted the authenticity of Muhlenberg's own letters of introduction. And all feared the financial implications of his arrival:

> Finally, some had also taken offense at the salary mentioned in the reading of the letter and said they would have nothing to do with the affair, for it might be that this would lay a burden upon them and their descendants which would not be so easy to throw off. The deacons and the elders are unable to do anything about it, for in religious and church matters each has the right to do what he pleases. The government has nothing to do with it and will not concern itself with such matters. Everything depends on the vote of the majority.[1]

This was going to be very different from church life in the established state churches of Europe. And for a long time the task of establishing the church would remain formidable, as waves of immigrants arrived and con-

138

tinued to be wary of committing themselves to the building of specifically Lutheran churches.

Things had not changed a great deal a little more than a century later in the Midwest, when Eric Norelius took up his work in Vasa (near Red Wing), Minnesota. At the end of 1856 the missionary pastor who had already known considerable hardship expressed great frustration at the task before him:

> Spiritual conditions in this area at the close of the year 1856 have not been very encouraging. Very few people give evidence of any genuine spirituality and even where there has been some interest shown in getting a congregation established, this concern has often been stifled by indifference and by the financial expenses involved in such an undertaking. When the first wave of curiosity has been spent, people are reluctant to attend services, and no one wants to submit to discipline.[2]

As we the descendants of Muhlenberg and Norelius, Elling Eielsen, Matthias Loy, and Carl Ferdinand Wilhelm Walther struggle to consider the catholicity of the parish in our own day, we might remember at the beginning the remarkable things that the American Lutheran congregation has achieved.

Money is a good place to begin, since both Muhlenberg and Norelius see that as a central issue. The organization and financing of parish ministries in the U.S. and Canada has been a remarkable accomplishment, and it is still stunning to many European visitors who wonder how the church could possibly survive without income from taxation.

Language is another important consideration. While there is still some diversity of worship language in American Lutheranism (with a strong and growing Spanish component), nevertheless it is remarkable that Lutheran parishes have lived through all the language struggles and language divisions, and even have discovered rather fine ways to worship God in the English language.

Theological Identity is a third achievement. American Lutherans have certainly struggled with and about theology, and some divisions remain. But the striking thing is that for all of the continuing problems, Lutherans in local parishes continue to treasure a distinct theology as Lutherans and are perhaps no worse informed—at the grass-roots level—about the content of the Lutheran confessions than earlier Lutheran generations.

Shared Leadership is a major accomplishment. Lutherans in North America had to learn to adapt to more democratic patterns of institutional life and to find a way to bring democracy into the parish without destroying the particular role of the pastor. Problems remain here too; however, they should not obscure the fact that to a large extent clergy and laity have learned to work together and that women and men have begun to share leadership in the local parish in a way that would have been unimaginable a century ago.[3]

This much at least has been accomplished by most Lutheran parishes in the U.S. and Canada and other changes seem well underway, if less completed. Many Lutheran parishes in recent years have had some success in reaching out beyond the family and ethnic ties which were their original base of strength. In order to help this outreach, many parishes have developed a more hospitable climate—needed to reassure those who are not part of the family that they are really welcome—and have begun to engage in more comprehensive and imaginative programs.[4]

Muhlenberg, Norelius, and others would be delighted at the vitality and diversity of Lutheran congregations in the U.S. and Canada today. But there is one abiding legacy of the conditions that they described so vividly. The strength of the Lutheran church continues to be at the parish level. Indeed, many parishes continue to be suspicious of any discussion of the church that suggests that the local parish—their parish—is somehow incomplete or even dependent on others for its reality.

To be sure we have not for the most part been congregationalists of an extreme sort.[5] We have had our synods and our districts with their complex histories, and we have had a number of institutions that have been able to evoke and sustain Lutheran loyalty over a long period of time. But we have seen most of this as a willing, voluntary cooperation with other Christians who were near-cousins. Most of us have felt the congregation to be the primary reality, and the wider church a secondary and more problematic matter.

As for the *catholicity* of the local congregation, we have not discussed that much at all, except in specialized theological and ecumenical circles. To tell the truth, it has only been in recent years that many American Lutherans could use the word *catholic* about themselves at all. Some still cannot, and they will find this whole topic a little distasteful.

But if the word *catholic* is new, the struggle to know how to connect the local parish with its own legitimate concerns and full life with the mission of the wider church is an old one for us. Conrad Bergendoff's lectures, *The Doctrine of the Church in American Lutheranism*, still ought to be widely read, for while the idea is not new, the struggle to understand the transcongregational reality of the church still continues in many parishes. Bergendoff argues to our generation—as to an earlier one—that:

    while the local congregation has the Word in its fulness and possesses the sacra-

ments, whereby it exists as a church, the nature of the Word and those sacraments calls for a fellowship of congregations without which we cannot understand
the fulness of the Word and the power of the sacraments.[6]

Perhaps in a changed ecumenical climate we are able to somewhat more
openly ask for the first time about the *catholicity* of our parishes. That
strong term can be the occasion for some searching self-examination of the
sort that ought to take place when new church structures are being formed.
However, I believe that we should guard against importing someone else's
definition of what catholicity means. Of course we will listen to non-Lutheran
voices, and they will help us struggle with this non-Lutheran question. But
we ought to stop short of imagining that the structure of the church in
another time or another place will give us the ideal model of how catholicity
can be strengthened in our parishes. Let us give three examples:

1. The New Testament understandings of the church have been much
discussed in recent years. There is a rich appreciation in biblical studies today of the diversity represented within and just beyond the limits of the New
Testament and a widespread ecumenical willingness to admit how much we
do not know.

But even if we knew everything, this would not settle the matter for us.
Our church situation is vastly different than what missionary congregations
faced in the first century. We are apt to learn most from them if we do not
start out looking for a justification of our own preferred arrangements in
one or more of the strands of the New Testament. We are likely to find principles but unlikely to find concrete guidelines for the structure of a new
Lutheran church.

2. In the same way the church situation of Luther's time can be a helpful
lens to help us focus certain themes and certain problems, so long as we do
not assume that the sixteenth century settled the matter.[7] Melanchthon's
single mention of the term "catholic" in the Apology does not seem a very
helpful basis for building an answer to the complex theological question of
the interdependence of the local parishes.

3. The writings of Jürgen Moltmann, for example, contain some of the
most provocative statements about the life of the congregation that we can
find today. But careful examination of Moltmann's assumptions about
church life show that his writings assume the European church-state situation with all the malaise that theologians since Søren Kierkegaard have felt
about those arrangements.

When Moltmann says, for example, that "the congregation is mature to
the extent that it no longer experiences itself as being taken care of ecclesiologically and tended to by ordained officials,"[8] he is both speaking and
not speaking to our American Lutheran situation. He would, to be sure,

find much of our congregational life lacking in vitality and too dependent on districts and synods for stimulation to mission. But we are not "taken care of" in the sense that we receive most of our funding from church-state structures.

The simple point is that while others can challenge us to examine our catholicity, only North American Lutherans can finally decide how the various theological arguments fit the realities and the struggle of parish life here. And even when we have decided that change is necessary, others probably will not have the precise model that we can adopt as the answer to our discovered needs. Ecclesiology cannot be done in private, and no one can do it for us.

SYMPTOMS OF THE PROBLEM

Before we examine the notion of the catholicity of the church in recent theological discussion, I would like to take a preliminary look at some of the ways the Lutheran parishes might be lacking in catholicity. This is a risky undertaking, but something is needed to keep the theological discussion from being too theoretical. I think there are four major ways in which we might find some or many Lutheran parishes to be deficient in catholicity:

1. *Exaggerated Homogeneity.* No parish can hope to be catholic in the sense that the universal church is catholic. No parish can hope to have represented in it all of the diversity found within the people of God. It is true that every parish has some degree of diversity within its membership—men and women, young and old, perhaps some diversity of economic circumstances. Nevertheless, many of our parishes still contain a very isolated spectrum of the human family, even of those living in the vicinity of the parish. Our continuing failure to be a racially inclusive church can be clearly seen in the composition of many parishes, even if there are reasons for hope in some locations.[9]

Of course many parishes have made real efforts in recent decades to reach out to a broader spectrum of the human family. And some parishes are in situations where the opportunities to achieve much diversity in membership may be rather limited. However, most deeply troubling as a sign of the lack of the catholic note of the church is the degree to which many congregations are quite content with their own isolation, their own lack of outreach, their own protection from the challenges that more diverse membership represents.

Hans Küng has argued well that the lack of catholicity for a local church does not come from its being local, but from its satisfaction with its particularity.[10] One strong form of this satisfaction is failure to engage in mission outreach in a local situation because the people are considered "unsuitable" for the Lutheran church. Failure in mission can be sustained by grace, but refusal of mission is a more serious sign of misunderstanding the real nature of the Christian message.

2. *Sole Focus on Local Needs.* A parish rightly sees itself called to be the church in a particular place and to develop a ministry to the people and the needs that can be found there. But no parish that lives in indifference to or contempt for the work of the church in other places can claim catholicity. Many parishes show in their program, their giving, and their self-understanding that the wider work of the church plays a very small role.

There are two forms of this malady—one more serious than the other. The less serious, more hopeful, way in which a church might lack catholicity would be in an overconcern for the needs of its own community so that it had little time or energy to spare (say perhaps only prayers to give) to the wider mission of the church. One can imagine an urban congregation, for example, so caught up in the survival of its neighborhood, the ministry to the indigent, the outreach to new people, that it could not be too concerned with other issues and problems.

The form of *incurvatus in se* would not be good, however it would be vastly better than the more serious—and I fear more prevalent—form of this manifestation. Many congregations in our time see their ministry as defined by the stated needs of their own members, of those already "on the rolls." The members, it is argued after all, are the church in this place, and what they want is what they get.

This indulgence is a terribly common and terribly dangerous phenomenon in American religious life, and Lutherans have not been completely spared. The church is seen as a voluntary association ("I might well join another one"), and giving is seen as an investment ("I want to get the most for my money"). On those counts, world mission, social advocacy, care for the vulnerable, and even simple local evangelism are not likely to be priorities. However, if the church is eager to grow, then it will not be able to resist the temptation to look around to see what is religiously exciting to people today, and to formulate quickly a Lutheran version of that religious opportunity.[11]

Once again certain mild versions of this phenomenon seem harmless enough. But very quickly the church is invaded with exaggerated notions of local control, human autonomy, and parochial definition of the mission of the church. Individual parishes need to engage in the most careful self-examination to see whether they are victims of this misunderstanding of the church. In fact they probably need to examine the ministry of other parts of the church in order to see their own life honestly and critically.

3. *Inadequate Teaching.* In one sense the teaching of the church is always inadequate. Luther found conditions in Saxony so shocking in the late 1520s that he was driven to write the catechisms. But inadequate teaching becomes a theological problem of catholicity whenever a local congregation goes off in a strange direction by its own preference and without discussion with others in the church.

Inadequate teaching is one of the hardest manifestations of parish life to measure, partly because one person's inadequate teaching is another person's marvelous diversity. I am not referring here to diversity of piety, worship styles, and hymn preferences. These may have even greater legitimacy in the church than we have permitted to date. And I am certainly not going to touch the complex issue of what curriculum to use in the Sunday school.

By inadequate teaching I make reference to teaching in a formal, theological sense. There are a number of Lutheran parishes, for example, that have abandoned using the historic creeds of the church and have replaced them with something more "contemporary." There are others that have given up on sin and now preach a gospel of success and human possibility which is popular in a number of places in our society. There are parishes where one still hears nothing but the preaching of law. There are even a few parishes these days where only gospel (in complete exclusion of any use of the law) is heard. And there are vast numbers of our parishes, and of our pastors, that are quite indifferent to theological issues of every kind.

I am concerned, therefore, to ask how in a confessional church it is possible for almost anything to go—well aware that in a few such cases in recent years synods, districts, or national bodies have had to step in. The question for the catholicity of the local parish is whether that parish has totally free reign in shaping the theology that is confessed there.

4. *Inadequate Practice.* Closely related to the problem of inadequate teaching are a host of inadequate practices that undercut both the message of the gospel and the unity of the church:

a. There are parishes that claim membership in the Lutheran part of the one, holy, catholic, and apostolic church, but that are inadequate in sacramental practice. I am thinking not only of those parishes where communion is infrequent (and there are many such parishes), but also of those where Holy Communion is offered grudgingly—with a sense that this is a duty that we must bear from time to time.

b. There are parishes that continue to limit severely the role that women can play in the leadership of the congregation, if not by formal rule, then by informal tradition.

c. There are a great many parishes that give nothing per year—and even year after year—to the mission of the church in the wider world.

There are additional examples the reader could supply. The problem is not that such things happen or that we should expect a perfect church, but whether we can claim to be catholic in our congregational life if we are quite free to do what we will in such issues without being truly accountable to anyone.

Many will rightly object that while many of these examples are real, they do not present the complete picture of church life in our time. This is correct. The local congregation would be a good deal less catholic were it not for the efforts of bishops, pastors, church executives, national and regional staff, and concerned people within each parish. We are not arguing that our parishes are completely lacking in catholicity, only that they could be seen to be somewhat deficient in one or more of these ways.

Others will say that much of what has been said is true, but in the end people will have what they want. This may be a partially true observation about fallen human nature, but it cannot be the working assumption of our doctrine of the church. Congregations are not free to be the church in splendid isolation, if by church they mean part of the one, holy, catholic, and apostolic church confessed in the creeds. Love and concern for others is not an option, but an assumption of Christian faith. As Althaus has said, "That love which accepts only advantages from the other but will not bear burdens is imaginary love."[12]

THEOLOGICAL REFLECTIONS ON CATHOLICITY

Perhaps many will now be ready to concede that there is some measure of a problem—whether there is more or less catholicity in American Lutheran parishes today, whether things could be better and more fully catholic almost everywhere. It in not surprising that discussions of catholicity should emerge, particularly in two contexts: in ecumenical discussions and in theological works that are especially interested in ecumenical reconciliation of Roman Catholics and other Christians. There is a great degree of consensus among theologians about the positive aspects of catholicity in the church and a considerable degree of agreement about how it could be furthered. With a view toward reforming the church in our own time, we look to recent theological discussions of catholicity for insights to help us shape concrete proposals.

Following the suggestions of Bultmann and others that the New Testament understanding of the church is both that of the local gathered congregation and of the total church, modern interpreters are included to begin with the argument that the local parish is not complete in itself.[13] The local congregation needs "fellowship and concord with the church as a whole"

(Moltmann); it needs to be "bound together in love" (Schillebeeckx).[14]

While this is a rather important traditional theme concerning the church, especially in Roman Catholic theology, there are some interesting contemporary accents in the theologians' presentations. Catholicity is seen as a gift from God, according to Küng, "a grace given to the church and constantly renewed by its Lord."[15] There is a recognition that such connection goes against the grain of human division and is not a "natural" attribute of the church, but something to which we need to be led by the Holy Spirit.

There is also no confusion of catholic with monolithic. The mark of catholicity cannot be achieved simply by subordination of the congregation to the hierarchy; catholicity includes diversity, including the local struggle for what catholic means not only from "above" but also "from below." Local congregations must concern themselves with the management of the universal church, even if the universal church also has an element of oversight of the congregations.[16]

Finally, catholicity cannot be a stagnant matter of including all times and all places in such a way that the church is universal in a neutral, or static, sense. Catholicity, especially for Moltmann, is not a present achievement of the church so much as an eschatological hope. But the church engages in mission now, often siding with the "lost, the rejected and the oppressed"—in the service of eventual catholicity, but by way of temporary partisanship.[17]

The local parish that happened to be in dialogue with these theologians would then ask a number of questions about its own life: Is our parish able to understand its life as part of the wholeness of the world church? Is our parish able to see that the ability to reach out beyond our natural limits is a gift from God—a part of the gospel for us? Is our parish willing to help shape the life of the wider church, rather than resisting all outside influence or waiting passively to be shaped by others? Does our parish understand the relationship of the church to justice and the inadequacy of any notion of the church that excludes large segments of the world from our concern?

Many of these questions would be enough to provoke considerable debate within most Lutheran parishes. But we have not yet come to the heart of the discussion of catholicity. There is a broad consensus beyond these general issues—emerging especially in the theology of the ecumenical dialogues—that "there is a need for a single, world-wide set of visible, ecclesiastical institutions, hierarchically organized on the basis of the historic episcopate."[18]

This is John H. S. Kent's strong historical summary of these dialogues, one that is not altogether friendly. But it does bring us to the issue that is lurking behind both the Lutheran–Roman Catholic documents and the recent report of the World Council of Churches on *Baptism, Eucharist and*

Ministry.[19] The preference for episcopal structure is implied in the general direction taken by the Lutheran–Roman Catholic dialogues—both in the U.S. and internationally—and is quite evident and boldly stated in the "Ministry" section of the recent Faith and Order report.

The argument goes something like this: unity is a difficult thing to maintain in the church. The churches with strong episcopates may have things to learn about freedom and diversity, but they have things to teach about "the continuity and unity of the church." It is the special role of *episcopé* (the function here—rather than the person necessarily) "to express and safeguard the unity of the body. Every church needs this ministry of unity in some form or other to be the Church of God, the one body of Christ, a sign of the unity of all in the kingdom."[20]

The challenge to Lutherans from these discussions is clear. How much have we been persuaded by the critique of our division, or inappropriate local diversity? How much would we be willing to change in the hope of bringing about ecumenical reconciliation? The "ministry" document implies a hope that we would be willing to go a long way:

> Today churches, including those engaged in union negotiations, are expressing willingness to accept episcopal succession as a sign of the apostolicity of the life of the whole church.[21]

It should be noted that there is something more implied in these suggestions than simply calling our presiding officers "bishops." There is a strong concept of the role of bishop as the keeper of unity and of the college and succession of bishops, and as the keeper of continuity in the church.

Even if the role of bishop can be agreeably defined, there is still a fundamental difference that probably separates most Lutherans from most Catholics and will continue to do so for some time. A Lutheran tends to start with the congregation and to ask what else may be needed for the fulness of the church. A Catholic has strong theological reasons—almost demands— to start with bishops and then to ask whether parishes are necessary.

Many Lutherans and many Catholics (and others) will quickly converge as they all admit the mutual necessity of parishes and of bishops. But the logical, traditional starting point for thinking is so different that true convergence will probably take a long time. A Catholic is inclined to say that "the bishopric is logically, intrinsically and historically prior to the parish."[22] A Lutheran in North America is likely to think that we have districts, synods, and bishops because local congregations were willing to have them. Both positions are logically and historically simplistic, in my view, but each position is held in such a way that it creates ecumenical worries on each side.

Nevertheless the strong affirmation of the episcopate as a major way of preserving unity and catholicity in the church is something that Lutherans must consider as they structure a new church. However, there are voices of dissent from the suggestion that the episcopate holds the major answer to the renewal of catholicity. Moltmann, for example, despite his concern about catholicity, sees the true future for the church in a radical congregationalism that breaks with the deadness of the old structures and is free to embrace the liberation of the world. "The future of the Reformation does not lie on the right wing with its Catholic tendencies but on the so-called left-wing of the Reformation."[23]

There is also dissent about the strong emphasis on episcopacy from certain sociologists of religion—or it might be better to say that they offer another interpretation of this new ecumenical consensus. B. R. Wilson in *Religion in Secular Society* offers a nontheological appraisal of the new stress on liturgy and bishops:

> The ecumenical alternative to sectarianism—is associated with the liturgical revival and the reassertion of the episcopacy even in denominations which began by disavowing both. Both have special appeal to the professionals of the Churches. They improve the claim to social status on the part of the ministry; they emphasize the antiquity of the religious role and hence reassure its performers of the legitimacy, permanence and usefulness of their chosen calling. Liturgicalism reasserts the monopoly of the professional, providing him with the equivalent of skilled techniques which he alone is licensed to practice. Episcopacy ensures the promotion prospects of the cleric, and perpetuates the claim to high dignity, association with ruling *elites*, and the maintenance of the religious institution in some nominal position of high social importance.[24]

It is clear that one takes certain risks in agreeing either with *Baptism, Eucharist and Ministry*, or with the explanations of the social scientists.

TOWARD GREATER CATHOLICITY

My hopes for this essay would be that readers might agree that there is some problem for Lutheran congregations in relation to catholicity and that there is some hope for working with that problem in the new church structures by paying close attention to the thinking about the church in recent ecumenical theology.

Now I would like to propose four ways in which I think that the catholicity of our parishes could be strengthened. Each of the four is very modest and they would therefore make the most dramatic impact if performed together.

Proposal One: Let bishops minister to the catholicity of the congregations. We are likely to have bishops of some sort in a future Lutheran church. There are plenty of proposals being made about what it is that bishops now do that is essential and what it is that they ought to be doing in a new church. Some see bishops as administrators, and there is much present reality to that. Some hope for bishops who are theologians. Some hope for bishops who will be pastors to pastors. The demands of modern bureaucracy are likely to ensure that whatever else bishops do they will spend most of their time in meetings.

I hope that American Lutherans will be willing to go at least this far with *Baptism, Eucharist and Ministry*—that we will structure the episcopacy in such a way that there will be freedom to focus great energy as the ministry document suggests—so that bishops "relate the Christian community of their area to the wider church, and the universal church to their community."[25]

I think that we could try this with greater effectiveness in our new church than we American Lutherans have done before. This would have to involve some real level of contact between bishops and congregation—not just in reference to raising benevolence and calling pastors, but in relation to the total life of the parish. This does not mean a great increase in episcopal power and authority. But it does mean that American Lutherans would give full support to the office of bishop and would be willing to try to adjust to the idea that the life of the congregation is neither the congregation's solitary burden nor solitary realm of privilege. The bishop would have to take on a difficult task of persuasion, since there would be no tradition or special prestige that would carry her or his will automatically against the congregation's refusal.[26]

I think this proposal actually builds on the trajectory of our American Lutheran experience—more and more willing to retreat from extreme congregationalism, more and more willing to admit that having bishops might be a good thing. It is to be hoped that we can now be serious about discovering what bishops can do for us and with us in an evangelical ministry of Word and Sacrament to unify the scattered Lutheran congregations.

Proposal Two: Let the church commit substantial resources to the theological education of the laity. This proposal has been suggested by many for a long time, but it has special relevance to the problem of the catholicity of the local parish. Negatively it is an important protection against any new clericalism in the church. And I think it is fair to say that there is something to B. R. Wilson's explanations of why we may be so interested in high doctrines at this particular time in our history as an institution.

A theologically educated laity is a good protection against any highhandedness from either pastors or bishops. As women and men come to be more confident in their knowledge of the faith, they can play a different kind of

role both in the congregation and in the world. Those who have a real
understanding of the doctrine of the church, for example, are not likely to
be happy with a narrow congregational focus on mission. Those who understand the inclusive nature of the gospel can play a leadership role in opening
up each congregation to be more inclusive of the people of God in that
place. My plea, then, is for a commitment of the resources of time and
money to make excellent programs available that are truly suited to the
diversity of congregations in the new church.[27]

Proposal Three: Let pastors rediscover the role of teacher in the church.
This is an important part of the Lutheran heritage, but it is in need of real
rediscovery and reemphasis at this point. The greatest problem with catholicity is not in developing an adequate theology of the church, but in working with local congregations to discover the theology that could rightly be
their own.

The ecumenical documents of recent years have given a great deal of attention to the problem of the *magisterium* at the international, ecumenical
level. This is a genuine problem, and Lutherans must be prepared to experiment so that churches can find a formal way to consider new theological
issues.[28]

However, I believe that there is another serious magisterial problem at the
level of the local parish. A part of the task of pastor is to teach the people of
the congregation the fulness of the gospel and its implications for the life of
that parish. Once again, people may not be "asking for it"—or they may.

At the same time that our parishes are reaching out—appropriately—to
learn from others and to discover opportunities for ministry in the world,
they are also in danger of losing their distinctive vision. This too is a part of
the problem of catholicity—how to preserve something distinctive about the
Christian message without settling for the merely parochial. George Lindbeck has argued that Lutherans are especially vulnerable at this point in
America to the loss of their distinctive identity:

> A word more needs to be said about the character of these pressures. They are
> of a peculiar intensity in a society, such as the American, in which religion is
> less and less a matter of familial or social tradition, and more and more a mat-
> ter of individual preference or choice. A mass market develops. Success comes
> to those with the widest rather than with the most discriminating appeals.
> Every church tries to serve the needs of everyone who has any chance of being
> attracted. Thus the mainline denominations, with their basically middle-class
> clientele, come to resemble each other more and more . . . The command to
> preach the gospel to all seems to require, in a mass consumption society, that
> one aim the message at the common denominator of religious interests so that
> it will be accessible to everyone; none must be turned away. Thus the desire for

institutional and communal expansion seems to combine with the biblical imperatives to undermine denominational distinctiveness.[29]

If bishops were free to visit congregations, if lay people were free to learn as much as they desired about theology, if pastors were free to teach, then some dent could be made in the parochialism and isolation of parishes. But some will say, rightly, that while these goals are worthy, they are not realistic with the current pressures of time in parishes—to say nothing of districts and synods. That brings me to a final proposal.

Proposal Four: Let parish structure be greatly simplified. I am more and more impressed—and depressed—that so much time in the parishes that I know best goes into the keeping of records, the running of committees, the making and distributing of reports, the shoring up of all aspects of the parish as a complete and well-run voluntary organization.

It is not surprising, then, that people have no time to study if they are already attending too many meetings, that there is no energy left to consider the concerns of the wider church when the shrinking pool of volunteers can barely fill all the "necessary" tasks, and that synod and district conventions are dull when they are simply congregational and church council meetings magnified to a higher and longer power.

I hope that radical thinking will be done about the structure of the parish in the new church. I hope that we all will spend less time going to meetings, writing reports, and listening to reports that others have written. I hope that we will have a larger vision and dare to be the church catholic in our local communities.

CONCLUSION

There is something pretentious about setting out to create a new church. But there is something wonderful about not wanting to settle for business as usual. Yet we end these reflections on the catholicity of the local parish more aware of limitations than hopeful about new plans. We also know that while the church can shape its own future to a certain extent, it is ultimately in God's hands. More immediately the church is influenced by social forces whose impact may not be understood until the effects are seen.[30]

Some of those forces may work to help the catholicity of the local parish, as even now television news of famine helps to raise church dollars for world hunger relief. However, some of the forces may work strongly against catholicity. There is a special danger, seen most clearly by Karl Rahner, that the slow decline of the institutional church may make us less catholic than ever—content to know little of the depressing story of what is happening elsewhere and focused more than ever on our narrow world of the local congregation.[31]

During all of these struggles, the church will continue to wrestle—among other things—with its own interconnections. Someone will remember how Ignatius of Antioch first used the term *catholic* in his *Epistle to the Smyrnaeans:*

> Wherever the bishop appears, let the congregation be present; just as wherever Jesus Christ is, there is the catholic church.[32]

There is a promise in this: we are still the church even when, to paraphrase Karl Rahner, we are part of a narrow and hardhearted particularly regional Lutheranism.[33] And there is challenge in this too: to be what God has called us to be—local manifestations of the one, holy, catholic, and apostolic church. I predict that the newness that we experience in creating our new Lutheran church will be largely proportional to the degree of success that we have in bringing that great ecclesiological vision to working reality for our congregations.

NOTES

1. Henry Melchior Muhlenberg, *Notebook of a Colonial Clergyman* (Philadelphia: Fortress Press, 1959), p. 9.

2. Eric Norelius, *The Journals of Eric Norelius* (Philadelphia: Fortress Press, 1967), p. 153.

3. Conrad Bergendoff, *The Doctrine of the Church in American Lutheranism* (Philadelphia: Board of Publication of the United Lutheran Church in America, 1956), pp. 58–59. The major recent study of ecclesiology in American Lutheranism—and in even broader Lutheran focus—is J. H. P. Reumann, "Ordained Minister and Layman in Lutheranism," in *Eucharist and Ministry,* Lutherans and Catholics in Dialogue IV (Minneapolis: Augsburg Publishing House, 1970).

4. The best description of the last traditional Lutheran parish of the generation—and of many still today—is found in Richard E. Koenig, *A Creative Minority* (Minneapolis: Augsburg Publishing House, 1971).

5. Bergendoff, *Doctrine of the Church*, pp. 75–76. Few went as far as the Lutheran Free Church, in its *Principles and Rules* (1897) which stated: "The congregation governs its own affairs, subject to the authority of the Word of God and of the Spirit, and recognizes no other ecclesiastical authority or government over itself." See Bergendoff, *Doctrine of the Church*, p. 63. This is a position that is still widely held, even if now less influential than at an earlier time.

6. Bergendoff, *Doctrine of the Church*, p. 79.

7. Helpful beginning sources for the congregation in the Lutheran Reformation include Jaroslav Pelikan, *Spirit versus Structure* (New York: Harper & Row, 1968),

and Gert Haendler, *Luther on Ministerial Office and Congregational Function* (Philadelphia: Fortress Press, 1981).

8. Jürgen Moltmann, *The Passion for Life* (Philadelphia: Fortress Press, 1978), p. 115.

9. Koenig, *Creative Minority*, p. 87.

10. Hans Küng, *The Church* (New York: Sheed & Ward, 1967), p. 300.

11. There is a splendid discussion of this matter in Douglas John Hall, *Has the Church a Future?* (Philadelphia: Westminster Press, 1980). This book raises questions about the structure of the parish that go far beyond the rather narrow focus on catholicity in this paper.

12. Paul Althaus, *Theology of Martin Luther* (Philadelphia: Fortress Press, 1966), p. 313.

13. Rudolf Bultmann, *Theology of the New Testament, II* (New York: Charles Scribner's Sons, 1955), pp. 96–97.

14. Jürgen Moltmann, *The Church in the Power of the Spirit* (New York: Harper & Row, 1977), p. 310; Edward Schillebeeckx, *Ministry* (New York: Crossroad, 1981), p. 37. See also pp. 73–74.

15. Küng, *The Church*, p. 313.

16. Schillebeeckx, *Ministry*, p. 74.

17. Moltmann, *Church in the Power of the Spirit*, pp. 349–52.

18. John H. S. Kent, *The End of the Line* (Philadelphia: Fortress Press, 1982), pp. 75–76.

19. See *Teaching Authority and Infallibility in the Church*, Lutherans and Catholics in Dialogue VI (Minneapolis: Augsburg Publishing House, 1978), p. 32. Also *The Ministry in the Church* (Geneva: Lutheran World Federation, 1982), pp. 19–20.

20. *Baptism, Eucharist and Ministry*, Faith and Order Paper No. 111 (Geneva: World Council of Churches, 1982), pp. 25, 29–30.

21. Ibid., pp. 29–30.

22. François Houtart and Ernst Niermann, "Parish," in *Sacramentum Mundi*, vol. 5 (New York: Herder & Herder, n.d.), p. 338. See also Karl Rahner, "Peaceful Reflections on the Parochial Principle," in *Theological Investigations II* (Baltimore: Helocon, 1963), p. 294. "The territorial parish exists because and insofar as Canon Law and the bishop desire its existence and the measure of its functions." Technically, of course, Rahner is only commenting on the parish system of church organization and certainly not denying a certain fundamental reality of the local worshiping community.

23. Moltmann, *Passion for Life*, p. 117.

24. B. R. Wilson, "Religion in Secular Society," in *Sociology of Religion*, ed. R. Robertson (Baltimore: Penguin, 1969), pp. 155–56. Ecumenism from weakness—often unconscious weakness—has been masterfully discussed in the writings of Peter Berger, for example, *The Sacred Canopy* (Garden City, N.Y.: Doubleday & Co., 1969), pp. 141–48.

25. *Baptism, Eucharist and Ministry*, p. 27.

26. Bishops who are nervous about too much power can take comfort from reading Karl Rahner, *The Christian of the Future* (New York: Herder & Herder, 1967), p. 98. See also Althaus, *Theology of Martin Luther*, p. 312.

27. Rahner discusses special reasons for this kind of lay theological education being necessary in our time in "Notes on the Lay Apostolate," *Theological Investigations II,* pp. 348–49.

28. *Teaching Authority*, pp. 33–34. See also Lutheran comments on p. 68.

29. George Lindbeck, "Lutheran Churches," in *Ministry in America*, ed. Schuller, Strommen, and Brekke (San Francisco: Harper & Row, 1980), p. 435. See also Hall, *Has the Church a Future?* p. 120.

30. Persons who wish to pursue this idea should start with Ernst Troeltsch, *The Social Teaching of the Christian Churches,* 2 vols. (New York: Harper & Row, 1960), beginning with vol. 2, pp. 515–75, 991–1013.

31. Karl Rahner, "Concern for the Church," *Theological Investigations XX* (New York: Crossroad, 1981), p. 129. See also Troeltsch, *Social Teaching*, pp. 1006, for the advantages of church-type over sect-type Christianity today.

32. Ignatius of Antioch, *Epistle to the Smyrnaeans* in *The Apostolic Fathers* I, Loeb Classical Library, trans. K. Lake (Cambridge: Harvard University Press, 1912), p. 261.

33. Rahner, "Concern for the Church," pp. 11–12.

9
Missionary Structures and World Struggles

ELIZABETH BETTENHAUSEN

There is an enduring, if only partly true, notion abroad that Lutherans are not really concerned about social ethics. When I mentioned to several of my friends that I would lecture on sanctification during a conference on "The New Church and Its Ministry: The Ecclesiological Challenge Facing American Lutheranism," one of them said, "Now that would be a *new* Lutheran church!" Many of my colleagues at Boston University School of Theology are Methodists and still as convinced as Wesley was that no one "was more ignorant of the doctrine of sanctification, or more confused in his conception of it" than Martin Luther, although no one had written more ably on justification by faith alone.[1]

The task before us today is not so much to redeem Martin Luther from this judgment (although a decent, small attempt may be made in passing) as to determine whether sanctification should and can be an important doctrine and reality in the life of the new Lutheran church. The task, as requested by the conference committee, is the consideration of the following claim:

> The holiness of the church is a gift, but it also summons the church to the pursuit of sanctification and thus calls for structures that engage the church in the struggles of people for liberation and justice.

SANCTIFICATION

To begin this consideration I pose three theses concerning the issue of sanctification.

1. Justification and sanctification should be distinguished but not separated from each other, and equal emphasis should be given to each.

155

2. The emphasis on justification by grace through faith highlights the inadequacy of all human works to win God's favor and to bring about the perfect reign of God in this world.

3. The emphasis on sanctification by grace through thought and action highlights the necessity for the church to pursue the reform of individual lives and socio-political structures in light of the present activity of the Holy Spirit to bring about the perfect reign of God in this world.

Several points of clarification and elaboration are made immediately. First, the phrase "the perfect reign of God" is my synonym for the more usual phrase "the kingdom of God." Second, the thesis on justification (thesis 2) affirms that the perfect reign of God always has a transhistorical dimension. It is not realized simply as the result of the gradual and eventually total perfection of human beings who become less and less sinful by the realization of their own potential. Sin in its personal form of unbelief and in its social form of destructive social systems of thought and action is real, serious, and in constant and continuing need of forgiveness and defeat.

Third, the thesis on sanctification (thesis 3) affirms that the perfect reign of God always has an inner-historical dimension. The Holy Spirit makes present in this world the new creation affected in principle by the life, death, and resurrection of Jesus the Christ. Thus the power of sin is defeated in principle. This is to be evidenced in thought and action as the church embodies the new obedience, in its individual members and corporately, not simply in itself but also for and in the world. Fourth, the first thesis thus implies that salvation includes both justification and sanctification, both the forgiveness of sin and the declaration of righteousness for the sake of Jesus the Christ and the new obedience which is made possible by Jesus the Christ mediated now by the Holy Spirit. The Christian life includes both new creation and new obedience. The new obedience is made possible by the new creation, not vice versa; but the new creation is evidenced in the new obedience.

The phrase "the new obedience" is taken from Article VI of the Augsburg Confession, as the heading was later added. It refers to the "good fruits and works" that "faith should produce" (German version), or to the good fruits that "faith is bound to bring forth" and to the "good works commanded by God" (Latin version). Article XX on "Faith and Good Works" makes the explicit connection with the Holy Spirit: "When through faith the Holy Spirit is given, the heart is moved to do good works. Before that, when it is without the Holy Spirit, the heart is too weak" (German version). "Because through faith the Holy Spirit is received, hearts are so renewed and endowed with new affections as to be able to bring forth good works'' (Latin version). The new obedience points to both the necessity of good works in that they are commanded by God and to the possibility of good works in that the Holy Spirit makes the person new.

Before turning to a more detailed specification of sanctification, mention should be made of two common confusions of justification and sanctification. The first confuses them by identification, reducing both to the forgiveness of sin and making no moral claims at all. Here is a good opportunity to quote Luther and redeem him in Wesleyan eyes.

> That is what my Antinomians, too, are doing today, who are preaching beautifully and (as I cannot but think) with real sincerity about Christ's grace, about the forgiveness of sin and whatever else can be said about the doctrine of redemption. But they flee as if it were the very devil the consequence that they should tell the people about the third article, of sanctification, that is, of the new life in Christ.

> They may be fine Easter preachers, but they are very poor Pentecost preachers, for they do not preach *de sanctificatione et vivificatione Spiritus Sancti,* "about the sanctification by the Holy Spirit," but solely about the redemption of Jesus Christ. . . . Christ did not earn only *gratia,* "grace," for us, but also *donum,* "the gift of the Holy Spirit," so that we might have not only forgiveness of, but also cessation of, sin.[2]

The second confusion arises when justification and sanctification are not only distinguished but completely separated. Here the common result is that Christian life is reduced to the moral task only, and righteousness must be achieved by building the perfect society or simply by "realizing" the self. To avoid both antinomianism (including its present form in the claim that justification by grace through faith entails no moral conclusions) and legalism, justification and sanctification must be distinguished but not separated.

Sanctification in its most general sense is the actual transforming of human life by the Holy Spirit. For Luther this meant the following:

> For Christian holiness, or the holiness common to Christendom, is found where the Holy Spirit gives people faith in Christ and thus sanctifies them, Acts 15 [:9], that is, he renews heart, soul, body, work, and conduct, inscribing the commandments of God not on tables of stone, but in hearts of flesh, II Corinthians 3[:3].[3]

This renewal is not so much an upward progression in an unbroken line, as a daily dying to sin and being raised to new life. However, the idea of progress and growth is not alien to Luther's understanding of sanctification:

> We need the Decalogue not only to apprise us of our lawful obligations, but we also need it to discern how far the Holy Spirit has advanced us in his work

of sanctification and by how much we still fall short of the goal, lest we become secure and imagine that we have now done all that is required. Thus we must constantly grow in sanctification and always become new creatures in Christ. This means "grow" and "do so more and more" [2 Pet. 3:18].[4]

Here, however, we must ask whether the goal toward which the Holy Spirit is advancing Christians is only transcendent and beyond history or rather transcendent and yet a fulfillment of history. How seriously, that is, does sanctification apply to the structures, as well as to the individuals, of this life? Are the former also to be transformed?

In his book *Christian Anthropology and Ethics,* James M. Childs argues that Luther's dominant understanding of the goal consisted in a restoration of the originally created image of God in the human form as it existed before history, that is the time of "fallen," sinful, human beings. From this he draws the following conclusion:

> When history is essentially fallen history and eschatology is a restoration of that which obtained before fallen history, then there will be a fundamental opposition between [hu]man's historical being and [human's] eschatological being; [humans'] destiny is discontinuous with [their] nature.
>
> This dichotomy and discontinuity are reflected in Luther's two kingdoms theology. . . . In two realms thinking there is a dualistic tendency to concentrate the ministry of the church on the inner man and to depreciate the value of historical existence, for if historical existence is replaced by rather than fulfilled by the eschatological kingdom, then little in the way of meaningful change can be anticipated in history.[5]

If we recall the combination of growth and re-creation images in Luther's comments about sanctification, it is clear that they refer to the life of the individual in relation to two points: daily renewal and a goal that is beyond historical existence. Because achieving the goal depends on faith, not on works, the first table of the Decalogue is "greater and must be a holier possession" than the second.[6] The works of the second table are certainly part of sanctification, but a "lesser" part.

Doesn't this serve to diminish the importance of sanctification in relation to justification? Is the perfect reign of God, the coming of which we pray for daily, only the reign of the Spirit in the individual heart? Paul Tillich, upon whose work Childs relies in developing his critique of the traditional Lutheran approach, lists several shortcomings in what he calls the "transcendental" interpretation of history. In it "There is no relation between the justice of the Kingdom of God and the justice of power structures." "After history has become the scene of saving revelation, nothing essentially new can be expected from it."[7] While this view protects against utopianism, it does not take seriously enough the doctrine of creation or history.

> Its most obvious shortcoming is the fact that it contrasts the salvation of the individual with the transformation of the historical group and the universe, thus separating the one from the other.[8]

José Míguez Bonino makes a similar point:

> If faith is to be lived in the realm of history, *as* history, we cannot imagine a "transcendental" self that would relate to God apart from a historical self that acts in history. Neither can we envisage a transcendental action of God that would operate in history outside of, or in the "gaps" between the chain of processes in which human beings are subjects.
>
> Traditional Protestant theology—and much Roman Catholic post-Vatican II thought, which follows a parallel line—is so concerned with the prevention of any "sacralizing of human projects and ideologies" that it seems to some of us to result in emptying human action of all theological meaning.[9]

Continuing the analysis, Tillich points to other shortcomings of this "transcendental" position, namely, that it "contrasts the realm of salvation with the realm of creation" in such a way that life itself appears to be beyond salvation. Both culture and nature are excluded from the saving processes in history.[10] Only individuals separated from their historical, cultural, natural identities are redeemed.

This view makes it very difficult to see the task of structural reform as an essential element of sanctification. More usually sanctification in so far as it is related to culture and history is viewed simply as the individual Christian acting out of love within the structure, but not impelled by love to change that structure. This leads to certain affirmations that seem essential to the development of a social ethic that takes sanctification seriously.

First, against the strict separation of the individual from her or his social situation, that is, against the notion of a "transcendental self," a social ethic must affirm that true humanity is always individual and social. This polarity of the human can be distorted in either direction. The human being, or self, who is justified and being sanctified is not an individual, autonomous and unrelated to social reality. Salvation is the fulfillment and perfection of the new creation already begun with history, not an additional new creation that begins all over again wholly beyond creation and history. Creation and nature (including the other than human) are thus also the objects of salvation. This does not necessarily mean a utopian or humanly created perfection of the realm of creation. It does mean that sanctification is to be embodied not only in human beings but in all being, especially as human beings can deter or promote that embodiment.

Second, the perfect reign of God (the "kingdom" of God) is not simply "a static supernatural order into which individuals enter after their death."[11] Rather, it is present now as the process of sanctification, a process that will be completed in God's future. This is in keeping with Luther's explanation of the second petition of the Lord's Prayer in the Small Catechism: "When the heavenly Father gives us his Holy Spirit so that by his grace we may believe his holy Word and live a godly life, both here in time and hereafter forever."[12] Clearly, in this explanation in the Large Catechism the kingdom does not consist in nor even work through "temporal things," but only through the Word and faith. Temporal things will, of course, be provided by God; but they do not partake of the kingdom. Thus, unlike Luther, the affirmation here is that the perfect reign of God is begun now through not only the process of sanctification but also through culture and socio-political structures and actions, as well as through individuals. The human cannot be separated from the social—from life in groups.

This brings us to the question of holiness as it is both given to the church as a gift and summoned to the pursuit of sanctification. The gift of holiness is given to the church in its foundation, Jesus the Christ. In this theological claim there is no ambiguity in the holiness of the church. Viewed sociologically, however, the church is in constant need of reformation, for as a social reality it never fully manifests the holiness of its foundation. Here sanctification may be seen as the process of reformation by which the church as an institution in the world is led by the Spirit into more adequate embodiment of the holiness that it already has in its foundation. As the body of Christ the church is the present manifestation of the new humanity that was realized in the life, death, and resurrection of Jesus the Christ. As "the Lutheran church" or "the Roman Catholic church" or "the Methodist church," the church is being sanctified, moving toward the destiny and fulfillment of the perfect reign of God which is the culmination of the new creation.

The churches are representatives of the perfect reign of God within history. Because God's reign is also transcendent, this representation is always partial and imperfect. However, there are elements of the reign of God, or, as Paul Tillich labels them, characteristics of the symbol of the kingdom of God, that can be posited and used to specify more closely the relationships between sanctification and the struggles of people for liberation and justice.

The reign of God has first of all a political characteristic. This includes both the spatial image of a realm and the power that is God's. The second characteristic is social and includes the ideas of peace and justice. The third is personalistic, an emphasis on the importance of the individual person. The fourth characteristic is universality.[13] Together these four characteristics point not only to the reign of God in its ultimate form but also to the foci of sanctification in the church as it represents that reign within history. For our purposes it is useful to look at each characteristic more carefully and closely.

To begin it is worth noting Tillich's basic point: "God as the power of being is the source of all particular powers of being, [so] power is divine in its essential nature.[14] Power as the capacity to be is a necessary and inevitable part of creation. The notion that power is evil or always immoral must be set aside. Turning from the theological point to a more explicitly political definition of power, power is "the ability to get others to act or think in ways they would not otherwise act or think, specifically in ways which maximize one's interests."[15]

One's interests do not necessarily run counter to the interests of others, of course. Equitable power relationships are those in which both parties have relatively equal resources that translate into power. At the extreme of asymmetrical relationships there is, on the one hand, violence, which is used when the "other" refuses to give an empowering response, refuses to enter into an exchange relationship at all. On the other hand there is powerlessness in which there is no ability (because of a lack of resources) to enter into a relationship that maximizes, or even acknowledges, one's interests. Indeed, the powerless are often at the mercy of others who have the resources of power which enable them to define the "interests" of the powerless for them.

Such imbalance of the resources of power is dehumanizing precisely because one's capacity to be is decreased and degraded to the level of sheer physical survival, or even death. The resources of power that enable the capacity to be thus range from the utterly prerequisite (such as food and shelter), to the useful (such as education and leisure), to the affluent (such as status and economic wealth).

Sanctification in this respect affirms the necessity of power, is increasingly aware of the dangers of the distortion of power, and uses the resources of power to empower the oppressed. Further, this emphasis on the necessity of power in society makes possible a useful distinction between power and coercion, useful because it protects against a tendency in some versions of the doctrine of the two kingdoms to portray power in the civil realm only as coercion. This view is based on a conflict model of social life arising out of the emphasis on the pervasiveness of sin, such that social and political order is maintained only by coercive constraint. Thus power is identified with police power, and justice is what is achieved when the deviant is "punished." If power is understood to be enabled not simply by the resource of coercion (with the threat of violence as a backup) but also by economic and educational resources, power in the social and political order can be viewed as consentual, not conflictual, and thus subject to the ethical principle of beneficence, as well as the principle of nonmaleficence. Sanctification, then, is the process whereby the church critically judges the identification of power with coercion alone, especially with the violent resources of coercion such as military weapons and capital punishment; uses its own resources of power to empower others; and so works to minimize the conflict that arises out of inequitable distribution of the resources of power.

This is directly related to the social characteristic of God's reign, expressed in the ideas of peace and justice. If power is essential to the process of being human, then liberation from powerlessness—that is, from the condition of being wholly under and a function of some other individual's or group's power—is prerequisite to peace and justice. The most minimal definition of peace as the absence of conflict (which can never be certain when millions have nothing to lose but their lives) and of justice—as not treating another human being (or groups of human beings) as an object of power only—depends on liberation. Liberation is the starting point, for neither peace nor justice is possible so long as structures of domination and oppression prevent the empowerment of people. This emphasizes that peace as the preservation of the status quo of domination, of gravely imbalanced resources of power, is not peace at all and is certainly not in the realm of sanctification. Given asymmetrical power relationships in the world, confrontation is necessary to disturb the status quo. The reluctance of Christians in the north and west to see this has been called the ideological screen of conciliation at any price.[16] Peace as reconciliation, on the other hand, recognizes the reasons for the confrontation and seeks to create a new situation in which the reasons are eliminated. In this sense the church in pursuit of sanctification is an agent of peace. Unless the new situation is characterized also by justice, reconciliation as peace will be short-lived.

For purposes of our question today it is necessary to choose a definition of justice, even though there is not time to justify that choice with an extended rationale. The formal definition of justice is that individuals who are equal in relevant respects should be treated equally and individuals who are unequal in relevant respects should be treated unequally. This definition avoids the idea that justice consists in equal treatment only, a view which makes distributive justice a covert maintenance of the status quo and undercuts attempts to rectify past injustice (through affirmative action, for example). The material definition of justice which seems compatible with the neighbor orientation of Christian ethics and hence appropriate within a discussion of sanctification is justice based on a criterion that each person receive according to need. However, in social ethics that can and should be expanded where appropriate to groups, as well as individuals.

The pursuit of sanctification here includes exposing distortions of justice that either reduce it to punitive justice only or use characteristics of equality and inequality which are in a particular case not relevant to the determination of treatment. For example, equal treatment with regard to health benefits or employment opportunity should not be frustrated by appeal to the irrelevant characteristic of sex or race. On the other hand, the unequal status of blacks in the U.S. or Namibia or of native Americans in the U.S. calls for unequal treatment in the sense of preferential treatment, since the unequal status is the result of unjust treatment based on an irrelevant characteristic in the past, that is, race.

Such judgments, of course, entail some normative determinations of human need and characteristics, determinations not universally shared. In the process of sanctification the church uses power resources to bring about justice on the basis of these characteristics, even if that flies in the face of opposing definitions of justice in the society at large, for example, justice based on the criterion not of need but of social merit or contribution. Confrontation may thus be unavoidable but may also be prerequisite to a more equitable compromise or reconciliation in the direction of justice which leaves no fundamental needs unmet. The difficulty in realizing this definition of justice based on need is obvious when it is viewed from an international, rather than local, perspective. This raises the third characteristic of the reign of God—universality.

The church as representative of the reign of God participates in the process of sanctification, that is, the church becomes more fully the representative of this reign by opposing parochialism and embodying the commitment to the whole world. The catholicity of the church and its worldwide actual extent should be of help here (so long as this is not translated into an imperial self-image). The task of the church is, on the one hand, to challenge parochialism which denies the humanity of persons not of "our parish," whether ecclesially, politically, economically, racially, or sexually defined. It is universality that enables the discernment of the oppressed and the oppressor, even when they are separated by oceans or political systems. It is universality that enables the discernment of injustice even when it is not happening to members of one's own parish. It is universality that enables the discernment of the false peace of conciliation at any price.

On the other hand, the task of the church in pursuit of sanctification in universality is to challenge the anthropocentric parochialism which views the human as the only valuable part of creation. The dominion of the rest of the creation by the human quickly becomes oppression. This parochialism is to be overcome not simply because the consequences of our destructiveness loop back upon ourselves. Overcoming this parochialism is part of the sanctification of the entire creation, for the universality of the reign of God includes the natural world.

Finally, the fourth characteristic is the personal. The reign of God does not and will not meld individual, personal life into an undifferentiated mass. The church's pursuit of sanctification involves political, social, and universal goals, but not at the expense of the identity and integrity of individual human beings.

STRUCTURES IN THE NEW CHURCH

The church in its historical form is always the church as a socio-political institution. The new Lutheran church to be created is not an exception. Thus the question of its structures in relation to the pursuit of sanctification must be viewed from two perspectives. First, the structure should make more rather than less likely the just and reconciling exercise of power within the institution. Second, the structure should make more rather than less likely the just and reconciling exercise of power outside the institution. This means the creation of structures that not only enable such an exercise of power, but also are susceptible to reform in the event that they encourage an unjust and divisive exercise of power.

Using the concept of power as the focal point for either perspective enables us to look at the question of structure in parts. In any power relationship there are, first of all, interests or objectives, both of the agent and the recipient. Second, there are the resources that are translated into power. Third, there must be the empowering response to the agent by the recipient, that is, the recipient must be "interested" in the positive or negative sanctions (benefit or detriment) posed by the agent of the resources.

The church, of course, has many interests and objectives. For the dimension of the mission and ministry of the church which is our topic, however, the overall objective is the pursuit of sanctification in the political, social, universal, and personal dimensions of the reign of God as developed earlier. More particularly, the church in North America today is called by the Holy Spirit to side with those individuals and groups who are the victims of the unjust use of power by other institutions, groups, and individuals in this society and in the rest of the world. In this sense, the interests and objectives of the church are determined by the needs of the neighbor, and in order to meet those needs the church must have resources of power.

A basic list of these resources includes the following: 1) the divine power of the church's foundation given through the Holy Spirit, prayer, hope, etc.; 2) material resources: money, land, buildings, equipment, etc.; 3) human resources: education, talent, commitment, energy, etc.; 4) social resources: generation of socially important values, reputation for beneficence, institutional form, etc.; 5) catholicity: the immediate presence in places of need and in other loci of power relationships, for example, government, industry, etc.

Several comments should be made about the process of translating these dimensions of power into structures. First, no structure will be effective unless there is commitment by significant numbers of individual members of the church, including those who are more powerful by virtue of offices of leadership, to the pursuit of sanctification as earlier described. The objective must also include interest by the individuals. The interest can, of course, be nurtured, which is part of the process of sanctification. For example, the seminaries become a resource of power in that they can provide or frustrate the theological legitimation of the objective and encourage or discourage the interest of future clergy. Thus, even if the structure of the new church leaves the seminaries fairly intact, it is necessary to ask whether, given the paucity of faculty and courses dealing with sanctification and social ethics in our present seminaries, it is necessary to build a compensating mechanism into the structure of the church locally and elsewhere.

Second, unless the neighbor gives an empowering response, none of the resources listed will be resources of power. To the degree, therefore, that the new church is viewed by the oppressed as in reality more interested in the maintenance of its own privilege, affluence, and so forth, any structure will be ineffective. The credibility of the church here depends in part on the degree to which it uses power internally in a just fashion. For example, racism internally diminishes power externally in relation to the racially oppressed.

Third, the effectiveness of internal structures to pursue sanctification in external action is directly and heavily dependent on the distribution of power resources internally. For our issue this means distribution primarily of people and money. For example, if the structure of the new church locally and otherwise includes no staff or operating budget for "social justice," even though structurally there is a "consulting committee" (or equivalent body), the structure will be rhetorical window dressing. The distribution of power resources is in part a function of the church's overall view of its mission and ministry, its interests and objectives. As Luther saw the first table of the Decalogue as more important for sanctification than the second table, so do many Lutherans in the U.S. today. Using the formal definition of justice, unequals should be treated unequally in the sense of preferential treatment. The laity and social ethics are two such unequals in the present Lutheran churches.

At this point in the development of the new Lutheran church it may be more helpful to pose some guidelines for the development of structures which will engage the church in the struggles of people for liberation and justice, rather than to pose actual structures. These guidelines will be stated fairly briefly.

1. The structure should enable, rather than frustrate, the liquidity of power resources. Liquidity refers to the extent to which the resources can be mobilized and deployed to exert influence. If, for example, a crucial vote is imminent in a state legislature on ratification of the Equal Rights Amendment, the church is relatively powerless if its first step is to try to find the names of people who may be interested in the issue.

2. The structure should embody power resources of a general, as well as particular nature. The greater the generality of the resource, the greater the power. Thus, for example, concern itself can be a resource of power, but if it is very narrow in focus, power is diminished. If the chairperson of a social ministry committee in a congregation is interested only in Meals on Wheels, her power is very restricted.

3. Structures should enable both individual and structural change. The choice between individual conversion and socio-political and economic structural change is a false choice. Just individuals do not necessarily result in a just social order, but structures that seem to be conducive to justice can be frustrated by unjust individuals. The concern for the sanctification of individuals should not be posed as an alternative to the concern for reformation of institutions and systems of meaning.

4. Structures should enable both direct aid and systematic change. There are situations in which immediate and urgent need must be met. However, the response of direct aid of this sort does nothing to change the situation of the powerless which often gives rise to such need, especially economic and political powerlessness. To rely on direct aid alone is thus unjust.

5. Structures should enable the church to exert influence on both government and nongovernmental institutions. Clearly the nature of sanctification outlined above assumes that the church should and must be involved in political processes. Although many institutions participate in decisions concerning distributive justice in the social order, it is government which by vir-

tue of the liquidity and scope of its power resources has the most power in this regard. However, the influence of the church should also be brought to bear on nongovernmental organizations and institutions. A structural issue here in particular is the specification of responsibility and accountability for this influence. It may not be helpful to try to specify these institutions by matching geographical structures of the church to geographical counterparts in other institutions.

6. Structures should enable strategies for influence that include both education and direct action. The temptation is to stress the former at the expense of the latter. Even when equal attention is given, however, action is ineffective in direct proportion to the absence of strategy. In a recent article James A. Nash, the executive director of the Massachusetts Council of Churches, wrote:

> Today, political activity is too often mistaken for political strategy. Theological-ethical reflections on political issues are surrogates for strategic action. Pronouncements alone are presumed to be effective deeds.[17]

The entire article is worth considering for its practical suggestions concerning the nature of sanctification.

7. Structures should enable strategies for influence which reinforce ecumenical rather than parochial structures. This has to do in part with the efficient use of power resources. The duplication of efforts created by the insistence on parochially owned resources and influence results in a decrease of actual power. The ecumenical emphasis, however, increases the liquidity of power resources and the perception of need which a more parochial perspective and structure may well lack.

8. Structures should reflect and embody a definition of the church which is more explicit in reference to sanctification than is Article VII of the Augsburg Confession. Article VII tends to reinforce the dichotomy of personal redemption and historical, social, and cultural life in this world.

Much more could be said on the questions before us. We could consider the effect of American cultural values, north and south, on the church's commitment to sanctification. We could consider the tendency toward social and political conservatism and quietism in American Lutheranism and the chances of significant change in this regard. We could consider the effect of the U.S. Constitution on the political life of the churches as it tends to define their relevance to the social order only in what they all hold in common. These and many other issues could and must be considered in the next several years as we move toward a new church. However, for this moment I leave us with a twelve-year-old recommendation from the Evian

Assembly of the Lutheran World Federation "for further study and appropriate action within the LWF and its member churches":

> The Church witnesses to its commitment in social change by its willingness to arrange its own structures so that they are not only sensitive to human need but also demonstrate the responsible use of power in the service of others.[18]

This is a summary statement of the pursuit of sanctification through structures that engage the church in the struggles of people for liberation and justice.

NOTES

1. John Wesley, "On God's Vineyard," in *John Wesley,* ed. Albert C. Outler (New York: Oxford University Press, 1964), pp. 107f.

2. Martin Luther, "On The Councils and The Church" (1539), *Luther's Works,* vo. 41 (Philadelphia: Fortress Press, 1966), pp. 113, 114.

3. Ibid., p. 145.

4. Ibid., p. 166.

5. James M. Childs, Jr., *Christian Anthropology and Ethics* (Philadelphia: Fortress Press, 1978), p. 30.

6. Luther, "On The Councils and The Church," p. 167.

7. Paul Tillich, *Systematic Theology,* vol. 3 (Chicago: University of Chicago Press, 1963), p. 355.

8. Ibid.

9. José Míguez Bonino, "Wesley's Doctrine of Sanctification From a Liberationist Perspective," in *Sanctification and Liberation,* ed. Theodore Runyon (Nashville: Abingdon Press, 1981), p. 50.

10. Tillich, *Systematic Theology,* vol. 3, p. 356.

11. Ibid.: the definition is attributed by Tillich to the "transcendental" interpretation of history.

12. Theodore G. Tappert, trans. and ed., *The Book of Concord* (Philadelphia: Fortress Press, 1959), p. 346.

13. Tillich, *Systematic Theology,* vol. 3, p. 358.

14. Ibid., p. 385.

15. Michael Parenti, *Power and the Powerless* (New York: St. Martin's Press, 1978), p. 5.

16. Quoted in José Míguez Bonino, *Doing Theology in a Revolutionary Situation* (Philadelphia: Fortress Press, 1975), p. 120.

17. James A. Nash, "Politically Feeble Churches and the Strategic Imperative," *The Christian Century* (October 6, 1982): 983.

18. Quoted in Ulrich Duchrow, *Conflict Over The Ecumenical Movement* (Geneva: World Council of Churches, 1981), p. 117.

10
The Social Sources of Church Polity

ROBERT BENNE

In his classic work on the sociology of American religion, *The Social Sources of Denominationalism* (1929), H. Richard Niebuhr employed the sociological approach to religious bodies in a way that startled American Christians who in their naiveté assumed that denominational differences could be attributed primarily to theological disagreements. He held up the mirror of sociological reality to the churches, making them view their divisions through sociological rather than theological prisms. Class, race, region, and ethnic identity were the shaping factors of denominational division, not theology.[1] We have of course lost that kind of naiveté. We know that social groups and their "interests" shape intellectual and organizational life. Indeed, our problem might be the opposite. We are deeply skeptical of the capacity for religious and theological notions to affect church organization at all, let alone secular organizations of infinitely vaster power. We are not startled to hear sociology reduce theology and religious organization to middle class, white, male interests and objectives.

However, this conference is dedicated to the fiction that theological notions do or ought to make a difference, especially in the organization of a new Lutheran church. I will go along with that fiction. But I will proceed in a different way from many of my colleagues. They, in my jaundiced view, will sketch a glorious picture of the way the church ought to be were it shaped by pure theology—as pure as can be expected given our knowledge of the relativity of historical and personal perspective. They will, in the inimitable words of one of my colleagues, "keep their heads above the water [presumably buoyed on great pontoons of theological air] and their eyes on the eschatological horizon, not getting pulled under by currents that surround them." Now this is one way to do things—lay out visions of what might be called indeterminate hope. Unfortunately, when such hopes run into reality, they often become nightmares of indeterminate judgment. The poor, messy concrete reality of the church's organizational life is lambasted for not measuring up to that hope.

There is another way to approach the subject before us. I call it the snorkeling approach. This approach has gotten me into a lot of trouble with regard to other intellectual pursuits, but nevertheless I will try it again. The snorkeler has his or her head in the water, definitely sustained by the fresh air of a living tradition. But instead of gazing at the far shores, the snorkeler watches below the surface for hidden rocks and sand bars so that they can be avoided. Further, he or she tries to sense the direction of currents that pull and push, aware that it is easier to move with them toward the shore than against them. In the case of contrary currents, the snorkeler knows when he or she is up against them and may wish to compensate for them in order to move toward the shore.

Thus, in this paper I will try to discern those social realities in which the new church will necessarily live—not, as Niebuhr, in order to shock us with the realization of our accommodation to these social realities, but to make us aware of them so that we can resist them, embrace them, or respond critically to them. The paper will move beyond simply an awareness of them to a commendation of how we *ought* to respond to these social realities as we shape the polity of the new church. It will therefore have a normative thrust to it, although the normative principles will be implicit rather than explicit. I claim this implicit theologizing as the prerogative of a lay theologian dealing with adiaphora. We laity are not expected to have full command of the historical and systematic tradition, and we are often assigned adiaphora as the subject of our reflections. I, for one, am willing to accept adiaphora as my subject if the theologians are willing to accept my implicit theologizing. For adiaphora, if understood properly, are not matters of indifference. While they may not deal with matters essential to the faith, they are essential to good practice. And the discernment of good practice is preeminently a task of the laity, who have always been more endowed with sound practical judgment than the clergy. I hope in this paper to live up to that tradition.

So, as we are reflectively poised before the act of shaping a new church, it behooves us to look at those realities of our political, social, and cultural environment that are unavoidable for a church on American soil. It is our destiny to be an American church. But it is also our freedom at this moment to decide which of those realities we wish to resist, or to embrace, or to modify and transform according to our own identity as Lutheran Christians. We cannot avoid the limits of our situation as American Christians, but we can shape them according to our own freely chosen purposes.

DEMOCRACY

It is scarcely imaginable that three American Lutheran denominations, which in fact accept that appellation for themselves, would construct a polity that was not democratic. Democracy is certainly an unavoidable reality in our environment that we cannot and will not resist. By democracy most of us would mean three things: (1) we have the right to participate in the selection of those who lead us (the consent of the governed); (2) we exercise our democratic rights through representatives fairly elected (representative rather than direct democracy); and (3) we insist that our elected leaders be constrained by a body of written law (constitutionalism). I find little contentious about these three elements that determine our polity. They are without doubt our destiny. However, there are three further issues that correspond to each of the above elements and that are certainly open for discussion: What kind of democratic model do we want? that is, how do we participate in the governance of the church? What kind of criteria for selecting our representatives should we choose? that is, who should represent us? Who will be in charge of interpreting both the form and content of our constitution for the ongoing life of the church? that is, how will our church transcend the will of the majority?

MODELS OF DEMOCRACY

In a study I did in the mid-1960s of the organizational patterns of the three major Lutheran church bodies, I concluded that there were three different organizational models at work in their polities.[2] While some of the findings are obsolescent because of later tinkerings with function and structure, the general outlines of the models are still clearly visible. I argued that the LCA was organized along federal-pluralist lines, the ALC along centralized-mass lines, and the Missouri Synod along traditional-communal lines. The Missouri Synod of the mid-1960s is no more, of course, but insights into its former polity are still very useful as contrasts, as I hope to show.

The LCA's federalist-pluralist character is still strong in spite of the centralizing tendencies in the merger of 1962. (The most important centralizing tendency was the takeover of home missions by the Board of American Missions which later became the Division for Mission in North America.) The synods remain strong loci of identity, power, and authority. LCA people are more likely to identify with and participate in the synod than they are the national church. The synod continues to be crucial in the support and governance of colleges, seminaries, and social service institutions. It is the prime gatherer of benevolence money beyond the congregation. It is a strong intermediate level of participation between the local congregation and the national church. The national church is also quite strong as it carries out the mission of the whole church through its divisions and offices. However, it is certainly checked and qualified by the synods and their bishops and staffs, which carry many regional interests and characteristics. (Districts, unfortunately, have never functioned particularly well as additional levels of identity and participation.) These various levels, as well as the agencies and divisions at each level, are held together by a rather precise and orderly constitutional framework. The agencies are specialized and guided by professional managers.

The ALC is marked by its centralized democratic style. While there are exceptions, most of the ALC districts tend to be weak. They are not the foci of identity, participation, and power that synods are in the LCA. All of the key functions of the church beyond the congregation were taken over by the national church in the merger of 1960. That resulted in a diminishment of intermediate participation between the national headquarters and the local congregation. This organization sometimes results in rather high levels of isolation and alienation of local congregations from the life of the broader church. This gives the ALC its "mass" character. On the plus side, however, the national organizations can be very effective since they do have a lot of power and are unchecked by recalcitrant regional organizations.

The Missouri Synod was a traditional-communal organization. It was held together by a familial-ethnic solidarity and a strong theological consensus. Its formal organizations were run by highly practical men who followed the directives given by tradition. The organizational framework itself was highly inflexible and archaic. But there were several characteristics of its polity that are very noteworthy—from which we can learn something. Because the Missouri Synod relied upon an ideological consensus shored by familial-ethnic solidarity, it was able to allow a remarkable degree of autonomy to its districts. These near-at-hand levels could exercise more functions than their counterparts in the LCA and ALC. They raised and controlled funds, and they established new missions, for example. Furthermore, the Missouri Synod circuit (about a dozen congregations with a circuit counselor visiting them often) was more effective as a pastoral presence than the district has been in the LCA. A second noteworthy characteristic of the Missouri Synod polity was that new challenges to the church were handled by semiautonomous associations outside the formal organization of the church. Because the formal organization was so traditional and inflexible, groups like the Lutheran Human Relations Association, the Lutheran High School Associations, and even the Walther League with its Prince of Peace

Volunteers sprang up to handle new opportunities for mission. The freedom and creativity of these associations were partly due to the fact that they were not absorbed by the formal organization of the church. As long as the ideological consensus held, they could be allowed their autonomy. However, as we all know, such a consensus did not hold and therefore these associations either did not survive or they had to dissolve their informal connection with the Missouri Synod.

If these are the models of the past, what variations and/or combinations do we wish for the future? I shall add further suggestions as we go along, but at this point I would like to put in my plug for a modified federal-pluralist model. We should have a strong national church, but it should be matched by a dispersion of power and participation in strong regional units. These regional units should be larger than most of the current LCA synods so that they can handle more crucial functions of the church's life than they currently do. Functions such as home missions, college and seminary education, continuing education, social service, and regional church and society issues should be devolved to the regional level if they are not already there. These "archdioceses" should be impressive centers of public presence with adequate staff and funds to get the job done.

The national church should also be a strong center. It would, as Bishop Kohn of the AELC has argued, "coordinate the regions, relate the church to the government and ecumenical matters, oversee world missions, develop materials, set standards for theological education, and administer pensions for professional leaders."[3] I would add to this list the following: research, public communication to church and world, and some form of theological guidance.

The larger regional units should be complemented with smaller units under them—"dioceses." These would be primarily pastoral and celebrative in nature and would be presided over by a bishop or dean. The diocese would have no further full-time personnel and would be of optimal "pastoral" size—perhaps one hundred congregations at the most.

The model outlined above follows the principle of subsidiarity—it encourages necessary functions to be carried out at the lowest possible level. There are two main arguments for this. The first is the argument from sin. A large centralized polity gives over too much power to one center. It encourages pretention and authoritarianism, if not idolatry. A federal model will mitigate those tendencies. The second is the argument from creativity and effectiveness. Locating as many functions at the lowest possible level increases the capacity for identification and participation in the life of the church by the people. People can "own" their church. This will lead to more vitality and creativity because people become involved at processes and issues nearer at hand. Further, it cuts down on the indirectness of much of the church's life, in which people are asked to imagine, identify with, and support causes that are distant from them, both geographically and psychologically. Bureaucratic rationalization, and the indirectness that characterizes it, has probably gone far enough and needs to be reversed through participatory models.

> The national headquarters could be in Chicago. There would be seven archdioceses—South Eastern, North Eastern, North Western, Pacific South Western, South Central, Middle Western, and Upper Middle Western. Each would have its headquarters in major cities and each would have a seminary. This would entail closing or moving several so that the South Central and Pacific North Western archdioceses would have seminaries. Several of the archdiocesan headquarters would have to be established at a scale far beyond that warranted by their present numbers. The South Eastern (Atlanta or a Florida city) and the Southern (a Texas city) come immediately to mind. All would need to be large enough to carry out their functions and to convey public "weight."[4]

REPRESENTATION

The most celebrated issue under this rubric concerns whether representation at synod conventions will be according to the LCA pattern (lay representatives of congregations and all clergy) or according to the ALC pattern (lay and clergy representatives from congregations). These differing means of representation flow from different ways of defining the church: the LCA with its "congregations and ordained ministers" and the ALC with its "union of congregations." There are important ramifications for the church's life implicit in each mode of representation. However, I feel neither competent nor motivated to tackle this difficult problem in this paper. To my mind, Arland Hultgren has given us the best public discussion of these issues in two related articles.[5] He takes us through the history of the problem as well as its theological and biblical dimensions. He suggests a compromise solution that seems to bend slightly to the LCA pattern in which all ordained clergy can officially participate in the deliberations of synod or district, thus recognizing this participation as a manifestation of the church to which all belong. The synod or district then elects representatives of equal numbers of clergy and laity to the national convention.

A second issue concerning representation has to do with the nomination and election process for membership on synodical/district and national boards and committees. I might include the processes for nominating and selecting representatives for synodical and national conventions, though I believe these to be more authentically representative than those for boards and committees. It seems to me that we have two unsatisfactory styles of representation *by ascription,* one traditional and one very modern, but neither one leads to the best results. This is not to say that many of the elected representatives are incompetent and uncommitted, but it is to say that we can do better if we diminish our reliance on ascriptive patterns.

The first ascriptive pattern refers to the traditional pool of names and persons that has become well known to the church. It is primarily the "old boy" network, though there are a significant number of "old girls" in it too. It is most visible in the "circulating elite," persons who become known to the professional staff of boards and committees and who move from one board or committee to the next when their terms expire. They continue to show up in many reaches of the church's organizational life. Often they are knowledgeable and devoted and would appear in these places on their own merit; but just as often they are there because they are known to be yeomen who enjoy the sociability of church meetings, and because they perform their obligations dutifully but are docile followers of the wishes of professional staff and elected officials. They are often what Mark Gibbs calls "type B" laity—laity whose primary way of serving God is to serve the institution. And in many cases they are laity whose livelihood is gained in church institutions (like me) or who are married to clergy. In any case, they are frequently very institutionally oriented with far too much awe for the institution's professional leadership, which leads them to accept bureaucratic direction and/or inertia too easily.

This pattern has of course been noticed by those who are in the forefront in demanding an "inclusive" church. The old ascriptive style is predominantly white, middle-aged, middle-class, and male. So new ascriptive styles of representation have been promoted. Minority persons—black, Hispanic, American Indian, oriental—and women constitute the new ascriptive groups. It is not very difficult to find women who are committed and competent, but the ratio of their presence on boards and committees to their membership in the church has a long way to go before it is in proportion. But minorities are another matter. Too often they are selected primarily because the board or committee or staff needs to fulfill a quota. Minority persons of all levels of ability and commitment to the church are in great demand and are often burdened with multiple claims from the church. In the worst cases an automatic posturing ensues, because it is perceived that they are there because of their membership in a minority group and they must without fail bring up their cause. I am not sure this is a happy result either for the church or for the minority persons involved.

Please do not misread me on this score. I find it a welcome direction to include varieties of people in the church; perhaps it is even necessary to go through a period of ascriptive representation. But it, like the more traditional mode of ascription, draws our sights away from selecting the most committed, knowledgeable, competent, and active persons to represent us. The new church should find ways of holding representative positions genuinely open and using relevant criteria of discrimination (one of which might be minority status) so that the full potential of its people is tapped.

A third issue concerning representation has to do with the distinction between authority and power. Many studies have been done to indicate the disjunction of these two elements.[6] Those who often have the real power to influence and decide are not the ones who formally, through written rules of procedure, have the authority to do so. Too much disparity between formal authority and informal power leads to hypocrisy and its attendant cynicism and/or anger. I believe we in the LCA are close to an unwholesome level in two instances. One has to do with the presumption that management committees shape the policy of divisions; the professional staff of the divisions actually do that. I will say no more about this issue now but will return to it later. A second has to do with the real power of the bishops and their council. They, it appears, have much more informal power than they have formal authority. I do not have objections to a major role for the bishops and the bishops council in decision making, but I would hope that in the new church such a role would be formally authorized.

INTERPRETATION OF THE "CONSTITUTION"

Even if representation is perfect in a constitutional democracy, there is a framework of law that transcends the will of the majority and protects the rights of minorities. In political affairs, the Constitution and Bill of Rights serve that function. Those documents, however, are not self-interpreting; a judicial body, independent as possible from the shifting will of various majorities, interprets that constitution for each new challenge in each new age.

There are of course major differences between sovereign political bodies and American denominations. But the analogy is helpful. Some body needs to interpret the "constitution" of the new Lutheran church, not only its formal rules but also its theological substance. For the Lutheran church does not believe that truth emerges from the vote of the majority; churches worthy of the name know there are limits to democratic procedures. We have a confessional tradition that we think needs to be contributed to the ongoing life of the people of God, and that tradition needs to be interpreted for all the activities and functions of the church. In secular terms, the ideology of the church must be stated, interpreted, and pressed into use as a guidance system for the direction of the body. The LCA has done this in a diffuse and informal manner. Diffuse in that theologizing goes on in many places—seminaries, colleges, bishops' meetings, the writing of educational materials, the setting of priorities, the life of local congregations, and the like. This is as it should be. But who sets the big clock from which others take their cue? The LCA has "set the big clock" by using an informal system of "court theologians." There are three or four or five theologians who have had the confidence of the bishop of the church and other key leaders. These theologians then provide theological direction for the church. Others are generally ignored. So the "formal" theology of the LCA is shaped in an informal way. The result is that while it has an amazing array of creative theologians at work, its own theology is rather staid and exclusive.

I would like to see two things occur in the new church: First, we could formalize the place of theology by constituting some sort of theological council at the national level of the church's life. Members could be elected or appointed from each of the archdioceses to ensure diversity. Second, this group would have the task of "setting the big clock" for all the little clocks of the church. It could provide or oversee theology for the constitution itself, the key educational pieces of the church, social statements, standards in theological seminaries, dialogue with other churches, and for the overall thrust of the church's self-definition. It need not *do* all these things; it just needs to oversee them. It need not insist that all the little clocks are set according to its signals; it just needs to provide direction that is clear and consistent with the tradition. It is important that interpretation of that tradition be at the center of the church's life.

DENOMINATIONALISM

If the spirit and practice of democracy are one social source for the new church's polity, the American denominational arrangement is another. The history and theory of American denominationalism have been analyzed by Sidney Mead in *The Lively Experiment*. In contrast to both the church and the sect, the denomination makes no exclusive claim to truth; it presumes that other denominations possess a measure of the truth. Therefore, it will recognize a certain amount of relativity of perception and will cooperate with other denominations. It believes that a fuller witness to the truth will emerge in interaction with other denominations. In short, it has an ecumenical stance. The classic notion of the church, however, makes a claim to sovereignty over both truth and territory. The sect claims an exclusive access to truth, but it abjures responsibility for territory or society, generally viewing them as demonic. Neither the sect nor the church believes in discussion among humble seekers of truth, or in cooperatively accepting responsibility for social care and action.[7]

The ALC, LCA, and AELC all fit the denominational pattern and as such are ecumenically concerned. The LCA and AELC belong to the National Council of Churches, but the ALC does not. Interestingly enough, perhaps the best suggestion for realizing the ecumenical promise in the American denominational system has been made by President Preus of the ALC. He has suggested that a new ecumenical body be organized to replace the National Council of Churches. Such a suggestion makes good sense to me. The full panoply of American denominational life has not been represented and expressed in the NCC. Several large evangelical groups and many smaller conservative denominations have remained outside the NCC. The Roman Catholic church, perhaps because of its involvement in the American denominational system, has moved toward accepting a more humble and more cooperative approach to church relations and common witness, yet remains outside the NCC.

Meanwhile, according to my reading, the NCC has been heavily conditioned by the theology and social perspective of the declining old Protestant establishment. It has not been able to provide the kind of context for ecumenical exchange and witness that would reflect the dynamic pluralism of American denominational reality. At any rate, as we participate in American denominational reality, why not press for a fuller reflection of that reality? Further, we should probably listen carefully to the Missouri Synod's plea for a new inter-Lutheran organization. Perhaps they are already tired of being a sect.

BUREAUCRACY

A third reality in the social landscape that cannot be avoided is bureaucracy. As Weber argued, bureaucratic organization is far superior to other forms of administration—collegiate, honorific, or avocational. "Precision, speed, unambiguity, knowledge of files, continuity, discretion, strict subordination, reduction of friction and of material and personal costs—these are raised to the optimum point in strictly bureaucratic administration."[8] Characteristics of bureaucracy are: there are the principles of fixed and official jurisdictional areas, which are generally ordered by rules; the regular activities of the bureaucratically governed structure are distributed in a fixed way as official duties; the authority to command such a structure is distributed in a stable way; only persons who have generally regulated qualifications to serve are employed.[9] There is little doubt that the LCA and ALC are thoroughly bureaucratized organizations—the AELC is less so because of its size and youth. The new church will be a bureaucratized organization; that is inescapable. However, it is within our freedom to shape bureaucracies that are efficient and responsive and to avoid some of the blind spots of bureaucratic organization.

Let me take up the first challenge—the challenge of efficiency and responsiveness. In a fascinating paper on the survival of different types of organizations, Eugene Fama and Michael Jensen examine "agency problems" in nonprofit bureaucracies.[10] They argue that since nonprofit organizations like churches are donor-financed, those organizations will have difficulty holding their bureaucracies accountable. There are several reasons for this. The "product" offered by the religious institution is not easily measurable so there are no easy ways to determine productivity. Further, the donors are not "residual claimants" in the sense that they have a claim on the cash flow of the organization. They can quit giving but once they do give, they have no ongoing right to the funds of the organization. Thus, they have little leverage on the management or control groups of the church; they cannot by law replace members of boards.[11]

There is in nonprofit bureaucracies, then, the danger of expropriation of donors' funds, not by the bureaucrats themselves but by the inefficiency and aimlessness of the bureaucratic-organizational process itself. Since there is no "bottom line" and there are no residual claimants, there are serious problems of agency efficiency and purposiveness. Who has not experienced such problems when attending meetings of the boards and committees of the large ecclesiastical bureaucracies? I am not suggesting that our officials are deficient or that our organization is seriously flawed. I am rather pointing to the inherent difficulty of a nonprofit bureaucracy.

This inherent problem puts a great deal of pressure on both the professional staff of the bureaucracy and the managing board or committee. There are several ways that commend themselves in attacking this problem. One approach is altering the kind of representation we have on the boards and committees. I observed above that we often are represented by institutionalists—both clergy and lay—who enjoy the sociability of meetings, who do their duties in yeoman fashion, but who often docilely accept the leadership of the professional staff and are all too patient with the inefficiency and aimlessness of the proceedings. Meetings then are reduced to ratifying the direction and production of the bureaucracy. Little room is left for deliberation on policy or authentic monitoring of the whole organization. The needs of bureaucratic organization then take over and achieve a kind of self-sustaining momentum. The gifts of the donors are expropriated by a kind of nonmalicious, silent complicity.

If, however, we were able to place a different kind of representative on the boards and committees, perhaps some of our agency problems would be mitigated. We should aim at "type A" laity, who have experience in the management of other kinds of organizations than simply nonprofits and who view their primary mission in their vocations, not in serving the institution. We have very few of these types of persons on our boards and committees except, perhaps, our pension committees. I doubt that such persons would tolerate the kind of inefficiency and aimlessness of nonprofit bureaucracy. They would, I believe, demand a more deliberative role for the managing board or committee and more space for its deliberations. Clergy, of course, can also help in calling our organization toward more accountability and purposiveness, but I believe the laity must take the leading role.

A second improvement has already been hinted at. I believe the control function (ratification and monitoring) of the boards and committees must be given a *pro*spective rather than a *retro*spective status. That is, the boards and committees must have the time and agenda freedom to ratify and monitor management functions (initiation and implementation) in an authentically critical way. To use a metaphor, they must be able to board the moving train and deliberate with the engineers about the speed and direction of the train rather than stand by on the platform as the train moves by, saying their "amens" to what has already been decided and implemented.

A second great challenge of bureaucratization in church life is its tendency to dampen the prophetic. As one goes over the characteristics of bureaucracy, it is evident that there are few places for radical critique and action to emerge. Life in the bureaucracy is just too regularized for the genuinely prophetic to emerge. So, how should the new church allow and encourage genuinely radical criticism and action?

Our earlier discussion of organizational models may be instructive here. The LCA and ALC, with their bureaucratic sophistication, have been able to construct significant social statements and, in consonance with them, shape their organizational life accordingly. But the most effective radical social criticism and action have not come from those formal bodies. They have come from autonomous associations outside the formal organization of the churches, organizations frequently spun off and staffed from Missouri Synod sources.

The more modern and sophisticated ALC and LCA bureaucracies tend to absorb, co-opt, and dampen the prophetic impulses of those who want to participate in radical witness. Such witness is unlikely in congregations. So, in a curious way, it is the voluntary associations—forced to independent status by the hidebound Missouri Synod traditionalism—that have carried on radical criticism. The Lutheran Coalition on Southern Africa is a perfect case in point. While LCA people have been active in that group, I suspect it may be former Missouri people from the Lutheran Human Relations Association, the Walther League, and the Prince of Peace Volunteers that are crucial.

The point is not whether the depiction just made is historically accurate. Rather, it is that associations must be free of the dampening effects of bureaucracy in order to carry on prophetic witness. Perhaps the best way to ensure the continued presence of such witness is to follow the old Missouri pattern. Let them raise their own funds and be authentically independent. Or should the new church support them through block grants or some other mechanism that gives financial support without bureaucratic control? If the Roman Catholic church has its orders that provide the radical witness, cannot the new Lutheran church provide some imaginative scheme for encouraging such a witness?

CURRENT TRENDS

In the following I wish to take up three trends in American society that are of long-term significance. The new church must respond to them in some way; they simply cannot be ignored without serious consequences.

1. If John Naisbitt in his *Megatrends* is correct, "the North-South shift is stronger than first thought and is irreversible in our life time."[12] More people are now living in the south and west than in the north and east. And when one recalls that the Lutheran churches are churches of the north and east par excellence, one envisions the last two dinosaurs mating. The vision could be that grim if we do not respond constructively to the trend. Constructive response might mean: establishing major regional headquarters in the Southeast, Southcentral (Texas), and Pacific Southwest, out of which vigorous home missions would be generated; the establishment of a seminary in Texas; gathering the considerable strength of the northern and eastern Lutheran churches for an intentional and concerted ministry in severely declining areas to indicate that the mission of Christ's church is not simply to the booming areas; and attending to the minorities who are also growing in those expanding southern and western areas.

2. If we are in the midst of a revolution in communication that will lead to an even vaster choice and accessibility of information, entertainment, and learning, the new church should establish an office of communication at the national level that will produce the learning materials appropriate to the new age of communication. Let us not leave the field open to the electronic churches.

3. If it is true that the diversity, complexity, and individuation of our society will continue to increase, the church will need to spend much more time and energy on *formation*—formation of its youth, clergy, and mature laity. Our society is already drowning in choices and the freedom to make them, but it is thirsty for the integrated personalities to make them wisely. Choices and options are cheap and plentiful, but persons of character devoted to profound religious and moral values are scarce. Without healthy communities having high values to inform such persons, *disintegration* of person and society is likely. Thus far the church has not responded to the challenge of formation with adequate wisdom and vigor. It has diminished the importance of confirmation; it has disbanded national youth organizations; it has relied too much on volunteers to educate and form the young; it has not fostered the development of an American version of the evangelical academies for the training of its laity; it has only begun to take lay adult education seriously; and it has not demanded the learned and able clergy that we must have for the future.

I believe we are in a whirlwind in which all traditional moorings are coming loose. They can no longer be passed through the loins of pious parents or through the allure of traditional religious institutions. We are in a struggle for the next generation, and the new church must gird for it.

NOTES

1. H. R. Niebuhr, *The Social Sources of Denominationalism* (New York: Meridian Books, 1960).

2. Robert Benne, *A Study of the Regional Organization of the Three Major Lutheran Bodies* (unpublished research project, 1963). This project was part of a much larger project under the direction of Gibson Winter, which was published under the title *Religious Identity: A Study of Religious Organization* (New York: Macmillan Co., 1968).

3. "Lutherans Uniting," *Partners* (December 1982).

4. The composition of the archdioceses could follow roughly these lines: South Eastern—Florida, Georgia, Alabama, Mississippi, Tennessee, Virginia, Kentucky, North Carolina, South Carolina, and the Caribbean (headquarters at Atlanta or

Tampa); North Eastern—New England states, New York, Maryland, Pennsylvania, West Virginia, and Ohio (Philadelphia as headquarters); Upper Midwestern—the Dakotas, Minnesota, and Wisconsin (headquarters at Minneapolis); Midwestern—Nebraska, Kansas, Iowa, Missouri, Illinois, Indiana, and Michigan (headquarters in Des Moines, Kansas City, or St. Louis); Southern or South Central—Texas, Louisiana, Arkansas, Oklahoma, Colorado, New Mexico (headquarters at Dallas or San Antonio); South West Pacific—Arizona, California, Utah, Nevada (headquarters at Los Angeles or San Diego); North West Pacific—Idaho, Alaska, Montana, Wyoming, Oregon, and Washington (headquarters at Seattle).

5. Arland J. Hultgren, "Reflections on the Constitution and Polity of the Church," (unpublished manuscript), and "Re-thinking Ecclesiology and Polity," *Lutheran Forum* (October 1982): 8–11.

6. For example, see Paul M. Harrison, *Authority and Power in the Free Church Tradition* (Princeton: Princeton University Press, 1959). Also, *Religious Identity* by Winter (already cited).

7. For a good discussion of the church-sect-denomination typology, see Chalfant, Beckley, and Palmer, *Religion in Contemporary Society,* (Sherman Oaks, Calif.: Alfred Publishing Co., 1981), pp. 120–36.

8. Gerth and Mills, ed., *From Max Weber* (New York: Oxford University Press, 1962), p. 214.

9. Ibid, p. 196.

10. Eugene Fama and Michael Jensen, "Agency Problems and Residual Claims," *Journal of Law and Economics* 26 (June 1983).

11. Ibid, p. 21–26.

12. John Naisbitt, *Megatrends* (New York: Warner Books, 1982), p. 210.